CW00591210

THE SAMBURU

First published in 1965, this classic ethnography examines the society of the Samburu, a nomadic Kenyan people clinging to a traditional way of life. Paul Spencer spent more than two years amongst the Samburu, during which time he became adopted as a member of the clan and observed the workings of their age organization.

Samburu society is a gerontocracy in which power rests with the older men. Men under thirty may not marry or otherwise assert their personal independence, and in *The Samburu* Paul Spencer reveals how young men are trapped in the vacuum created by this gerontocractic regime. This delayed development leads initially to resentment that is expressed in delinquent tendencies, but as the young men mature and acquire a greater stake in the system, they learn to support it.

In his new preface to this important work, Paul Spencer describes how he came to profile the Samburu at a time when they were relatively unknown, and explains the relevance of the study of age organization in anthropology.

Paul Spencer is Honorary Director of the International African Institute and Emeritus Professor of African Anthropology at the School of Oriental and African Studies in the UK. He is a world authority on the peoples of East Africa and author of *The Maasai of Matapato* (1988, 2004) and *Time, Space and the Unknown* (2004).

ROUTLEDGE CLASSIC ETHNOGRAPHIES bring together key anthropology texts which have proved formative in the development of the discipline. Originally published between the 1930s and the 1980s, these titles have had a major impact on the way in which anthropology, and most particularly ethnography, is conducted, taught, and studied.

Each book contains the text and illustrations from the original edition, as well as a new preface by a leading anthropologist explaining the book's contribution to the development of anthropology and its continuing relevance in the twenty-first century.

ABORIGINAL WOMAN
Sacred and profane
Phyllis M. Kaberry

WOMEN OF THE GRASSFIELDS
A study of the economic position of women
in Bamenda, British Cameroons
Phyllis M. Kaberry

STONE AGE ECONOMICS
Marshall Sahlins

THE MAASAI OF MATAPATO
A study of rituals of rebellion
Paul Spencer

THE SAMBURU
A study of gerontocracy
Paul Spencer

HUNGER AND WORK IN A SAVAGE TRIBE
A functional study of nutrition among the southern Bantu
Audrey Richards

CUSTOM AND POLITICS IN URBAN AFRICA
A study of Hausa migrants in Yoruba towns
Abner Cohen

THE SAMBURU

A study of gerontocracy

Paul Spencer

Routledge
Taylor & Francis Group

LONDON AND NEW YORK

First published 1965 by Routledge & Kegan Paul

This edition first published 2004
by Routledge
11 New Fetter Lane, London EC4P 4EE

Simultaneously published in the USA and Canada
by Routledge
29 West 35th Street, New York, NY 10001

Routledge is an imprint of the Taylor & Francis Group

British Library Cataloguing in Publication Data
A catalogue record for this book is available from the British Library

Library of Congress Cataloging in Publication Data
Spencer, Paul, 1932–
The Samburu : a study of gerontocracy / Paul Spencer ;
[with a new preface by Paul Spencer].
p. cm.
"First published 1965 by Routledge and Kegan Paul"–T.p. verso.
Includes bibliographical references and index.
ISBN 0–415–31725–8
1. Samburu (African people) – Social conditions. 2. Samburu (African
people) – Kinship. 3. Samburu (African people) – Marriage customs
and rites. 4. Aged – Kenya – Samburu District – Social conditions.
5. Gerontocracy – Kenya – Samburu District. 6. Samburu District
(Kenya) – Social life and customs.
GN492.1 .S6 2004
306/.089/965 21   2003046999

ISBN 0–415–31725–8

TO MY PARENTS
BROTHERS AND SISTERS

CONTENTS

Contents

ix

ILLUSTRATIONS

TABLES

PREFACE TO NEW EDITION

The Samburu was first published in 1965 and this new edition is linked to a reprint of *The Maasai of Matapato* (1988) by Routledge and the publication of a further volume on the Maasai entitled *Time, Space, and the Unknown* (2004). These follow in a logical sequence to form a set of three works that span my involvement in this area.

When I first started along this track, there had been an upsurge of interest in the age-based pastoral societies of East Africa. Anthropological studies on this topic were few, and each newcomer was expected to seek out an unclaimed group – a tribe – as uncharted territory. In 1957, I was at the tail-end of this trend and had at first proposed to study the Maasai, only to find that there were already two other social anthropologists in the area: Alan Jacobs among the Maasai proper and Philip Gulliver among the Arusha, both in Tanzania. This led me to turn my attention to the Samburu of Kenya, where the field was quite empty.

The Samburu were the most northern group of nomadic pastoralists within the Maa-speaking cluster. In effect, they could be regarded as up-country cousins of the Maasai proper, sharing traditions of joint ancestry and just managing to survive into colonial times over a period when the Maasai dominated the plains further south. The Samburu were an idyllic society for an anthropological novice and this switch in focus from the political centre of this group to the periphery was a stroke of good fortune. The literature on this area was fragmentary compared with the Maasai, present-ing an open pasture for research, and, as it turned out, an altogether less elaborate and confusing set of practices.

The present volume focuses on the Samburu age system as a geronto-cracy. A number of people – including some well-seasoned colleagues – have suggested that it is a book about old men; and I have been tempted to con-gratulate them for getting as far as the subtitle. Some reviews even substi-tuted the term 'gerontology' in the title. The point to stress is that this work is not primarily about old or middle-aged men, but about young men who are trapped in the vacuum created by a gerontocratic regime, where their alterna-tive lifestyle has a mesmerizing quality. It concerns the social construction of adolescence. Age systems structure the politics of ageing, and the Samburu provided a particularly well-defined version. The Maasai system had some gerontocratic aspects, as I later found, but the power of the *moran* (or warriors) in carving their own independent arena and the problems of senior age-sets declining into old age suggested that 'gerontocracy' was not quite the right label to summarize my later volumes on the Maasai.

I wrote this study when I was still fresh from an extended period among the Samburu, aware that they had given me every opportunity I could wish for and an unrepeatable experience. The text went through numerous drafts before I was rescued by a structure that seemed to do justice to my material (a habit that persists). Apart from correcting some obvious errors, I have left this text as it stands. I was enchanted by the Samburu, like so many others who have had dealings with them. There was a charm in their manner that seemed to stem from the warmth of their community life. But this involvement also raised some awkward contradictions. Readers of this work may note the odd contrast between the initial pages, where I expressed my affection for the Samburu, and later chapters where I exposed my ambivalence over the brutality of arranged marriages between older men and barely mature girls. On the one hand, this practice was a fundamental premise from the outset of a study that aimed to convey a total way of life, and no self-evident part of this could be ignored or expunged. On the other hand, my attachment to the Samburu as a people managed to gloss over this issue. The resolution was to aim at a morally neutral account that sought to learn from the Samburu experience rather than defend it. But the deeper my involvement with them, the more uncomfortable the moral dilemmas. My case study of one of these marriages, where I had been drawn to play a symbolic role, was a critical experience. It added so much to my understanding of family and gender relations for the sake of my study, but at the cost of colluding with a practice that I abhorred for its gross unfairness. Again, there was a discrepancy between my assertion at the end of this work, that the Samburu could contemplate no alternative to their way of life, and my sense that everything would change when Kenya achieved its independence in 1963, adding to the urgency of this study and the need to break the spell it held over me. The tortuous process of writing this volume raised these contradictory aspects and much more besides. It was time to place the Samburu as I had experienced them on record for posterity. The moran of my age-set were at last moving on in a society to which they belonged, and I needed to do the same in order to give my career the chance of a new start.

I only returned to social anthropology in 1971 after a break of nine years, when I decided that the academic world seemed more promising than anything I could achieve elsewhere. The next six years were the most productive period of my career. Much of the substance of what I have been writing since then stems from this period. As a lecturer at the School of Oriental and African Studies in London, I had an opportunity to work among the

Maasai, where the field by now was wide open. It was my double fortune to have cut my teeth among the Samburu, where I had been drawn into a community from whom I learned the rudiments of the Maasai language and culture – and of fieldwork – and then to find a niche among Maasai studies – which was an altogether more crowded field. In this sense, my subsequent book on the Matapato Maasai followed directly from *The Samburu*.

The clearer structure of the Samburu age system provided a stepping stone towards a greater awareness of the more dominant Maasai edifice in Matapato. At the time of my fieldwork, age-set restrictions on initiation and marriage were rather more rigorous among the Samburu. The Maasai, by contrast, laid more stress on loyalty between age mates, and their moran were encouraged to display an excessive regard for accountability towards one another and to develop their debating skills. This led them towards the finesse of elderhood, which was characterized by these loyalties, provoking striking tensions between age-sets. By comparison, the Samburu moran in this volume are cast into a limbo for up to fourteen years, facilitating polygyny among the elders but also slipping too readily out of control. Once out of this limbo, their lifestyle as married elders appears more tranquil and mellow than in Matapato. These differences were matters of degree up to a point, but generally there was a greater elaboration and variety in the Maasai age system, and I would have found this too complex as an initial study.

The Samburu also have a place in the most recent book of this series, which addresses the Maasai perception of their universe and the wider pattern of variation. In the first place, aspects of Samburu cosmology are less opaque than among the Maasai; this requires some explanation and it also throws light on the Maasai system of beliefs. While the Samburu are generally less eloquent than the Maasai over a wide range of topics and their ritual behaviour is less elaborate, they are at least more explicit on metaphysical explanations associated with guardian spirits and the operation of the elders' curse. Second, the Samburu are characterized by strong clan loyalties and interclan rivalries. Gossip infects their conversation within each dispersed clan community, constantly updating news over a network stretching up to one hundred miles or more from end to end. Correspondingly, there is a general ignorance of and lack of interest in the affairs of neighbours of another clan. This contrasts with the Maasai, where local community relations cut across the bonds of clanship. However, there is evidence that the Maasai may have had stronger clan loyalties in the mid-nineteenth century, before they developed a more formidable warrior system. Partisan feeling among clansmen appears to have been undermined by adopting an overarching loyalty within each age-set as a basis for unity and military aggression. Transferring my attention to the Maasai gave an impression that the Samburu were closer to an ancestral prototype of Maa social organization, when clans had been stronger and age-set loyalties weaker. This lay beyond the scope of my research, but the evidence was striking, especially taken alongside oral traditions and some of the earliest writings on the Maasai. From this point of view, the Masula of Mt Ngiro may be regarded as a sector of Samburu society that is closer to Maasai in various ways. In the present volume, I refer to them as 'Samburu-Dorobo' and describe how they conform less to 'Samburu' ideals: there is less concern for local clan unity and an easing of age-set restrictions on early initiation and marriage. It was only later that I realized that these are also Maasai characteristics. Revisits to the Samburu area in 1973 and 1976 indicated some exceptions to these age-based restrictions in areas affected by change, but the integrity of clanship remained strong. Since then, there has been substantial change in the grow-ing townships and on the Leroghi plateau. But in the vast barrenness of the low country, nomadic Samburu have continued to display the strong trad-itional features that are described here.

The third volume also explores another telling feature, which concerns an ox that a Samburu boy should slaughter for a feast after his initiation to become a moran. This ox is known as *loolbaa*, and I refer to the ceremony in the present work as the *ilmugit of the arrows*. This corresponds to the ox-feast that is mounted for each Samburu girl as the most critical part of her bridewealth when she is married; and regardless of sex, these feasts should be mounted for brothers and sisters in strict order of birth (pp. 87, 239). Turn-ing to the Maasai, a highly prestigious ox-feast bearing the same name – *loolbaa* – is performed much later in a man's career (and only after his older brothers). Similarly, the formal bridewealth is paid for a Maasai wife and a fine ox is slaughtered for a feast many years after her marriage (and again only after her older sisters). Historical evidence suggests that each of these ox-feasts may have previously been held at an earlier stage in the careers of Maasai men and women; and these practices now appear in the process of slipping into disuse, beyond the point of recovery with a mounting backlog of delay and unperformed ceremonies by older siblings (and parents). The Maasai do not suggest that they once staged these ox-feasts as early as the Samburu, where they follow initiation, but extrapolating the evidence backwards makes this a logical inference. The extended process of slippage suggests a cumulative decay in the ideals of family propriety and reputation among the Maasai, again linked to the erosion of bonds of clanship. In other words, this slippage could be one more side-effect of the uncompromising constraints that were imposed on the Maasai age system during the nine-teenth century. It is the Samburu evidence above all that suggests a historical dimension to these trends.

The study of age systems has had a chequered career in social anthro-pology. It has appealed to those who have encountered it – mostly in East Africa – but has barely touched the subject as a theoretical topic. A second-ary theme that I consider in this volume concerns the exploitation of women, which I noted above. Audrey Richards's *Chisungu* (1956) could be read as a pioneering study of the dignity and confidence that the ordeal of initiation bestows on a girl around the time of her marriage. However, this did not prepare me for the stark experience of Samburu girls facing arranged marriages to men who were up to four times their age. Since that time, gender and concern over the status of women, ranging from their exploitation to their inviolability, has grown into a major topic in the anthropological literature. Whereas ageing, as a further dimension of universal experience, remains in the doldrums, and the structuring of this experience through age systems arouses even less interest: it is widely regarded as esoteric and quaint rather than challenging. If bringing these three volumes together raises awareness of the topic of age organization, then it will have served a useful purpose.

'The Survey' that is cited in these pages was subsequently published in an abridged form as *Nomads in Alliance* (1973). My fascination with the dancing of moran (pp. 120–7) led me to elaborate on this theme and to edit a volume entitled *Society and the Dance* (1985). There are also several unpublished pieces that I would willingly offer to any reader on request. Foremost among these is a census that I compiled for Pardopa clan, involving over 600 adult males and their wives (pp. 318–19). The structuring of this genealogy by age has enabled me to use it for further exercises, extrapolating to the Maasai (*The Maasai of Matapato*: 178) and further afield (1998, *The Pastoral Continuum*: 105). Clearly, this material could have relevance for other researchers who require raw demographic data to feed into simulations for societies of this kind, where adequate material is sparse, polygyny is high, and age is a crucial variable. I can also offer copies of earlier papers on the 'Dynamics of Samburu Religion' (p. 185), and on 'Samburu Notions of Health and Disease and their Relationship to Inner Cleanliness' (pp. 269–70).

In addition to all those to whom I have expressed my thanks in these pages, I should add Edmund Leach, who first suggested that I might consider the topic of age systems in East Africa for my research; Jack Trevor, who then steered me towards the Maasai and gave me a priceless first-edition copy of Merker's *Die Masai*; and Alan Jacobs, who encouraged me to turn to the Samburu instead. Since then, my career has led me to consider each of these subjects, though in reverse order. For this new edition of *The Samburu*, I am grateful to Benet Spencer for the new cover design and to Julene Knox, who was the commissioning editor for anthropology and religion at Routledge when I first submitted my latest typescript for publication. It was Julene's suggestion that these three works should be published as a trilogy, bringing the various strands together to form a coherent series. This was wholly unexpected and a long way beyond the horizon of my ambitions, and I owe a special debt of gratitude to her for this idea.

Paul Spencer
2003

Bibliography

Merker, M., 1904, *Die Masai: Ethnographische Monographie eines ostafrikanischen Semitenvolkes*, Berlin: Dietrich Reimer (Ernst Vohsen).

Richards, A.I., 1956, *Chisungu: a girl's initiation ceremony in Northern Rhodesia*, London: Faber and Faber.

Spencer, P., 1965, *The Samburu: a study of gerontocracy*, London: Routledge and Kegan Paul.

—— 1973, *Nomads in Alliance: symbiosis and growth among the Rendille and Samburu*, London: Oxford University Press.

—— (ed.) 1985, *Society and the Dance: the social anthropology of process and performance*, Cambridge: Cambridge University Press.

—— 1988, *The Maasai of Matapato: a study of rituals of rebellion*, Manchester: Manchester University Press on behalf of the International African Institute (reprinted 2004, London: Routledge).

—— 1998, *The Pastoral Continuum: the marginalization of tradition in East Africa*, Oxford: Clarendon Press.

—— 2004, *Time, Space, and the Unknown: Maasai configurations of power and providence*, London: Routledge.

ACKNOWLEDGEMENTS

THIS study would never have been possible without the help and good-will of a large number of people. This is a welcome opportunity to express my warmest thanks.

The research was initially made possible through my being awarded the William Wyse Studentship by Trinity College, Cambridge: this financed a preparatory year at Oxford and my first two years in East Africa. It was supplemented by a research grant from the Colonial Social Science Research Council, and a travel grant from the British Council. My third year was covered by a research grant from the Emslie Horniman Anthropological Scholarship Fund. Two final years were spent mostly at Oxford in preparing a report for the Kenya Government and writing a thesis for a D.Phil. degree; these were made possible by a State Studentship from the Ministry of Education.

Throughout my stay among the Samburu, members of the Administration and of other Government Departments showed a great willingness to help me in every conceivable way. Mr. C. P. Chenevix Trench, as District Commissioner for Maralal District during the greater part of my stay, gave me every assistance and suggested certain lines of research which proved both interesting and invaluable for my study. During the early days of my field work, in particular, I owed much to the help and hospitality of Mr. David Lambert, and Mr. and Mrs. Tom Powell at Wamba, and of Mr. and Mrs. Gerard Prior at Isiolo. While staying among the Samburu I had no permanent base, and my greatest personal debt is to Mr. Robert Chambers who offered me unlimited hospitality at Maralal, and whose immense enthusiasm for the Samburu gave an increased stimulus for my work. Many of the points treated in this study were first discussed in embryonic form with him. I must also thank Mr. A. M. daCruz, Mr. Leonard Waithaka and Mr. David Adams for their help in many small ways.

At Makerere College, Kampala, during two breaks in my field work, Professor Aidan Southall generously extended the facilities and accommodation provided by the East African Institute of Social Research. Here we discussed aspects of my work, and it was largely through his help that I was able to extend my field work to cover the Rendille. Dr. Gerry Shaper set up two medical research expeditions to the Samburu where we collaborated together. The second of these was a stroke of good fortune from my own point of view, as it enabled me to return to East Africa during the final phases of my writing up period at Oxford, and make up for the many omissions of my earlier field work which had by then come to light. Dr. John Lock showed an interest in Samburu herbal lore, and I am grateful to be able to quote some of his findings in Chapter Nine of the present study.

Writing a work of this kind, knowing just where to start and what to include is inevitably a formidable task, especially after several years away from a purely academic environment. I was guided during my two final years at Oxford by my supervisor, Professor Evans-Pritchard whose work among the Nuer remains the first and foremost study of pastoral peoples. I also owe much to the many informal discussions I had at this time with members of the staff and students at the Institute of Social Anthropology at Oxford. In publishing my thesis in its present form, I have taken careful note of the points raised by my examiners, Dr. John Beattie and Dr. E. L. Peters, and by Dr. John Middleton who read the manuscript on behalf of the present publishers.

My work has been influenced by several writers. My debt to Professor A. N. Tucker is only implicit in these pages: he showed an early interest in my work, and armed with the Masai Grammar he had prepared in collaboration with Mr. J. Tompo Ole Mpaayei, it was possible to dispense with interpreters and an initial knowledge of Swahili from the very start; the exact value of this in terms of field-work time that was saved is inestimable. Dr. P. H. Gulliver has not only given me sound advice since my period of field work, his earlier work among the Turkana has also proved a stimulating model of pastoral life in this part of Kenya, and I constantly found myself using it as a comparison and contrast with my own work. During my field work, I was generally intrigued with the emphasis that the Samburu placed on their ceremonies and the anxiety verging at times on chaos and panic that they displayed during such occasions. Dr. W. W. Sargant's book, *Battle for the Mind*, provided a vital clue to appreciating these phenomena. Dr. Sargant has since visited the Samburu and has endorsed the general line of argument put forward in Chapter Nine of the present study with some helpful comments.

And finally, my greatest debt is to the Samburu themselves, not only for their co-operation in my work, but also for making what might have been an arduous period of my life into one of the most delightful ones I am ever likely to experience. Choosing a virtually unknown tribe for study is a risk many anthropologists have to take, but few can have been so fortunate in their blind choice as I was. From a purely academic point of view, theirs was a fascinating social system for any anthropologist to study; but my fascination inevitably covered all aspects of their society, and above all the people themselves: *they* demanded it. I was drawn compulsively into the society so that I became less of an outside observer, and more of a member subject to many of the pressures and frustrations of their daily lives as well as to the warmth and the charm of their community existence in that harsh environment. By adopting me into their numbers, Pardopa clan gave me insights that it may well have been impossible to obtain as an outsider. By accepting me as a member of the Kimaniki age-set at the time of change-over, and hence as a *moran* on the verge of elderhood, they opened the way for me to gain first-hand impressions of the two distinct worlds of the *moran* and of the elders. Friends that I made, particularly of my family and clan, appear pseudonymously in the pages of this study, and they were mainly responsible for my education, leaving me only with the problem of trying to convince myself afterwards that there were other ways of life besides the Samburu. While Africa to the south of us was in the throes of an industrial revolution struggling towards a golden age of the future, we were living – foolishly perhaps – in the golden age of the present. Time meant something quite different; and under this spell, three years of my life slipped past unnoticed.

If I am to single out any individuals for special thanks, they are Ledumen Lenaibor and his brother Letapawa who as camp

Acknowledgements

assistants at one time or another during my stay shepherded me from the time that I was hesitatingly trying to find my feet to moments when I was in danger of losing my head. Even if a private retreat was never a really practical proposition when living among the Samburu, a well-organized camp to lean back on was essential, especially when there were guests to be looked after or a move to be made. In entering fully into the spirit of our rather odd assignment, these two were in many ways my closest friends.

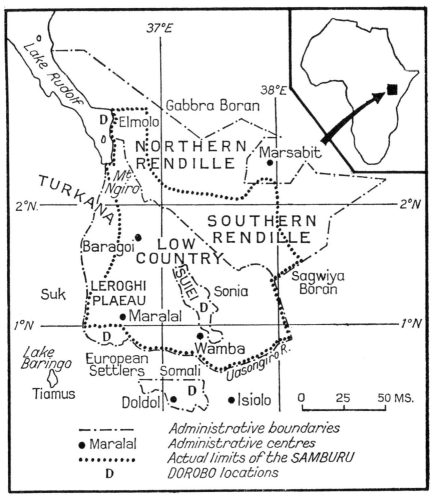

Map of the Samburu District, with Neighbouring Tribes Referred to in the Text.

INTRODUCTION

IN their language and culture, the Samburu are very similar
to the Masai. In fact, it is commonly accepted by both Africans
and Europeans that they are a branch of the Masai people and
were originally of the same stock. This popular tradition
should not be taken too seriously in view of the extent to which
intermarriage and intermigration have taken place between
the tribes of this area for countless centuries; but it does
underline their similarities.

In other respects, the two tribes are rather different, especially
when considering their social systems and recent histories. The
legend which has grown up around the Masai concerning their
aggressive and domineering behaviour towards other tribes,
especially during the nineteenth century, has not been extended
to the Samburu. There seem to be a number of reasons for this.
In the first place, the legend was partly inspired by the audacious raids of the Masai against the less warlike agricultural
tribes along the East African coast where Europeans first heard
of them; whereas the Samburu, who lived farther inland and
to the north, were surrounded by other pastoral nomadic
tribes who were all belligerent in character; the Boran and the
Turkana, in particular, were formidable enemies with whom
they had to contend. Secondly, the first contact which Europeans made with the Samburu occurred at a time when they
had lost almost all their cattle in an epidemic in the 1880s
(probably rinderpest) and they were found scattered among
the surrounding tribes. Those who remained as pastoralists
associated closely with one of their oldest allies, the camel-
owning Rendille, took part in raids to rebuild their lost herds,
and carefully bred their sheep and goats in order to exchange
them for cattle with other tribes. The oldest living Samburu
still remember this period and refer to the epidemic as *The
Disaster* (*e-mutai*); they look back to it with disgust in contrast to

their history earlier in the nineteenth century when they claim to have captured Mount Ngiro and Mount Kulal from the Boran and Mount Marsabit from the Laikipiak Masai – a powerful tribe who were later routed and scattered by the Ilpurko Masai. And thirdly, the Samburu did not have a military organization comparable with that of the Masai. The arid regions in which they lived could not support 'manyattas', or warrior villages, containing some 3,000 warriors as reported by Thomson for the Laikipiak and other Masai;[1] the *laibonok* (diviners) who appear to have had considerable influence among the Masai in organizing inter-tribal warfare were viewed by the Samburu with distrust and those that lived among them at the end of the last century had only a moderate influence. Living survivors of this era are generally proud of their own achievements in a difficult time when the very existence of the Samburu as a tribe was threatened; but they did this, they say, without substantial help from their *laibonok* who gave inconsistent and bad advice and never had the power to initiate important raids.

It was a critical time for the Samburu. After The Disaster in the 1880s there was a smallpox epidemic in the 1890s. Their enemies to the north were now getting some firearms from Abyssinia; as a result, the Turkana were becoming an increasing menace in the north-west and a series of raids against the Boran in the north-east ended in serious defeats for the Samburu. The fighting strength of the tribe was low: too low to defend the herds they were trying to build up. The appearance of the British from the south at this time was an undisguised piece of good fortune. The Samburu needed protection and the British were prepared to give it. In 1914 they were moved south from Marsabit after they had asked for protection from Boran raiders, and in the same year they joined a British army punitive expedition against the Turkana as levies and made this an opportunity to regain lost cattle and land.

After this initial help, the new British colonial administration experienced all the difficulties of trying to govern a nomadic tribe that had no indigenous chiefs worthy of the name and was dispersed over the arid wastes of northern Kenya. Few people

[1] Thomson, 1885, p. 347.

who knew the Samburu doubted their loyalty and their general desire that the British should remain and continue to be their allies, but for years it seemed impossible to introduce any improvements to the area under the banner of 'progress'. Practically all the Government appointed chiefs were either disloyal to the administration or uninfluential among their own followers. The Samburu asked for nothing more than a *laissez faire* policy to be adopted towards them; and apart from the punishment of periodic disturbances and the curbing of the needless murders committed by the young men it looked for several decades as though they would have their own way.

The partial ending of this state of affairs after the second world war probably owes more to the development of the Land-Rover, a motor vehicle capable of traversing rough country, than to any other single factor. Between 1950 and 1956 the first grazing scheme in the district was successfully installed on the Leroghi Plateau in order to recover land that had been devastated by years of over-grazing. This covered nearly 8% of the 8,000 square miles of the administrative district of Samburu. So rapid was the spread of these schemes that by 1960 26% of the district area was under strict control and plans for further schemes were being laid. At this point, the recent drought which had affected the whole of Kenya made it necessary to modify the strict principles on which these schemes had been run, and in 1961, by the wish of the tribal elders, they were abandoned altogether and the only control that remained was over certain areas which were closed to grazing until they were needed.

The period during which I carried out my twenty-seven months of field work between November 1957 and July 1960 was one in which the administration's policy was focused on imposing new grazing schemes against the general will of the Samburu people. But I would stress that one of the most important reasons for the quick success of these schemes which allowed for their rapid expansion to new areas was that the immediate change for the Samburu was only superficial. Apart from a phase of the Leroghi scheme from about 1956 to 1959, the Samburu were not unnecessarily restricted in their movements or their way of life. Any scheme which aimed at modifying their habits could have been successfully carried out only at the risk of considerable expense and friction.

Strictly speaking, they are no longer a non-centralized society: the imposed system of administration interferes in any matters which come to its notice and are thought not to be in the best interests of all concerned. It effectively maintains a somewhat uneasy peace between formerly hostile tribes such as the Samburu and the Turkana or the Samburu and the Boran, and it interposes in any serious affray within the tribe itself. Reported stock thefts and murders are investigated, new laws against killing game, damaging forests and grazing cattle in forbidden areas are introduced and where possible enforced. Taxes have to be paid, certain numbers of cattle sold through official channels, and until recently new areas have been converted into regulated grazing schemes. The Samburu are under an imposed system of administration which, though it lacks the means of being highly efficient, has nevertheless altered the lives of the people considerably and has taken over ultimate responsibility for what might otherwise be serious and recurrent problems for the Samburu themselves.

Yet, as should become evident in the course of this study, the Samburu appear to rely on the administration only to a very limited extent in managing their own affairs and this draws attention to their own indigenous system. While undertaking field work, I was constantly aware of the presence of the administration, but it was at the same time quite possible to almost ignore its existence when collecting case material: it seemed to belong to another world. It was the elders who among themselves decided their own courses of action, and government innovations impinged on the society in much the same way that some ecological change would impinge: it was accepted almost as an incontrovertible fact and the social system adjusted itself accordingly. My main interest of research therefore turned to the indigenous system to which the Samburu themselves subscribed and not to the total political system which would inevitably include these extraneous factors.

Perhaps one of the first occasions when the Samburu have learnt that government innovations are not necessarily incontrovertible facts was when they were empowered in 1961 to retain or abolish the grazing schemes. They chose to abolish them. When I revisited them at the very end of the year, far from regarding the drought they had suffered as a second Disaster, they regarded it as accompanying one of their greatest moments of triumph in recent years: a definite step towards a return to their traditional way of life.

This occurred only two years before Kenya became independent and administration of the Samburu passed from the hands of the British Colonial Office to the Kenya Government. Thus, when Kenya was on the verge of becoming an emergent nation, the Samburu were very definitely non-emergent. It is for this reason that, even though my last visit was before independence, I have confidently kept this study in the present tense. I find it inconceivable that the people I describe in these pages can change substantially in the foreseeable future; while all evidence suggests that the changes taking place elsewhere in Kenya will continue to bypass them for many years to come, and may even encourage them to take several more steps in the direction of a return to tradition.

This tenacity of the Samburu to tradition is a theme which is considered throughout this work. A striking aspect of it is the *moran*. The *moran* (s. *lmurani*, pl. *lmuran*) are the young unmarried men who would at one time have been the warriors of the tribe. Why is it, Europeans keep asking, that they still wear their traditional apparel and observe their traditional customs? Are they an anachronous relic of the past when the tribe really needed warriors? In the course of this study, I hope to answer these questions and to explain how it is that the *moran* have survived more than 40 years of comparative peace in the area and show no sign of abandoning these habits. But it would, I agree, be anachronous to call them warriors today, for apart from minor affrays and odd murders that occur from time to time they play no martial role in the society. I have therefore retained the popular East African term *moran* (singular and plural); for if they are less than warriors, they are at least more than just youths and they deserve close attention in this study. In fact, they are a very necessary part of the society as it is today, regardless of what it may have been in 1900.

In this study, I am primarily interested in analysing Samburu society as a gerontocracy, that is, as a society in which power is essentially in the hands of the older men. Such a society inevitably exhibits certain strains between young and old, and in the present instance these strains are largely contained within the age-set system, which is strong and restrictive. But in addition, the gerontocracy must be supported by appropriate social values, the ecological balance of the society must allow it, and other institutions must be related with it in some way. Polygamy, for instance, which is encouraged by the high regard for autonomy and economic independence among older men, can only be practised on a wide scale when the younger men, the *moran* in fact, are prevented from marrying; and the monopoly of the older men in marriage becomes another aspect of the gerontocratic situation as does the tendency for delinquent behaviour among the younger men.

In handling their affairs, there is one social value which embodies almost everything that the Samburu expect of a mature person. This value, *nkanyit*, acquires different shades of meaning in different contexts: it may be rendered variously as respect, a sense of shame, honour, a sense of duty, politeness, avoidance, or decency. The nearest English equivalent is perhaps *a sense of respect*. The Samburu repeatedly emphasize the virtues of this quality. It is a quality which many of their neighbours do not have: prominent among these are the Dorobo, the small tribes of Masai speakers who until recently lived by hunting and gathering. To the Samburu they are immature and behave like children. It is the proximity of such tribes which makes the Samburu keenly aware of their own individuality, and the contrast in values has to some extent hindered a closer social relationship from developing between them.

These particular problems became my chief topic of interest because the patrilineal clan in which I did most of my work, Pardopa clan, conformed so well with the Samburu ideas of corporateness, polygamy and *nkanyit*. But Pardopa clan was typical of less than a half of the Samburu clans, and in order to obtain a more balanced view of the whole society I had to carry out some field work among these other clans. I have left a discussion on the variations that occur between the Pardopa extreme on the one hand and a distinct inclination towards a

Dorobo extreme on the other until Chapter Ten. Here, I would only point out that while the description I give in this book is essentially one of Pardopa clan, it is broadly applicable to the Samburu as a whole, and the problems I discuss are shared to some extent by all sections of the society.

In writing the book, it seemed more logical to stress certain aspects of the society, such as the corporateness of the clan, the degree to which a stock owner is truly autonomous, the extent of polygamy, and friction involved in marriage, before giving an outline of the social structure. In this way, certain salient features of the society are stressed at the outset: the clan clearly emerges as more important than the other levels of segmentation, individual stock owners are seen to be largely dependent on one another, and the nature of Samburu marriage is discussed (Chapters One to Three). It is only when the discussion cannot be developed further without introducing the segmentary descent system and the age-set system that these are presented (Chapter Four). It is then possible to turn to the principal theme of this book which is the strains exhibited by a gerontocracy and its relationship to the various social institutions. This leads directly to a consideration of the *moran* on the one hand, and the elders on the other (Chapters Five to Seven). These are supplemented by a chapter on the status of women (Chapter Eight) and one on the function of ceremony (Chapter Nine). A comparative survey of some other tribes in the area (Chapter Ten) reinforces the main arguments of the book and serves also to reiterate them.

In the illustrations in the text, I have distinguished between incidents I actually witnessed (marked with two asterisks), other incidents that occurred during my period of field work (marked with one asterisk), and incidents that occurred before my visit to the area (no asterisks). The last of these three types are likely to be the least accurate; but in most cases I knew the main protagonists and was able to check with a number of reliable informants on details: the general consensus of opinion was on the whole fairly good, and I have avoided including examples where there appeared to be a serious discrepancy. In so far as there have been elaborations, these examples can still be regarded as statements of ideals and attitudes even if they are no longer strictly accurate on facts.

Unfortunately I was unable to collect material illustrating a single community over a period of time: the nomadic life of the society constantly brought different families into and out of contact, so that over the brief period of my field work, the development of a relationship between persons was not really a suitable subject for study. Moreover, if two people quarrelled then they generally moved apart and kept apart throughout the remainder of my stay. On the other hand, the problems and material I do discuss were ones which constantly absorbed the Samburu in their gossiping and discussions and reflect what were for them crucial issues in their society, and the clan rather than the community emerged as being more relevant.

The present use of the terms *phratry* and *clan* may conceivably give rise to some confusion and an introductory note on the differences between them should help prevent this. The Samburu have eight ideally exogamous patrilineal segments which I refer to as *phratries* (*lmarei*, pl. *lmareita*). Within these phratries there are 17 segments which I refer to as *clans*: ideally the *moran* of each clan perform certain ceremonies together to the exclusion of outsiders and form what I refer to as a *Club*. However, only four of the eight phratries are internally segmented into two or more clans, and in the other four the same social groups emerge both as phratries (in their practice of exogamy) and as clans (in their residential preferences and their *moran* Clubs). In short, the terms phratry and clan are used to refer to levels of segmentation which correspond to definite patterns of behaviour rather than to internal segmentary divisions; and in a general discussion of Samburu society, it is convenient to distinguish between them, in spite of the fact that for four phratries no such distinction exists.

It is also worth noting at this stage that although the segmentary descent system is a patrilineal one, members of any of the more inclusive segments do not normally extend the principle of patriliny to its logical extreme and assume that they are all ultimately descended from one ancestor. They may refer to each other as 'brothers' (*lalashe*, pl. *lalashera*), but they use this term in a very broad sense and frequently assert that they have a diverse ancestry. To any Samburu it is important that he was born into a particular social group and has been brought up to observe its customary obligations. But it is less important to know how this tradition arose, and any details of ancestry are not matters of intense interest so far as he is concerned.

For convenience in the text and easier reading, the term *kinsmen* (unless specifically qualified) has been used to refer to agnatic kinsmen, and the term *polygamy* has been used for polygyny. The constant emphasis on male descent and plural marriage among men should preclude any ambiguity which this usage might give rise to. The marked asymmetry in the relationship between a man and his affines has made it necessary to distinguish between his *wife-givers* (the kinsmen of his wife) and his *wife-receivers* (the husbands of his kinswomen). These terms refer to specific marriages, and are not intended to imply a permanent asymmetry based on a succession of marriages between the same social groups.

A more systematic account of the various customs and ceremonial observances of the tribe has been drafted as a report to be submitted to the Kenya Government, entitled 'A survey of the Samburu and Rendille tribes of Northern Kenya'. I refer to this in footnotes as *The Survey*, and details of the various chapter headings are given in the bibliography at the end of the book.

Chapter One

THE PASTORAL ECONOMY

THE Samburu live in an area of some 11,000 square miles between Lake Rudolf and the Uaso Ngiro river. The south-western region of this country is open savannah lying on a plateau, the Leroghi Plateau, which geographically at least is a part of the Kenya Highlands inhabited formerly by the Masai before it was taken over by European settlers earlier this century. Maralal, the administrative headquarters of 'Samburu District', is situated on this plateau. To the north and the east the land drops away sharply to less hospitable scrub desert with large patches of thick thorn bush and frequent rocky out-crops and it is here that most of the tribe live. This scrub desert, or low country as it is called, is broken up by intermittent hills and forested mountains. In the north-eastern parts of the country, conditions are rougher, water is scarcer and the land is strewn with lava boulders; here the Samburu live interspersed with their traditional allies, the Rendille, and they come under the administration in Marsabit. By the term Samburu, I understand all those who regard themselves as such – about 30,000 people – and not merely those who belong to the 'Samburu District' for administrative purposes.

The rainfall on the Leroghi Plateau is of the order of 20 inches a year, but in the low country it is probably less than 10 inches and is far more unpredictable: it is never certain when or where or if the rain will fall: occasionally there may be floods, but it is more usual for the wet season to fail completely leading to a serious drought in the area. When the rain does come, it is very often the wrong sort of rain: showers are generally heavy and only a fraction of the water falling may be regarded as effective rainfall: the remainder is not retained by the eroded soil and it rapidly flows out of the country taking more soil with it. Soil erosion and a general scarcity of water are the two harshest limitations affecting Samburu economy. The people themselves do not view these as problems which increase with the years as more top-soil is washed away and less water is retained, but as problems which have always been with them and which are to be accepted as basic features of their environment.

The rainfall and the condition of the soil do not allow the Samburu to practise any form of agriculture in the low country, and even on the plateau where they might conceivably attempt it, it is absent. They live mainly off the products of their herds, occasionally adding certain roots and barks to their soups, and occasionally selling stock at government sales and auctions in order to supplement their diet with small supplies of grain bought from the handful of shop owners in the district. The larger part of their money obtained at these sales, however, is spent in paying government fees, taxes and fines, and with what remains of it they also buy such luxury commodities as loin-cloths, blankets, tobacco, sugar, tea and beads.

Livestock

The livestock of the Samburu consist of cattle, small stock (sheep and goats) and donkeys. Of these, it is the cattle that give most in return for the time and energy put into their care. Sheep and goats are very useful for their meat at the height of the dry season when the cattle no longer give adequate supplies of milk. While the donkeys are only used as pack-animals.

On average each homestead has a herd of about 80 cattle (i.e. 11 or 12 per person). But the range is considerable: one herd in five is less than half this size, and one in 15 is more than double. The poorer homesteads must inevitably rely on the richer ones for some of their food, depending on the size of the family and the number of cattle actually in milk.

Milk is the main diet of the Samburu. Only when it becomes scarce in the dry season will blood taken from living cattle be added to it or stock be slaughtered for meat. This stock will normally be sheep or goats. Oxen are saved for ceremonial occasions or when the dry season absolutely demands a substantial supply of meat; they are regarded as the final security against severe drought. Any cow that dies naturally is eaten without delay.

The emphasis in social values is placed on cattle, at times almost to the exclusion of small stock. 'A man who has cattle is important,' they say. 'He can have many wives and many sons to look after his herds. When he wants small stock he can easily exchange an ox for many sheep or goats. But if he has only small stock, then he is like a Dorobo[1] and it is hard for him to become rich.'

Despite this emphasis on cattle, the combination of the two types of stock is a happy one. The low country, where dry seasons are harsher and small stock are more important for their meat, is also the area where they thrive best. On the whole, goats are better adapted than sheep because they prefer browse which is abundant in the low country, whereas sheep prefer grass which is scarce. At the same time sheep breed rather more quickly than goats and there are more of them.

Strangely enough, the cattle also thrive best in the lower more arid altitudes, partly because salt is more plentiful. Those living on the plateau suffered more in the drought of 1959 to 1961; and when it was over, they generally gave less milk and were in poorer condition than those in the hotter drier areas of the low country. Thus, while it is sometimes said that the Samburu lived in a harsher, dryer area than the Masai because they were a weaker tribe, unable to assert themselves enough to live on the rich pastures of the Kenya Highlands; it is also true to say that they are better adapted to the low country with the stock they have, and that in some ways this may have been a mixed blessing, helping them to survive The Disaster of the 1880s (and incidentally, the recent drought).

The breed of their cattle is generally known to Europeans as Boran, and it has – or has acquired – a high resistance to many of the diseases endemic in the area. Mortality among the Samburu herds is high at times; but this also means that the surviving cattle can be given more individual attention, that

[1] Dorobo: the poor tribes in the vicinity that have only recently begun to acquire cattle. See p. xxii.

3

there is more grass available per head, and that the hardiness of the breed is maintained and even improved by natural selection. With patience and skill, a man who has lost many of his cattle in this way can rebuild his herds over the years.

The economic and social value of having large numbers of cattle is unquestioningly accepted by most Samburu. It is this principle which determines their total number of stock and not the more sophisticated one put forward by the administration that controlled numbers of cattle and small stock would ultimately yield more milk, meat and (today) money. The Samburu argue that with large herds of cattle, they can afford to lose considerable numbers in a drought or an epidemic, whereas with small herds such losses could be catastrophic. They are very sensitive to their own poverty and to the slender margin which separates them from utter starvation. Compared with many other Kenya tribes, they may be rich, having in their stock a nourishing source of food and a valuable commodity for trade. Yet the severity of recurrent misfortune has left an indelible scar on the minds of most of them resulting in an inflexible attitude towards the problem. Between the years of 1939 and 1961, there was nothing that did more to impair the generally cordial relations between the Samburu and the British administration than the question of limiting the total number of stock and restricting grazing in certain areas. With the administration this control was a major issue of policy in order to reclaim the land and improve the quality of the herds. With the Samburu it was the main issue of resistance and non-co-operation. The drought of 1959 to 1961 did more to solve the problem of over-stocking than 20 years of spasmodic control by the administrators, *and* it left the Samburu more convinced than ever of the logic of their own point of view.

It is the present carrying capacity of the land, the endemic cattle diseases, and the limitations in Samburu techniques of cattle husbandry which control the sizes of their herds. If a stock owner has too small a family to be able to manage his stock adequately, or if he is personally too lazy then his herd will only increase gradually, if at all. If he has too large a family and allows his wife to take too much milk from the cattle to feed her own children, leaving too little milk for the calves,

4

then again his herd is likely to suffer and may actually decrease in size. It is the man who rates the well-being of his herd almost as highly as that of his own family who ultimately has the large herd, which in turn is the basis of negotiation for more wives and the foundation of a larger family. A point to be stressed in this chapter is that family and herd are essentially dependent on each other and have what may be described as a symbiotic relationship.

The Ownership of Land and Water

There is no explicit ownership of land among the Samburu. In theory any stock owner has a right to live with whom he pleases where he pleases. Certain areas may be associated with certain clans which are well represented there, but any person is free to migrate to these places: 'This is our land,' they say, 'it belongs to us all.' This ideal is modified only slightly in practice. If a man wishes to migrate to an area where he has not been before and where he has no close friends or kinsmen, then the other inhabitants will accept him without question provided that grazing is not too scarce. If it is scarce, but he approaches the other inhabitants first to put his case to them, then they can hardly object. It is only when he ignores such social conventions at the height of the dry season that his action is liable to lead to bad feeling. A man whose stock has certain contagious diseases should warn his neighbours and take care to restrict his cattle to certain tracts of land and water points, preferably not leading them through areas where others are likely to herd their own cattle.

In discussing the ownership of land, then, it is more relevant to speak of the duties the individual stock owner is expected to observe towards other local inhabitants, than of rights he can claim.

At certain places in many dried up river beds, water can be be obtained by digging a few feet. Such places are referred to here as *water points*, and the wells dug in the sand at these points are referred to as *water holes*.

By digging a water hole and maintaining it, a man exerts an explicit right to use it as he pleases. He can make any arrangement he likes to share it with another stock owner who waters his stock on different days and helps in its upkeep. Any casual user should try to get his permission before watering his stock, and if he misuses it a fierce quarrel and even fighting may ensue. On the other hand, a quarrel may also break out if the original digger of the hole tries to refuse permission. Examples of both types of quarrel are relevant to later chapters, and they show how even the work of digging a water hole does not give the digger exclusive rights of ownership; rather, it gives him certain privileges. Once the hole is neglected, perhaps after being fouled by a wild animal, or after it has been destroyed by a spate of the river, the spot is open to anyone who cares to start digging.

The Pattern of Nomadism

The Samburu live in small settlements which typically contain between four and ten stock owners, and their families and herds. A herd is taken to the water point daily in the wet season, every second day in the dry season, or even every third day in the really dry parts of the country; and then it is driven to areas which afford as good grazing as can be obtained. The spread of the settlements over a wide area ensures that all those herds which are centred on one water point compete as little as possible for grazing.

Each man manages his own cattle as he thinks best, although there may be some difference of opinion as to what is best. The grazing close to a water point is inevitably exhausted before other areas, and the stock owner must choose between living close to the water point so that his cattle can have water every day and living some distance from it so that they can exploit the less heavily grazed areas. Regular salt is an asset to cattle and essential to small stock, but again the salt licks have become the most heavily grazed parts of the country and the stock owner must decide for himself whether his cattle would benefit more if he lived near to the salt lick or in some other part of the country. At some point, when the area he is in has been exhausted of grazing, he must migrate and has to choose for himself which area he will move to.

6

The irregular and unpredictable rainfall results in migrations of large parts of the population in similarly irregular and unpredictable ways. Dispersed clusters of settlements form as people group and regroup themselves at various points over the countryside. An independent stock owner generally confines himself to certain areas and migratory tracts which he knows well. When possible he will move to a site close to the ones he previously used where he knows many of the advantages which the countryside has to offer: grasses, browse, water points, paths, dangerous places to be avoided and so on. His nomadic pattern is affected by the size of his herds and the labour force at his disposal. In theory the Samburu are free to move as they please; in practice their freedom is limited to several choices.

In so far as any broad pattern of nomadism is discernible for the tribe as a whole, it may be said that as the dry season advances, there is progressive migration towards those water points which have not yet dried up. And the settlements already around these points tend to move outwards in search of better grazing. With the onset of the rains there is a wider choice for nomadism and the population tends to disperse more evenly over the countryside.

In order to give greatest benefit to the stock, it is often advisable for the homestead to split seasonally into two, or very occasionally three, parts. Three herds which emerge from this division of the stock are the *flock* (of sheep and goats), the *subsistence herd* (of cattle) and the *surplus herd* (of cattle). The *subsistence herd* is a herd which is just sufficient to sustain the less active members of the family, especially old people and young children; this herd consists almost entirely of milch cattle. The remaining cattle form the *surplus herd,* and this is driven at certain times by some of the more active members to a more rigorous area where it is likely to benefit considerably. The *flock,* unless it too is taken to a separate area, generally remains in the same settlement as the subsistence herd.

A common arrangement is for the young males of the homestead (the moran and older boys) to look after the surplus herd and build a *camp,* a stock enclosure with no huts. The advantages of this arrangement are that those who live in the camp are physically active and the whole unit is mobile; in wet periods they can migrate to an area where a shower has just fallen and in dry periods they can put up with considerable hardship in order that the cattle shall benefit. It is inevitably in the rougher parts of the country farther away from the water points that good grazing is available for anyone willing to live there, and it takes the more energetic young men to exploit these under-grazed areas.

A settlement is less mobile. Moving entails considerable hard work for the women; old and sick people inevitably cause delays; and owing to the limitations of donkeys loaded with movable belongings, the distance a settlement can travel in one day is generally less than 15 miles. Some active women, unencumbered by small children, may also accompany the surplus herd and put up their huts converting what would otherwise have been a camp into a partial settlement. Mobility is inevitably impaired by this, but it is the course often adopted when the herd is divided.

By choosing different cattle at different times to go with the surplus herd, the stock owner can ensure that they all obtain adequate supplies of salt and equal chances of good grazing. Whether he chooses to live near a salt lick and to send his surplus herd away to the better grazing areas, or to live in the better grazing areas and send his surplus cattle to the salt lick periodically will largely depend on whether he has a large flock of small stock which require regular salt or not. Distant migrations towards permanent water points in the dry season and away from them in the wet season tend to involve cattle rather than people and camps rather than settlements.

The division of the herd in the dry season strains the available labour force to its extreme: there are two herds of cattle to be herded, watered, milked etc. The settlement with the subsistence herd does not move too far from the water point, and the cattle of this herd, often tended by a rather small boy, are not driven too far away. The future prosperity of the homestead ultimately depends on the surplus herd being well looked after during the dry season and it is as important not to waste valuable labour on the subsistence herd as it is to keep as many people as possible with the surplus herd, so long as their presence does not impair its mobility. While the more active males are run-

8

ning the camp, the stock owner generally spends most of his time with the settlement and uses his skill and experience to look after the subsistence herd. Because of the close interdependence between homesteads at such times, those who live together in one settlement during the dry season tend to have formed close bonds of friendship in the past and are frequently quite closely related. In the dry season there is a greater emphasis on the purely economic aspects of social life, ceremonial activity is rare, and only really pressing visits are made to distant parts of the country.

The individual stock owner may solve other problems in his own way. He may prefer sparser open country which makes herding easy, or he may prefer bushy country where he himself has to help his sons to protect the herd and look out for strays. He may prefer to keep his cattle in a heavily over-grazed area which is free of disease instead of feeding them elsewhere. He may prefer to belong to a larger settlement which will provide a fuller social life and a greater protection from wild animals, or a smaller one which will not exhaust the grazing close to the settlement so quickly and will make it easier for him to manage his own affairs without interference and to keep an eye on his wives. Until recently he could choose between belonging to a government controlled grazing scheme where certain of these problems were solved for him, and the freer though harder life of the uncontrolled areas: since 1961 these schemes have been abandoned and all Samburu have to fend for themselves. Rainfall, existing concentrations of population, local preferences, and also social factors influence his decisions when he may have a choice of four or five distinct salt licks and as many dry season pastures near at hand. He acts at each point so as to make optimum use of what exists and what is expected.

The Division of Labour

The homestead is the basic economic unit in the society. At times it may be divided between settlement and camp as described above; but when conditions are more favourable, the young men in the camps will bring the surplus herd back to join the rest and the family will be united again.

9

Children belong to the active labour force of the homestead from a very early age. Already by the time they are six years old they may be required to herd small stock and calves close to the settlement. Boys from the age of about 8 to 17 are given the task of herding the cattle, and girls and older people assist if necessary. Watering the cattle requires at least two people, one to control the herd and one to scoop the water from the hole into a trough. The second is arduous work and is undertaken by some older male. In this way, the boys are kept fresh for the day's herding which lies ahead. But there are other good reasons why responsible people should be present at the watering. One of these is that boys left to themselves cannot be trusted to respect the rules for using the water point correctly and they may get involved in a dispute. Another is that young and thirsty cattle sometimes become troublesome at the water point, and this is the right time to train them to keep under control. A well-disciplined herd can be watered quickly and then be taken without delay to a distant spot where there is good grass or browse. A badly disciplined herd wastes time at the water and straggles when being driven to graze; this increases the chances of losing animals through straying and it is more likely that the herd will return home hungry and give little milk. The secret of building up and maintaining a large herd is to train both the herd-boys and the herd to react to each other. A well-disciplined herd will keep together, and a well-trained herd-boy will keep it in hand, beating those animals that seem likely to stray and occasionally going ahead to look for good patches of grass and to watch for signs of dangerous wild beasts.

At first, when he has a family of his own, a man takes his sons with him herding cattle and teaches them the techniques of husbandry while making sure that the herd does not return home hungry. Later, when he can trust these sons to look after the herd competently and to hand their skill on to their younger brothers, he merely sees to the watering of the cattle. As he grows older, his role in the economic running of the homestead becomes still less active; but he continues to direct its herding and nomadic activities so long as he remains mentally active, and his broad experience is invaluable.

The daily tasks of the women are to milk the cattle in the morning and evening, and to fetch water as required. By using their donkeys it is possible for them to bring back enough water to last two or three days. When the settlement moves, on average about once every five weeks, each woman is responsible for moving her hut and rebuilding it. All the necessary movables, including hides, wooden containers and important struts in the framework of the hut, can normally be carried by two donkeys. Older women rely on their daughters, their younger co-wives, and their sons' wives for help in all these tasks.

The sizes of a homestead and its herd are limited by the symbiotic relationship between people and stock. Unless a family has a labour force of a certain size, with at least one adult male, one adult female, one fully grown boy and two smaller boys or girls, it must to some extent rely on other homesteads to help it out in its daily routine.

As the size of the herd increases, so do the problems of management. A herd with, say, 300 cattle cannot easily be well looked after: watering it may take up so much time that it has too little left for grazing; and when it does graze, it may exhaust each spot so quickly that it must be constantly driven in search of fresh pasture. Either of these shortcomings will affect its milk production at the end of the day.

Men with herds of this size normally solve the problem by dividing their stock into two separate herds with different wives and their families allocated to each half; so that what was one homestead now in effect becomes two, although there still is only one stock owner. In a split homestead of this kind, the two parts may migrate independently as the stock owner sees fit. In this way, the general mobility and ease of management of the herds is substantially raised. This is a permanent arrangement and is quite different from the seasonal split between settlement and camp.

A man who splits his herd in this way will generally have at least one fully grown son to help in the watering. On the other hand, if his wives tend to quarrel, he may decide to split his homestead prematurely in order to keep them at a greater distance from one another.

The Pastoral Economy

The Composition of the Homestead

In order to examine more closely the actual composition of various homesteads and the ways in which their members tend to be related to one another, it is first necessary to define a number of terms used here. The *stock owner* is the senior male of a *homestead* who directs its activities. Each married woman has her own hut in which she sleeps together with her husband and children. The area surrounding these huts where the cattle are kept at night is the *yard* (*mboo*); and by the yard there is an opening in the thorn fence surrounding the settlement which is the *gateway* (*oltim*, pl. *iltimito*): a stock owner's livestock are driven through his gateway when they leave the settlement in the morning and when they return in the evening, and it is closed at night.

A deep-rooted Samburu ideal is that each man should have his own herd and ultimately be able to manage it independently. Even a poor immigrant from another tribe is expected to try to achieve this. The inescapable fact that no Samburu can be entirely independent of his fellows, that to a large extent theirs is a collective economy in which each man must continually seek help from his neighbours does not weaken this ideal; but it does give an enhanced prestige for those who normally have enough surplus to be the givers rather than the receivers in this interdependence. Those who are forced to rely on the generosity of others would never admit to being scroungers and would still try to retain their social autonomy. Expressed in another way, this ideal is that a man should aim at increasing his herd and the size of the family he founds until it can form a homestead in its own right.

The tendency for men to assert their independence as they mature is reflected in the following tables. These are based on a survey carried out in 1958 of 66 Samburu settlements containing altogether 230 homesteads.[1] In analysing the compositions of these homesteads five types were discernible, representing typical stages in the development of the male as he attains independence from his brothers and builds up his own homestead. The five types were as follows:

[1] Details of how this survey was carried out and further notes on the tables are given in the appendix (pp. 317 and 322).

The Composition of the Homestead

A. Widows with young (uncircumcised) children.
B. Widows with adult (circumcised) unmarried sons.
C. Homesteads consisting jointly of a married elder and his unmarried brothers living in their mother's hut.
D. Married elders, their wives and children.
E. Split homesteads (as described in the previous section).

The first table shows how these types of homestead varied in size, as measured by the number of people in them:

Type of Homestead Related to Size

Number of persons within a homestead	Type of homestead					Total
	A	B	C	D	E	
0– 3·0	2	8	–	10	7	27
3·1– 6·0	6	8	–	52	15	81
6·1– 9·0	–	5	7	48	16	76
9·1–12·0	–	1	3	15	9	28
12·1–15·0	–	–	2	9	3	14
over 15	–	1	–	2	1	4
Total number of homesteads	8	23	12	136	51	230
Average number of persons per homestead	4·0	5·5	9·4	7·2	6·8	6·9

It is evident from this table that type A is generally smaller than average and this accounts for its uncommonness: widows are more often attached to the homestead of an elder. Type C, as a composite form of types B and D naturally tends to be rather large; that it does not occur very often indicates the extent to which married elders prefer to assert their independence from their brothers as soon as possible. Type D and type E are of comparable size, as might be expected: when the homestead of an elder reaches a certain size, he usually splits it. It will be seen that a considerable variation of size is possible: this is largely because ecological conditions do not determine too precisely the optimum size, and also because the larger homesteads have a high proportion of small infants that can easily be contained. The average number of huts to each homestead in the sample was 1·6.

13

The second table shows how a man's ability to build up his herd and attain independence increases with his age as measured by the age-set he belongs to:

Types of Homestead Related to Age of Stock Owner

Age-set and approximate age range of stock owners		Type of homestead					Total
		A	B	C	D	E	
Terito and							
Marikon	over 70 yrs.	–	–	–	7	14	21
Merisho	57–70 yrs.	–	–	–	21	18	39
Kiliako	42–57 yrs.	–	–	–	64	13	77
Mekuri	31–42 yrs.	–	1	11	35	6	53
Kimaniki	17–31 yrs.	–	22	1	9	–	32
uncircumcised – junior		8	–	–	–	–	8
Total		8	23	12	136	51	230

Ultimately, independence, a large herd and a large family are obtained through marrying several wives; and with this goes considerable prestige among the other elders. In the next table, the degree of polygamy of Samburu elders is compared with their age. Column I shows the average number of wives of all the elders recorded in the survey. It will be seen that those men who live to a really old age (i.e. members of the Terito and Marikon age-sets) tend to have *fewer* wives than, for instance, the Merisho age-set, since their wives now begin to predecease them and they stop taking on new wives when their sons begin to marry. On the other hand, these sons frequently remain in the homestead of the father and their wives are effectively women belonging to his, *the father's*, homestead, even though they are not his actual wives. Column II shows the corrected figure giving the effective number of wives (excluding widows and stray women) and this demonstrates clearly how these increase in number with the age of the stock owner.

However, in these instances where a married man is living in his father's homestead, it is often he who directs its affairs, either because the father is staying elsewhere in another of his homesteads, or because he is a very old man and has allowed this son to take over these responsibilities. When the father

Numbers of Wives Associated with Age of Stock Owner

Age-set and approximate age range of stock owners		Column I Average number of actual wives	Column II Average number of effective wives
Terito and Marikon	over 70 yrs.	1·65	2·30
Merisho	57–70 yrs.	2·04	2·16
Kiliako	42–57 yrs.	1·56	1·56
Mekuri	31–42 yrs.	1·19	1·06
Kimaniki	17–31 yrs.	0·10	0·07

dies the homestead would automatically become of type C or D with the married son as the stock owner. But until then, it is nominally the father's homestead and his intervention into any of its affairs should not be disputed.

The Settlement

The settlement is another well-defined social unit. It consists of a collection of homesteads arranged in a crude circle. In their day to day dependence on one another, stock owners inevitably rely on other members of their settlement. Other things being equal, a man has the strongest claim for support with his closest kinsmen. In the 230 homesteads of the previous sample, the closest relationships within the settlement were as follows:[1]

Closest Degrees of Kinship between Families of a Settlement

1. Another homestead of the same elder
   (i.e. a split homestead)   22   (10%)
2. A closely related kinsman   71   (31%)
   (living father   9)
   (independent son   7)
   (full brother   42)
   (half brother   13)

[1] For purposes of analysis, the homesteads with no adult males (type A above) were classified as if the father was still alive. Terms used in this table such as linked clans, phratries and clan-associates are defined later.

3. A man associated with the same clan   84 (36%)
    (of the same sub-clan 47)
    (of the same clan   31)
    (clansman and clan-
       associate   6)
4. An affinal kinsman   28 (12%)
    (a wife's kinsman   18)
    (a close kinswoman's
      husband   10)
5. A distant kinsman   9 (4%)
    (of the same phratry 5)
    (of a linked clan   2)
    (of the mother's clan 2)
6. Others   16 (7%)
    (no apparent relation-
      ship   7)
    (no other homesteads
      in settlement   9)

                       —
                    230
                       —

    Membership of a common age-set may also encourage men to live together. Of the 209 stock owners in the sample who shared residence with others: 94 (45%) were also age mates of their closest relatives: a further 42 (20%) had age mates present in the same settlement; and 11 more (5%) had adult dependents (sons or unmarried brothers) who had age mates there. Such ties through age-set system are significant, but in the matter of sharing residence they are not as important or persistent as ties involving kinship.

    These associations in one settlement are in a continual state of flux. Men living with their brothers at one time may be living with their affines or other members of their clan at another time. Only the most general statements can be made concerning the pattern of residence: that a man who is living with an affine will probably return to his own clan very shortly; that a man living with his own brother will probably do so at intervals throughout his life. Rivalry over cattle and the need to remain in small mobile units tend to separate kinsmen, but warm friendships do sometimes develop between brothers which encourage them to live together. There is absolutely no indication in these figures to suggest that it is normal for brothers or close kinsmen to live together or apart at any stage of their lives. A man frequently lives with his father if he has one: of 24 elders in the sample whose fathers were alive, 12 were still members of their father's homestead, nine lived in the same settlement but had homesteads of their own, while three were living in some other settlement.

The following settlement has been chosen for illustration as fairly typical in its composition and internal relationships. (See map and kinship diagram on page 18):

Letuluai lived in a settlement with three other stock owners. Two of them, Lekiso and Loyan, were members of his clan, while the third, Keneti, was his half brother's brother-in-law who was hoping to beg some stock from him. Letuluai and Lekiso were the only two members of the settlement who regularly lived together. This was at the height of the dry season and only Letuluai had most of his stock here (note his larger yard in the map); Loyan's cattle were mostly with his junior wife, whom he visited several times, some 15 miles away; and the other elders had surplus herds in camps elsewhere. As the map also shows, each homestead had its own enclosures for calves, small stock and donkeys in the centre of the settlement. Because Letuluai's wives tended to quarrel over the stock allotted to each of them, he made them keep these stock in separate enclosures; but he had not actually split his homestead.

The settlement was joined unexpectedly by Partuala, a daughter of Letuluai's clan who had run away from her husband and wanted to live with her brother. While she was seeking refuge and waiting for him to come and fetch her, she built her hut in Lekiso's yard and depended on him for support.

After the settlement had been at this spot for four weeks, the browse became exhausted and it was necessary to move. And after two further moves in two months, each of the stock owners was living in a different settlement: Lekiso was with his brother about a mile away from Letuluai's settlement; Keneti had returned disappointed to his own clan without any gifts from Letuluai; and Loyan had moved in another direction after his wife had quarrelled with one of Lekiso's wives.

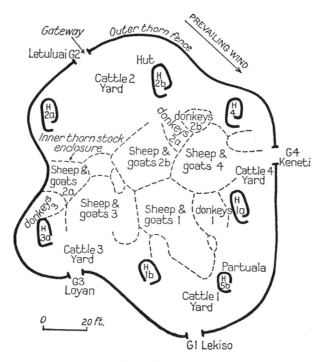

Map of Settlement.

Map and Kinship Diagram of Lekiso's Settlement.

This settlement has been chosen as a typical one in size and composition. Many aspects of the settlement and hut layout are stereotyped and may be seen anywhere in the country. Thus, in each homestead, the senior wife builds her hut to the extreme right and each wife in order builds to her left; if she is a very old woman relying on much younger ones (often her own daughters-in-law) then she may build her hut more towards the centre of the settlement. In ceremonial settlements (see map on page 92), the basic layout of each homestead is essentially the same. The layout of the hut is in many respects invariable: there are always two halves; the first is the hearth (*lturin*) next to the entrance in which there is a fire-place, and the second is the sleeping part (*ruat*) covered by hides and raised slightly off the ground. Older women build their own personal sleeping place, generally on the far side of the fire-place, and this leaves the sleeping part free for use by her children and their peers. On the Leroghi Plateau where there is less migration and the climate is colder, huts tend to be more solidly built and have more compartments; cowdung is used to protect them from the weather instead of hides and mats which are used in the low country.

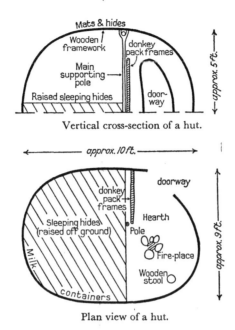

Vertical cross-section of a hut.

Plan view of a hut.

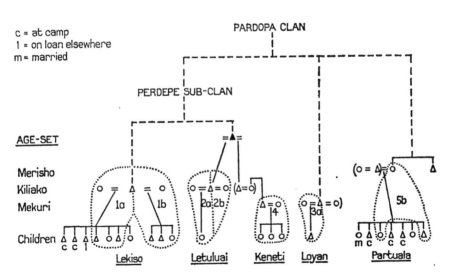

Diagram of Settlement.

As the kinship diagram shows, only Lekiso had enough children to maintain a surplus and a subsistence herd without relying on others for help; he had even lent out one of his sons to a clansman elsewhere. As matters stood, there were too few children in the settlement for herding, and it seemed inevitable that sooner or later these elders would have to disperse to settlements where there were more children.

Local conditions may affect the sizes of settlements. In parts of the country where wild beasts are a menace or where raids are expected from other tribes, settlements are generally large for safety. Conversely, where the ground is difficult and the distance that cattle can go to graze is limited, settlements have to be small and dispersed.[1] Apart from these restrictions, the Samburu may choose between larger settlements where social life is richer, and smaller settlements where the grass is less easily exhausted and where it is possible to remain on one spot for a longer time. Inevitably, the dry season favours smaller settlements.

The Local Clan Group

The map (on page 21) of a locality suggests a diffuse clustering of certain clans in that area, which corresponds in a broader sense to the clustering of clans in most settlements. This is typical of the whole country. The tendency for clansmen to associate together is even more marked and explicit in their behaviour, especially when they require help or have serious matters to discuss. The aggregate of all those members of one clan who live in one area at one time and share in these activities is referred to here as the *local clan group*, and the elders of this group as the *local clan elders*. The other settlements in the area associated with other clans may have their own local clan groups. There is generally less interaction between members of different clans.

---

[1] The following figures have been collected on settlement sizes: around Mount Ngiro (difficult country) – 2·9 homesteads; typical low country areas – 4·8 homesteads; dangerous low country areas – 9·0 homesteads. On the plateau around Maralal, settlements are often larger than 10 homesteads because of the easier conditions.

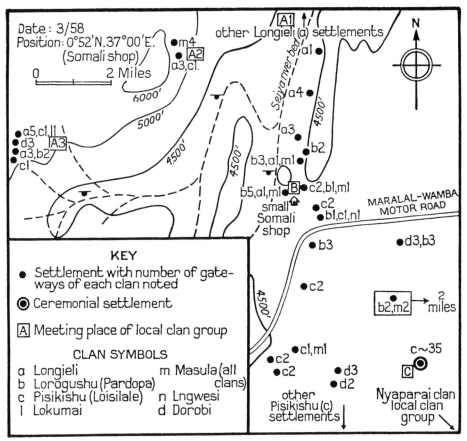

Distribution of Settlements in the Upper Seiya Area: March 1958.

Three clans were particularly well respresented in this area and formed three discernible local clan groups. Longieli clan (A) tended to be clustered in the north and members would frequently go to one of several places where they had members: these were Muru (A1 – off the map), Soito-ngiro (A2 – where a locally influential man and several others lived) and Lengoiro (A3 – where among others there were two very old and respected members of this clan). Pardopa clan (B) tended to be clustered around Lodungokwe where there was a small Somali-owned shop. Loisilale clan (C) tended to be concentrated in the south and frequently visited a ceremonial settlement built for their *moran* who were performing the *ilmugit of the bull* ceremony in this particular month. There were other Loisilale settlements further south. Masula phratry were present in considerable numbers, but they belonged to different clans which did not tend to associate as a group in this area, and there was no really evident local clan group. Another clan, Nyaparai were present in large numbers in an area about seven miles to the south-east of this map where they formed another local clan group.

21

A local clan group is also transitory. When there is a migration, it does not necessarily stay together; though individual members who move off on their own will normally join their clan in some other local group. This individual freedom encourages widespread communication between the members of the dispersed clan, balancing any tendency for it to segment into local clan groups. In addition, this communication is maintained by men's periodic visits to kinsmen living some distance from their normal paths of migration, by the occasional migration of a man to an entirely new tract, and, today, by the visit of many Samburu from over a wide area to government cattle sales held periodically at each of the administrative centres.

The dispersal of any clan is not entirely uniform; certain areas in particular are associated with it. Over the years it may migrate to new areas and develop new tracts. Thus a clan can be thought of as a continuous web of migratory paths along which at any time there are concentrations at various points: these are the local clan groups. In the course of seasonal migration along this web, local clan groups may disperse in several directions and form new local clan groups with other portions of the same clan. In this way, there is an almost continuous shuttling and changing pattern of interaction within the clan, and its corporateness triumphs over its dispersal.

Summary and Conclusion

The semi-desert conditions in which the Samburu live preclude any form of agriculture and make nomadism essential. This nomadism is not limited by any developed concept of land ownership, but by purely practical considerations and by the ideal that each man should achieve an autonomy in handling his own affairs even though it is unlikely that he will be able to attain complete economic independence. Settlements have to be small, and for one settlement to have exactly the same composition before and after migration is more the exception than the rule; on the other hand, for any two stock owners to belong to the same settlement before *and* after a migration is the rule rather than the exception. If two stock owners seek different areas or settlements at one migration, they are quite likely to come together in the future.

The salient points of this chapter which have considerable bearing on later chapters stem from the nature of livestock as a form of property. A herd of cattle may increase in size quite steadily or alternately decrease rapidly according to the care with which it is handled. It is important that the size of the homestead should be well adjusted to the size of the herd if it is to enjoy a measure of independence: there should be enough active people to tend the cattle properly, but not so many that the demand for milk would be harmful to the calves. It is rare that such an exact balance exists and neighbours must rely on one another for help so that, while it is ideal that each homestead should be a self-contained unit, it is more usual for it to be dependent on other homesteads of the settlement, and economically it is the settlement which emerges as a more self-contained unit. The necessity for this wider co-operation is increased by the unpredictable demand for hospitality by frequent visitors and the frequent absence of the stock owner or another member of his family engaged on some errand. Neighbouring families are essentially interdependent, and, as we shall see, this lack of real economic independence within the homestead is concurrent with a lack of social autonomy: to a significant extent each Samburu is answerable to others for his actions and in the final resort the running of his homestead is not solely his concern.

Another aspect of cattle as property which should be taken into consideration is the high value of each animal as a basic unit of exchange, gift or negotiation. A cow cannot be divided between a number of people except at a meat feast after which it ceases to have any tangible value. This means that those social relationships which are clustered around the ownership of cattle tend to be expressed in multiple and often diffuse rights which different persons can claim in certain beasts or in the whole herd, and inevitably all the hazards and bounties that accompany the stock economy affect the nature of these relationships. If Samburu society were oriented towards its small stock instead of towards its cattle, then it might be totally different from what it is: small stock are more expendable and they increase at a faster rate. At the same time, the marked orientation towards cattle has considerable economic justification; beyond this it must be accepted as one of the indisputable values of the society.

And finally, this is a nomadic society. Different people and sets of people are continually being brought into and out of face to face contact with one another. This is probably an important factor in maintaining the cultural homogeneity throughout the tribe. This kind of nomadism also constantly brings virtual strangers together, and their attitudes and behaviour towards one another are initially determined by their structural relationships regardless of any personal friendships or hostility that subsequently arise. In this context, then, formal relationships between social groups are particularly relevant. The two institutions which are especially striking in this respect are the segmentary division of the society into clans and the age-set system. The clan, which has been shown to be so prominent in residence choices, emerges as a social group which affords the individual a security and a means to fulfilling his ambitions, even although it inevitably restricts his freedom in other ways. The age-set system is related to certain strains that arise between old and young and is discussed in later chapters after a close analysis of the clan and family.

Chapter Two

CLANSHIP AND EXOGAMY

BY way of an introduction to Samburu clanship, more must be said of their social values in the context of the pastoral economy.

As compared with other forms of property, cattle herds are subject to unusually high and unpredictable rates of increase and decrease. Even under primitive conditions of management it is quite possible for a herd to double in size over five years. It is also possible that in the course of a stock epidemic, it will be reduced by more than one-half in a matter of months.

Because of the hazards he faces, a Samburu cannot afford to relax the careful watch over his herd even for a short period of time, for this may be sufficient to ruin the work of building it up over a number of years. The ability of different stock owners varies considerably. The size of one man's herd may remain constant because of the smallness of his labour force, because he tends to make serious errors of judgment or simply because he is lazy. He may just be able to maintain a herd of that size, but the extra labour and skill required to build up and maintain a larger herd are beyond him.

The success or failure of certain men in stock keeping is widely known. Kalasi, for instance, is well known for the substantial increase in his herd over the years. When he first married in about 1946 he had less than 30 cattle; but by 1959 they numbered more than 170. This was equivalent to an annual rate of increase of more than 14%.

Another case concerns the reversal of fortunes of two brothers, Nakuru and Dorian. Nakuru, the elder, was lazy and greedy; through neglect and slaughtering, he went through two herds of cattle, one inherited from his father and the other appropriated from a childless stepmother. At this time Dorian was in prison for trying to steal stock from a European ranch. When he was released, Dorian begged 10 head of cattle from some clansmen and herded these diligently. Within 20 years he had a herd of 100 cattle and two wives; while his elder brother Nakuru depended on him for support.

Kalasi and Dorian are well known as prudent men who have turned fortune in their favour; and Nakuru is a fool.

The ideal man who lives up to all expectations of the society is the *worthy man (lee, pl. lewa)*, and his opposite is the *mean man (laroi, pl. laron)*. The worthy man has a marked sense of respect *(nkanyit)* and he is generous to the point of self denial. But he is not expected to pursue his generosity to the extent of being unduly harsh on himself or his family, for this would be unreasonable. When there is a limit to his generosity towards his guests, he can always emphasize the reasonableness of his behaviour in the circumstances, just as the others normally emphasize the reasonableness of their requests. The social behaviour of most Samburu gave me the impression that they were acutely aware of public appraisal and constantly acted to maintain a pose of worthy men. Spontaneous generosity and respect were perhaps present to some extent in most men, but in public there seemed to be a slight exaggeration in behaviour where these were concerned. At meat feasts, for instance, younger men would insist on giving their seniors the best pieces of meat, and affines would be treated in a similar way. Even among age mates, whose equality was beyond question, there was a continual battle of politeness in which the man who seemed to eat the least and encourage his neighbours to eat the most was the moral victor, the truly worthy man.

The mean man is despised. He gives his own personal interests priority over what others consider to be his social obligations; no man would seriously admit to being mean. He would justify his behaviour as reasonable under the circumstances as would any worthy man; but he would fail to convince other people of his worthiness or good faith, and they would not be prepared to show good faith in their dealings with him. Where mean men are concerned, there is a shift in the limits of what is reasonable and worthy.

A mean man would tend to find that if he wished to accompany others in their nomadism then he could follow them, but they would be less prepared to follow him. In a discussion his

26

opinion would carry less weight. He would tend to be the last person to hear of some recent news or of a meat feast; but he would never be openly snubbed or denied an equal share.

Meanness is a favourite topic of the Samburu: only mean men do not care for their cattle; only mean men refuse to help their close kinsmen; and only mean men are jealous or curse out of sheer spite. The same term, *laroi*, is used of a coward or someone who lacks the determination to pull his weight in community life. It is extended whimsically to undersized or fragile objects: a cup that only holds a small amount of milk, a water bucket that leaks, a spear that shatters, or a Land-Rover that breaks down. It is the untrustworthy aspects of these that makes them a liability and gives rise to these not too serious allegations.

Stock Friends

Prudence and skill are not the only factors which affect the size of a man's herd. There is also an element of luck. Substantial loss through enemy raids (mainly in the past), confiscation (more recently) or epidemics may affect any man regardless of his skill. It is necessary for him to insure himself by developing a wide range of social ties so that he can rely on others more fortunate than himself in times of difficulty. Those who develop a relationship based on mutual help in times of need are referred to here as stock friends (s. *sotwa*, pl. *sotwatin*).

At first, a man turns quite naturally to his closest agnatic kin for support. He has formed his earliest social ties with them, and they are and remain his stock friends almost by definition. As he grows older, he looks further afield and turns to more distant clansmen for additional help. Again this is natural since he has certain vaguely defined rights in their stock. The interest he shows in their herds and they in his are a part of the diffuse sharing of stock and of fortunes within the clan. Only occasionally are stock friendships beyond the clan formed.

A stock friendship is formed when one man is given a beast by another: normally he will have to ask for it first.[1] In future,

[1] This is totally different from a debt (*sile*) between casual acquaintances, where the exact repayment is agreed upon at the time of the borrowing. The most common form of debt is the promise of a heifer in return for an immediate gift of a fat ox for slaughter. Obviously, for the creditor this is a very good investment.

either of them can turn to the other for support. Each Samburu can relate the gifts that have passed between him and each of his stock friends and the extent to which he feels he is on the whole the creditor or the debtor. If a stock friend proves to be mean, then his requests would be treated with diffidence and the relationship would dwindle. Whereas with a generous man, it would be strengthened by returned generosity.

A clear cut picture in which all worthy men have worthy stock friends and all mean men have none, is expressed by the Samburu in general terms. But it is only an approximation to the truth. There is a relativity about worthiness and meanness: a man is likely to be generous to some and unyielding to others; and they form different opinions of him. A wide consensus of opinion that he is worthy implies that his generosity almost knows no bounds, whereas a consensus of meanness implies that his generosity is severely limited. Few men are close to either extreme.

Again, different men have mean and worthy traits. Two such persons have already been mentioned. Kalasi, whose herds increased so rapidly, was generous, an indulgent host and an undemanding guest: in fact a worthy man. Yet others pointed out how reluctantly he gave away stock and this was mean: he had few stock friends. Or again, Nakuru, who lost all his herds through neglect and never offered to help his kinsmen, was seen as mean. And yet whenever he killed his stock, he was most generous in giving away meat, which was at least a worthy trait.

Apart from the prestige in being regarded as worthy, the Samburu recognize the long-term economic benefits: when a worthy man needs food, or stock or help with his herds, he can always expect these. In this way he is insured against exigencies and can more easily afford to continue to be generous and worthy. They clearly recognize that any increase in his wealth may be due to his sound economic policies.

They also see a religious significance in such reversals of fortune. Everyone blesses a worthy man and invokes God (*Nkai*) to bestow upon him large herds. Whereas they despise a mean man, and this, they say, amounts to an unvoiced curse bringing with it disaster.

28

The Clan and Marriage

Stock friendships are most common between members of the same clan. Clansmen are drawn together by their reliance on one another, by their shared good fortune in times of plenty and their shared hardship in times of want. To be members of the same clan, however dispersed, is to have an identity of interests.

Another aspect of this clan solidarity is the general exclusion of members of all other clans from its intimate affairs, and the mistrust, amounting at times to hostility, between clans. Members of other clans are *outsiders* (*leshing'a*); any man may form close personal ties with an outsider, but this is unlikely to happen between groups.

The bonds of clanship contrast strikingly with ties created through marriage. Strains which accompany marriage in all its phases from the initial proposals of a suitor to his later relationship with his affines inevitably cut across the social barriers surrounding each clan, as marriage within the clan is forbidden. Affines are outsiders; as affines they have rival claims in a man's stock, and as outsiders they may try to exploit these claims ruthlessly. Apart from certain extensions of clan exogamy discussed in Chapter Four, marriages between any two clans are numerous, and all outsiders are in a broad sense affines related by a web of close marital ties. Marriage among the Samburu implies conflicting interests; and exogamy is seen as protecting the basic unity of each clan.

The remainder of this chapter is concerned with the interests which different parties have in various aspects of any marriage and the extent to which they try to exploit their own positions. It is a topic which brings the relationships between clans and within each clan into sharp focus. In order to portray Samburu society more vividly at this stage, a considerable number of examples are used to illustrate the discussion.[1]

Marriage Negotiations

In contrast to the ties with fellow clansmen, the relationship

[1] In these examples, one asterisk indicates that at least a part of the incident occurred during my period of field work, and two asterisks that it occurred when I was an onlooker.

with a wife's clan is essentially asymmetrical to the general disadvantage of the husband. The initial gift of a wife is regarded as creating a debt which can never be entirely repaid. The bridewealth is accepted as an initial payment to be followed by an indefinite number of other gifts of stock; and behind their claims, a man's affines can always threaten to use their power to curse his children by this wife. In spite of the reciprocal term of address between them, *lautan*, the husband is never allowed to forget that he is the 'wife-receiver' and they the 'wife-givers'. A Samburu once told me that he had more respect for his affines than for any other people because they had given him his wife, implying that he was always under this obligation towards them. Tension which may exist between affines adds to and is reinforced by the general antipathy between clans.

In seeking a wife, a man may consult his own clansmen on the wisdom of his choice; they may be able to tell him something of the worthiness of the family he proposes to marry into. But in order to find out more about the qualities of the girl herself, her sense of respect, her morals and her skill in domestic duties, he may feel obliged to consult a kinswoman who has been married into the other clan and knows her, or a friend of that clan. He does this secretly before approaching the closer kinsmen of the girl with his request. There may be as many as ten of these whose consent he must obtain: these are elders of her father's lineage, often dispersed over a wide area. The suitor must take care to ask these men in an order and a manner which will offend none of them, and he may present them with small gifts of money, tobacco, tea, or even cloths and blankets. The elders will be non-committal at first and will tell the suitor to find out how their kinsmen regard the proposal: 'Tell them that I have heard (your request)' is the normal reply and is as close to positive support as he can hope to be given at this stage. Frequently he is accompanied by one of his own clansmen who acts as his spokesman or at least gives diplomatic support during this extended process.

In due course, it emerges that certain of the wife-givers support the suit and others oppose it. Ultimately, the decision to allow the marriage must be unanimous. Any elder who resolutely opposes it has an effective veto unless the suitor can persuade him with gifts and promises to change his mind. The various shades of opinion on the matter emerge in the discussions held by local clan groups of the wife-giving clan. Particularly important are the opinions of those elders who know something of the suitor, his family and background. They can give useful advice on the chance of the marriage being a success: a success, that is, in so far as it is likely to be lasting and profitable for the wife-givers. The more distant clansmen of the girl share a right to veto the match, but they are only likely to do so when they have some personal grudge against the suitor.

The suitor may visit a particular friend, often an age mate, of the girl's clan to enlist his support. In this way he has an ally who will speak in his favour:

> 1. Damayon, a popular worthy man, consulted a friend of another clan about a certain kinswoman he proposed to marry. He was told in confidence that she would make a bad wife, and was advised to wait and then ask for another closely related girl who would probably make an exceptionally good wife.
>
> The advice turned out to be sound, and Damayon maintains it was the influence of this friend that led to his successful marriage. He has given him several gifts in gratitude.

Polygamy is common and there is normally considerable competition between suitors for a particular girl. Competition may be especially keen for a girl who is likely to make a good wife, and her kinsmen will want to give her away to the contestant that they would most like as an affine. Competition for an unpromising girl may be correspondingly low. A mean man stands little chance of marrying a girl who is highly sought after, and, as was evident in the above example, a worthy man may be discouraged from marrying an unsuitable girl.

> 2.* Lemakeri wanted to marry a daughter of Seletu. It was generally held in Seletu's clan that Lemakeri was a mean man and hence an unfavourable suitor; at the same time, Seletu and his family were regarded as mean and the girl in question was no exception. She was unlikely to make a good wife, and her kinsmen could not really expect to benefit from her marriage. It was therefore argued that as Lemakeri was a fairly wealthy man, they could hardly hope for a better match for her. One of the

elders even went so far as to say: 'If her husband will not give us stock when we ask for it, we will curse the girl: she is mean and we do not think of her as one of our daughters.' It is rare that Samburu would admit such willingness to curse a kinswoman on the strength of the shortcomings of her husband. Seletu was in favour of the marriage and it was allowed to take place.

In marrying off a girl, there is more than the mere bartering of her person in return for what her clansmen can get out of it, but nevertheless this is an important aspect of marriage and of the relationship between affines. The girl's close kinsmen, and in particular her own father, may be genuinely concerned that she will be happy and well looked after, but they tend to associate such benefits with marriage to a rich and worthy man who will look after her in addition to being an asset to them.

Competition between several suitors may also bring certain kinsmen of the girl into dispute over the final choice, and they must resolve their differences in favour of one suitor before the marriage can take place. The compromise that is reached is a part of the give and take that typifies their relationship. The kinsman who agrees to withdraw his support for one of the suitors in favour of another may claim a gift, often a heifer, from the latter after his marriage. Or he may use his compliance on this occasion to justify a more uncompromising stand on some future marriage of a kinswoman, or possibly to strengthen his case when he or a son wish to marry into the other clan, thus reversing the roles of wife-givers and wife-receivers.

The Husband's Clan

A suitor's clansmen advise him on his choice and his strategy, but their role is non-manipulative and altogether different from that of the girl's clansmen. He looks to them, in particular his stock friends, for help in building up his herd for the marriage, for support in the negotiations, and for assistance during the wedding itself. As clansmen, they should give him this material and moral support at this point, just as he should give it when they too wish to marry.

The concern of his clansmen does not end once he has finally got himself a wife. They argue that they all helped him to marry her, and in a sense she is their wife and they are all wife-receivers, bound to show the same respect for his affines and bound to help him cope with his new problem of managing a wife. He can rely on them at moments of crisis. Thus it is almost a daily occurrence that some Samburu, seeing the wife of a fellow clansman some distance from her home, assume she is running away from her husband and escort her back.

On the other hand, clansmen will openly criticize a man who maltreats his wife, for jeopardizing his marriage. This criticism would normally take place when there are no outsiders present.

> 3.** Kimiri had been irritable with his junior wife for some time and one day when he found she had lost an armlet he had given her, he beat her. As she started to leave the settlement, apparently to run away, two other clan elders stopped her and promised to discuss the matter with Kimiri. This discussion took place later in the day. The other two elders pointed out to Kimiri how unreasonable he was being on this as on other recent occasions with his wife. They suggested that he should now buy her a new armlet to replace the lost one, in order to show his good will. He accepted this advice.

It is significant in this example that no attempt was made at confining the discussion to the mere loss of an armlet, or Kimiri might have persuaded the other two that he was justified in beating his wife. As it was, a number of other minor incidents in his homestead were brought up and he was criticized for his moodiness. The other elders did not ignore the very real possibility that unless Kimiri changed his attitude towards his wife, his marriage might come to an abrupt end. Their loyalty to Kimiri was in the marriage itself and not in helping him to save face on one issue.

The next example is one where sterner pressures were brought to bear:

> 4.** Letuno heard that his wife had slept with another man and beat her fiercely. He would not listen to the other clan elders, and a meeting was called by the local clan group. The woman was called, and Piliyon, Letuno's elder brother, chided her in front of the others and urged her to be more loyal to her husband in future. He also urged Letuno to treat her more gently in view of her youth

33

and to overlook the incident. Letuno started to argue but was shouted down by the other elders. Under pressure he blessed his wife as a sign of assent to the elders; and then they, led by Piliyon, blessed the couple. This signified that the matter was at an end. As one man remarked, 'Piliyon is a great and wise man. Letuno had to obey him.'

In this case, it was particularly suitable that Piliyon should have spoken in defence of the girl. Apart from the fact that as Letuno's elder brother he was in a position to command respect, he had also played an important part in arranging the marriage. The girl's father was, in fact, a member of his age-set, and Piliyon therefore had a quite explicit duty to look after her 'as a father'. His dual role as well as his age gave his arguments considerable weight in the discussion. If anyone could qualify for the role of 'guardian' of this particular marriage, it was he.

Clansmen may realize that certain members will never stop bullying their wives and may resort to more violent measures. In one recorded case they seized a man by surprise and beat him because he persistently beat his wives and drove them to run away. In another case they beat a man because he ignored their advice and slept constantly with a widow so that his own wife was on the point of running away in exasperation.

At other times, some form of compromise may be achieved. The following is an example:

5. Chilen was very brutal with his wife, and she ran away to her parents. Chilen's clansmen did not expect him to treat her any better if she returned, and they agreed that she should remain with her parents together with her children and some stock from Chilen's herd to feed them. It was made quite clear that when Chilen's behaviour became more moderate she would have to return. She returned after about two years.

The arrangements for Chilen's wife to stay with her parents in the above example appear to have been concluded by his clansmen and his affines. Chilen himself played very little part.

In Chapter One, we saw that in spite of the Samburu ideal of self-sufficiency for each stock owner, real economic independence is seldom achieved. We now see that there is also a limit in the extent to which a Samburu has complete social autonomy from his clansmen. In his own interests, they will interfere in his

34

family affairs and help to stabilize his marriage, especially in its early stages. In the final resort, these clansmen are concerned with their own interests, for the success of the domestic affairs of each of their number is a part of the prosperity of the clan as a whole; and also the reputation of the clan among other clans is enhanced by its ability to make good marriages and keep its more unruly members in check. In this way, it is easier for them all to marry into good lineages, for they belong to a clan which is on the whole a worthy one.

The Wife's Clan

Concern for their reputation as a worthy clan also prevents members of the wife's clan as wife-givers from exploiting the husband unduly. At first sight, they hold a strong hand: the bridewealth actually paid at a marriage only amounts to some six or eight cattle according to the custom of the bride's lineage; beyond this the wife-givers can demand endless gifts of cattle and small stock. The exact number is not defined by custom or discussed during the marriage negotiations, and this introduces a running sore into the marriage that can never be finally resolved.

But if it becomes generally known that they are ruthless wife-givers making unreasonable demands on their affines and threatening their curse freely, fewer people will want to marry their women and those who do will tend to be less worthy men of inferior lineages. They will have shown themselves as an unworthy clan, and when they in their turn wish to marry, they may find more worthy lineages and clans in competition with them.

A popular lineage, therefore, and to a lesser extent a popular clan has an interest in curbing its meaner members from exploiting the husbands of their kinswomen unduly. By augmenting his own herds too freely, a mean man is lowering the reputation of the lineage, which is damaging for all of them. To some extent he is immune to the criticisms of those he threatens as he is an outsider, but he is not immune to the criticism of his own lineage and clan.

Occasional requests by the close kinsmen of a wife for gifts

35

of one kind or another are expected and may be granted readily: the husband also has an interest in maintaining his own reputation for generosity and worthiness towards his affines if he wishes to marry other wives from popular families in the future. When such a request is made, both sides show respect for they are – or at least they always pose as – worthy members of popular lineages whose requests, concessions and refusals are always couched in polite terms and made to seem highly reasonable. It is only when they are with their own clansmen that Samburu talk freely and with disgust of their predatory affines.

A man who lives with his wife's kinsmen is at a considerable disadvantage: unless he is really poor, they have an explicit right to exploit his herds by begging from him, whereas he has no defined right to beg from them. It is only when he can convince them of the hardship which his wife and children suffer owing to his own poverty, that he can expect their help as a matter of common concern: they have a duty to their kinswoman.

But there are situations where a man may be tempted to live with his wife's kinsmen. If, for instance, she does not show enough respect towards him he may do so. In the presence of her own natal family and clan, she is obliged to modify her behaviour and act as a model wife out of respect for them. It may be that her father only agrees to the marriage in the first place on condition that the husband lives with him until the daughter is used to her new status; and the husband in his turn is constrained to treat her with moderation in the presence of his affines. Following this course acts as a check on both husband and wife and may effectively convert an uncertain marriage into a stable one. There are a number of men who live for long periods with their wives' kinsmen and ostensibly benefit from this. But the majority who are well established in their own clans disapprove: they point out that a man who is in difficulties should turn to his own clansmen for help rather than to those of his wife: that is what 'brothers' are for.

When other forms of coercion have failed to induce a woman to respect her husband, her clansmen may resort to a public beating as an extreme measure. Several cases have been recorded of this. In a further case, it was the husband who was beaten by his wife's kinsmen for treating her brutally. The last straw was when he drove her from his home and then followed her to her parents' home and beat her there. This showed so little respect for them that they did not hesitate to mob him and to threaten to do so again if he did not treat her more tolerantly. The Samburu claim a very high degree of success in these public beatings which may be carried out over several successive days.

Marriage, its success and prosperity are seen to be matters which concern not only husband and wife, but also their respective clans. Elders of these clans will not only try to prevent the husband or the wife from spoiling their marriage, but they will also try to check one another from exploiting it unduly, and this is particularly true of the wife's clan and lineage who have certain rights in the husband's herds: the future success and prosperity of their clan and lineage depend on the extent to which they can curb the selfish impulses of the more irresponsible members and maintain a reputation of worthiness.

The Mother's Clan

Any man is susceptible to exploitation by his wife's kinsmen, and this liability is inherited by his sons. The exact relationship between these sons and their maternal kin varies from one of mistrust resembling that between affines to a cordial friendship in which the maternal bond is regarded as justifying a reciprocal attitude of trust and good will resembling that between agnates. The precise nature of the relationship of any man with his maternal kin depends largely on the way in which it has developed during his lifetime. On the whole his relationship with his closest maternal kin is expected to be and tends to be tinged with genuine sentiments of mutual affection derived from the link through the mother, and his relationship with more distant members of his mother's clan tends to be tainted with mistrust.

A meeting between a man and one of his maternal kinsmen is on the face of it bland and affectionate. The term *abiyo* with which they address one another is intended to imply this. But when they describe the relationship, it is the power of the mother's brother's curse which the Samburu tend to stress, and his desire to exploit the herds of his sister's sons, in rather the same way as he did when these herds belonged to their father as wife-receiver of their mother. The following example illustrates the way in which the Samburu regard this relationship:

6. When Perean was a mere boy, he asked Taragi, a 'sister's son', for a cow and was refused. Shortly after this Taragi lost some cattle and the elders warned him that although Perean was many years his junior, his disappointment may well have amounted to the unvoiced curse of a mother's brother: he had in fact started to cry. Taragi therefore offered Perean a cow.

Many years later, Perean twice asked Kadede, another sister's son, for a sheep. Kadede was not wealthy and refused him the second time. Perean cursed him. The elders of Perean's local clan group intervened, and being unable to persuade him to withdraw his curse, they persuaded Kadede to offer him a heifer for his blessing. One of these elders said: 'We now know that Perean is not a really great man: he cursed his nephew for nothing, and then refused to listen to his clansmen. We do not now respect him.'

The asymmetry which exists in a man's relationship with his maternal kin is modified and eventually it may be virtually eradicated if he lives permanently among them, but the process may take many many years before it is complete. A boy who grows up among his maternal kin, whether it is because his father has gone to live among them or, more likely, because his mother has returned there, must sooner or later decide whether he wishes to remain among them or return to his own paternal clan. If he remains with them, then it is unlikely that he will have any of his father's stock with him and can only build up a herd of his own by begging from them. They may not at first be prepared to give him much stock in case he decides to return after all, taking with him the stock he has acquired, as he has every right to do. If, on the other hand, he returns to his paternal clan then he must form an entirely new set of personal ties within it and to some extent abandon those which he as enjoyed up to this point. But in returning to his proper clan he also overcomes the permanent disadvantage of being with maternal kin and he can form truly reciprocal friendships and expect substantial help in building up a herd. Frequently the elders of his father's clan send their initiate sons to recall him by coercion shortly before his circumcision in order to maintain their strength in numbers. Nyaparai clan was entirely dispersed after The Disaster of the 1880s, and most of the survivors lived with their mothers' brothers; when in the 1920s elders of this clan tried to re-establish it, they often resorted to this form of coercion.

The histories of five men who grew up among their maternal kin illustrate ways in which this relationship may develop:

7. Damayon grew up with his mother's clan Lokumai after his father's death. When he was about to be circumcised, elders of his paternal clan, Pardopa, sent their initiate sons to fetch him. They sang their circumcision song, *lebarta*, as a means of coercion: this would have amounted to a curse by his future age mates if he had not followed them. At first Damayon did not want to go, and his mother's brother Kotet refused to let him. At this point, other Lokumai elders pointed out to Kotet how vulnerable he was: he had two wives who were daughters of Pardopa clan, and in addition to the curse which threatened Damayon from his age mates, there was also the curse which the Pardopa elders could use to threaten Kotet's children, their sister's children.

Damayon was circumcised inside Pardopa clan after all, and has lived with it ever since. But he is still very friendly with his close maternal kin, and remembers the cattle they gave him and the excellent way they taught him to manage cattle as a herd-boy, which has been useful ever since.

8. Parsola, also a son of a widow of Pardopa clan and also brought up inside Lokumai, needed less encouragement to return to his paternal clan when called for circumcision in 1936. He had not been given any stock by his maternal kin. His present attitude towards them is one of formal respect, and his only contact with them is when they come to ask him for gifts.

Parsola's attitude towards his maternal kin and his relationship with them is fairly typical of most Samburu who have lived from birth inside their paternal clan.

9. Letore stayed with his maternal kin of Pardopa clan from his boyhood until he was an old man. It was only when three of his sons were involved in three separate affrays with Pardopa moran that he decided to return with his family to his paternal clan and

was immediately accepted by them. His younger sons were later circumcised in this clan.

10.* Kosoya also stayed with his maternal clan, Pardopa, from boyhood until he was an old man. Only then did some of his paternal kinsmen of Longieli clan suggest that he should return to them. To everyone's surprise, and disappointment in Pardopa, he at first agreed, but later changed his mind. It is generally thought that his wife and adult sons persuaded him to remain, and being senile he is highly dependent on them.

It now seems unlikely that Kosoya's descendants will ever return to Longieli clan where, in any case, all their closest kinsmen are dead.

The following example is of some interest as it suggests that the incorporation of a man into his maternal clan is not simply achieved implicitly over the years, but may be subject from time to time to dispute, and the outcome of each dispute may mark a definite stage in the transition. In other words, just as he may find that some crisis precipitates his return to his paternal clan, as in examples 7 and 9 above, so it may equally well confirm his position in his maternal clan:

11. Majaina and Lopodo were both members of Nyaparai clan who had grown up in their mother's clan, Pardopa. Lopodo later returned to Nyaparai while Majaina remained and consolidated his ties with Pardopa.

Some years later, Lopodo wanted to score off an adversary by vetoing his marriage to Majaina's daughter. Majaina reluctantly gave way. At this point, other Pardopa elders interfered as they supported the suit. Under the threat of their curse, Lopodo was obliged to withdraw his veto since they were his mother's brothers.

It appears to have been this incident that finally sealed Majaina's full membership of Pardopa clan, and all the bridewealth of the marriage was given to Pardopa elders closely related to Majaina's mother, since he had no close relatives left in Nyaparai.

The meagre economic value of bridewealth in this society has already been noted. But in marginal situations such as in this example the handing over of bridewealth may be a positive indication of the direction in which clan affiliations lie. For the husband, it also makes it clear which clan is likely to come and beg further stock from him in the years to come.

Radcliffe-Brown has suggested that the curse of the mother's brother is feared in some societies because the maternal bond is so strong that he will be the last person to use this power and will only do so in exceptional and serious situations.[1] This does not appear to be valid for the Samburu. Much depends on the relationship actually developed by individuals: if a cordial relationship is established then the mother's brother will be unwilling to use his curse and it will not be feared; and conversely, if such a relationship has not been established then certain mother's brothers may be more prepared to use their curse and it will be feared. The one person who will be most unwilling to use his power of the curse because of a strong and affectionate bond is the father; in any case, any curse he pronounces would affect his own cattle and the lineage he is founding. But the Samburu do not stress the father's curse for the very reason that it would be so disruptive and unlikely to be used.[2]

In another publication, Radcliffe-Brown is closer to expressing this relationship as it appears among the Samburu. He writes: 'A person's most important duties and rights attach him to his paternal relatives, living and dead. It is to his patrilineal lineage or clan that he belongs. For the members of his mother's lineage he is an outsider, though one in whom they have a very special and tender interest.'[3] However, in this context, Radcliffe-Brown is considering the ambivalence of joking relationships in which the sister's son can behave with a privileged disrespect in certain societies. Now the same ambivalence and asymmetry is present among the Samburu, even though they do not have any such joking relationship: the mother's brother can bless *or* curse his sister's son. But it should be noted that in the joking relationships referred to by Radcliffe-Brown, the hostile element is repressed in a joke and initiative lies with the sister's son; whereas among the Samburu, it is the hostile element, the curse,

[1] Radcliffe-Brown, 1950, p. 37.
[2] This is also the case among the Nuer (Evans-Prichard, 1956, pp. 165–6).
[3] Radcliffe-Brown, 1952, p. 98.

which is emphasized by informants and initiative lies with the mother's brother.

These differences may well be related to different patterns of property rights between the Samburu and these other societies. Fortes and Goody, for instance, have suggested that in parts of West Africa a man may take 'joking' liberties with the property of his mother's brother because he would have had property rights in that lineage if his mother had been a man: he is acting on her behalf and asserting her submerged rights.[1] The Samburu, however, view this relationship quite differently. It is the mother's brother who is concerned with his property rights and not the sister's son; and far from being submerged rights they are explicitly acknowledged so long as he only asserts them with moderation. But he may differ with his nephews over what demands are moderate and this introduces an uncertainty that can provoke hostility. The hostility is not submerged in a joking relationship, but is, I suggest, overtly expressed in the popular belief that the mother's brother should be feared for his curse. As one man described it: 'I am afraid of anyone's curse. But only my mother's brother would curse me "for nothing" (*peshau*). When he asks me for something, I dare not refuse.'

Forced Marriages

In this chapter we have seen how conflicting interests in a man's marriage tend to be curbed by clansmen who are concerned with the well-being of the clan and its reputation for worthiness. The next two sections are concerned with critical times when the general urge to assert an individual's rights overrides prudence. These occur when he has difficulty in marrying or in keeping his wife.

The concern of a man's clan in his marriage is most vividly demonstrated when he cannot obtain a wife and turns to them for support. At such times they rally to his side. Word spreads among members of the local clan group and farther afield summoning them to a secret meeting. Any man who stays away after he has been personally called by the others might be

[1] Fortes, 1949, pp. 305–6; Goody, 1959, pp. 81–2.

42

cursed. The Samburu stress the compulsion of this summons: 'The call (*siamu*) of the elders is very strong indeed,' they say. The term *siamu* implies collective strength and coercion: it is more than a mere invitation, it is a command backed by the threat of the curse. To be called is an honour from which a man cannot excuse himself in normal circumstances.

In *marriage by coercion* (*siamu*), elders of the suitor's clan collect together in this way, and without warning go to the settlement of the bride-to-be's father. They sit in a group, their heads cowled by their blankets in silence; they do not enter the settlement and they do not accept food: to do either of these would render their curse harmless. They sit there until the girl's father agrees to her marriage. This may take many hours while his own clansmen try to coerce him to accept and avoid the curse.

Such marriages are only carried out in exceptional circumstances, as the following example shows:

12.* After the death of his first wife, Sopoitan remarried, and this wife also died. His clansmen obtained him a third wife by coercion. As one man pointed out, 'Sopoitan has lost two wives already, and other people might think that he is under some curse. We know this is rubbish, but it would be hard to get him a third wife in any other way.'

Blindness, idiocy and other maladies do not lessen a man's rights to marry, and the duty to obtain him a wife and support him in marriage falls on his clansmen who take the initiative in finding a suitable bride and getting her through coercion. In one recorded instance, a blind and virtually deaf man was thought of so highly by his clansmen that they supported him in two marriages by coercion, the second occurring after the death of his first wife. In another case, however, this same clan did not help a blind member to marry a second time: he had lost most of his stock and had irresponsibly divorced the first wife they had obtained for him by coercion. They argued that he had shown himself ungrateful and that to repeat this would be too disruptive.

A second type of forced marriage, *marriage by fait accompli* (*nkunon*), can be achieved by the groom and a few close friends; it is therefore not necessary to obtain the general consent of the clan beforehand. All the wedding party have to do is to force their way at night into a settlement where an unmarried girl has been circumcised, and perform two ritual acts of the wedding ceremony. These are killing the marriage ox and leading a sheep to the circumcision hut. They can then claim an exclusive right to marry the girl, since it would be mystically dangerous to allow any other person to perform these same acts.

> 13. Lekiso's proposal to marry his first wife had been accepted by all members of her clan except her father's brother who had vetoed it uncompromisingly. At the suggestion of two other members of his clan and age-set, Lekiso successfully forced his way into the settlement one night and performed the necessary parts of the ceremony. When they realized what had happened, members of the settlement started to mob Lekiso and his companions. But after the initial fury had subsided, they agreed that the remainder of the ceremony should be performed and the girl be taken away.
>
> Shortly after the event, Rikasi, the brother of Lekiso's bride, was rejected in his suit for a girl of Lekiso's clan, and he forced his marriage in precisely the same way, shouting 'Repay the debt. Repay the debt' (*entala sile*) as the others came out to mob him.

In both cases, the girl had been circumcised but not married. It is because the interval between circumcision and marriage is a vulnerable one for any girl in that she may be married in this way, that the Samburu normally postpone her circumcision until the day of the wedding that they have planned for her. Certain families, however, have a custom of circumcising their children in the evening, whereas the marriage cannot take place until the next morning. This results in a night of suspense:

> 14.* One of Tamaruk's daughters had been promised to an elder, Naracha, and she was circumcised one evening in order to be married the next day. During the night, moran of another clan tried to force their way into the settlement and force a marriage by *fait accompli* for one of their number. Naracha, however, had brought some moran of his own clan to guard against any such attempt. The alarm was raised and the intruders were prevented from killing their ox and were kept at bay until Naracha had himself killed his own ox and ensured his marriage to the girl.

44

Forced Marriages

The Samburu support their belief in the danger of rejecting a marriage by *fait accompli* by reference to an occasion when this occurred: the father threw the *fait accompli* marriage ox into the bush and married his daughter to the suitor of his own choice; within a year, the girl died. But at least one man seems to have got away with it:

> 15. Kingeyo tried to force a marriage by *fait accompli* with a daughter of Kotet. Kotet, a stubborn though intelligent man (cf. example 7 above), refused to allow the marriage to continue, but insisted that he and the other elders should eat the ox that had been killed as in any normal marriage ceremony. He then demanded that Kingeyo should accept a heifer in return for the marriage ox: he was in effect acknowledging the marriage and insisting on an immediate divorce.
>
> There have been no major tragedies in Kotet's family since this time and opinion is at present divided: some believe that he has found a new way of evading the mystical consequences of ignoring a marriage by *fait accompli*, and others believe that it is too soon to judge the issue (twenty years after the event) and point out that Kotet has lost several small children which could be due to his unpropitious action. Few Samburu would be willing to follow his suit.

On the whole, irregular forms of marriage are avoided as they are only likely to increase tension between clans and may even lead to reprisals. Of 87 marriages recorded in one clan segment, only two were achieved by coercion and two others by *fait accompli*. The latter method lends itself to impulsive bravado on the part of a few irresponsible young men, while the former method is a calculated move on the part of the elders of a clan. When a suitable occasion presents itself, even elders are prepared to resort to *fait accompli* methods, but they are very critical of young men who take matters into their own hands without extreme justification.

The customs of forcing marriages draw attention to the difficulties that arise from the Samburu form of marriage and the wide consensus that is demanded. In order to satisfy the needs of each man in marriage, clansmen are sometimes forced to commit a deliberately hostile act which can only antagonize some other clan and invite repercussions.

45

Divorce and Remarriage

Marriage is brittle in its early stages. The Samburu say that children alone can bind a man and his wife together, and that 'a wife without a child has one foot inside the settlement and one outside': in other words, she is quite likely to run away from her husband.

Custom relating to divorce and remarriage is simple in theory, although rather more complicated in practice. In theory, divorce is impossible once a married woman has had a pregnancy or after her husband's death: widows can never remarry. Apart from this, the husband may force a divorce by demanding the return of all marriage payments: that is, the bridewealth given at the wedding, subsequent gifts of stock, and the increase of all this stock. When the woman is remarried, her new husband pays an equivalent bridewealth and further gifts of stock, but these are likely to be inferior in quality and prestige to the original bridewealth.

The complication in practice is not so much due to divorce occurring after a pregnancy (this would be unpropitious), but to the bids which the first husband may subsequently make for the return of his wife *and* her children by her second husband. Until the oldest of these children has been circumcised in the homestead of the second husband, these bids to reclaim the wife may recur. After this circumcision, the second husband has an indisputable right to keep the wife.

That there are loopholes in these customs is evident from the extent to which men with irregular marriages have gone to the administrative courts to seek official confirmation of their marriages. These have not been excessive in number, but the fact that they have taken place in a society which has not as yet exploited the courts to uphold or challenge its customs does suggest that certain men are not altogether confident that they can retain or regain their wives by relying solely on tribal custom and clan support. This dilemma over remarriage appears to be a long-lived one. There is no evidence to suggest that it is necessarily the result of a recent change or weakening of custom.

In order to secure the return of his divorced wife, a man may enrol the services of his clansmen. They may either use a form of coercion similar to marriage by coercion, or they may use force. Two examples illustrate this:

16.* A woman had four children by her second husband, after her first husband, Selemit, had procured an early divorce and reclaimed the bridewealth. Then Selemit and a group of his clansmen approached her father by coercion and offered him twice the original bridewealth for her return – or their curse. They later went without warning to the second husband's home to collect the wife and children by force if necessary. The second husband offered no resistance, but went to the woman's father to demand the return of the marriage payments that he had made. The matter was at an end.

17. After his second wife had run away, Leipa reclaimed all the marriage payments, and to clinch the matter he demanded the total increase of the original cattle plus a heifer for each animal that had died. This did not improve his relations with his former affines, but he was at least within his rights. However, when he asked for an additional heifer for the marriage ox that had been killed, he was bringing in an innovation which could lead to misfortune.

At the time Leipa's action seemed final. But many years later, some of his clansmen seized the wife and her son by her second husband without warning and led them back to Leipa, who then had to make an exceptionally heavy payment to her father.

It is not clear from my material exactly how the affines or the second husband can stop a determined first husband if they object to his retrieving his wife. I can only assume that like marriage by coercion or by *fait accompli*, it is a disruptive form of behaviour which is limited to exceptional circumstances so that bad feeling between clans does not build up into a vicious circle and the reputation of the husband's clan does not suffer too seriously. Where the first husband does succeed in getting his wife back, he must pay heavily for it or risk the curse that his affines can evoke on his children.

Thus divorce among the Samburu is in the first instance separation between the spouses, and only becomes divorce in the stricter sense after the circumcision of the wife's eldest child. It is generally felt that if the first husband does not insist on the return of all the marriage payments, confining his demands to certain stock, then he has a better claim for his wife's return in future. Such moderation also indicates that the divorce has been achieved with less bad feeling, and that the husband does not want to show undue hostility towards his affines over a matter arising from domestic incompatibility.

Frequently, it seems to be the decision of the wife's clansmen which is final in deciding the issue of her return and not the determination of the first husband:

18. Lekiso's second wife had previously been married to a man of Longieli clan, and later this had ended in divorce. When the first husband had asked her father for her return, he had been refused. It was not quite certain, however, whether the first husband would allow the matter to end here. Lekiso and his father-in-law therefore took the matter to the local native court and obtained their official ratification.

Is the matter at an end? Lekiso asserts confidently that it is. But other elders of his clan are less certain: they point out that Lekiso is himself the son of a girl of Longieli clan, and that if the first husband ever threatens to curse him as a sister's son, then Lekiso will not dare to oppose him. Lekiso's close maternal kin happen to sympathize with him in the matter of his marriage, but there is nothing they can personally do to prevent their clansman, the first husband, from resorting to the curse, nor can they nullify that curse.

Lekiso now has a son aged about 7 by this second wife. His best way of ensuring that he retains her and her children is to have this son circumcised as soon as possible.

If the husband demands a divorce, he can hardly be refused by his wife's clan as he can drive her from his home (if she is still there) and she cannot be remarried until the marriage payments or at least a part of them have been returned. However, the wife's clan cannot force the husband to accept a divorce, nor would they threaten to use their curse since this would also affect the wife whom they want to help.

19. Keseker is a hard man (*kogol*). After his wife ran away from him, his affines persistently tried to persuade him to accept a divorce. He refused, and one night he went to their settlement and led her back to his home by force.

48

If a woman has run away from her husband to live with another member of his clan as a concubine, then the affair can be settled within the clan:

20.** When Leperin was a young boy, he was castrated by some Boran raiders. A wife was subsequently obtained for him by coercion. This woman ran away and lived for a time with a number of men. Eventually she became a concubine of Dupua, a member of Leperin's clan. Other clansmen urged Dupua to return her to her husband, and under pressure from his half brother, the senior member of his lineage, he promised to do so. Shortly after this, several of Leperin's local clan elders came to collect the woman and Dupua willingly let her go.

One of his clansmen was particularly critical of Dupua: 'We arranged Leperin's marriage by coercion, and we do not want to have to find him a second wife. If Dupua had not returned her, then we might have cursed him.'

The following figures give some indication of the general stability of Samburu marriage. Of 80 recorded marriages of the men of one clan segment: 13 wives have run away to their parents' home at some time and have all returned; five have run away to live for a time as another's man's concubine and have returned; two have run away and have since been divorced; and eight have been previously married to another man and divorced – it is generally considered that the matter is now at an end in six of these eight cases and that the women will not return to their former husbands. These figures are not yet final since they concern living marriages: in due course of time it is fairly certain that more of these 80 wives will be divorced or will run away. Moreover, in addition to these 80 recorded marriages, there are almost certainly others which have ended in divorce which I did not record: a wife who has since been married elsewhere tends to be overlooked or forgotten. These figures, however incomplete, certainly suggest the considerable risk that is involved in any marriage; in so far as they are inadequate, they underrate the true state of affairs.[1]

It is in everyone's best interests that a marriage should be successful, and if divorce seems inevitable then it is best to

[1] Cf. a discussion by Barnes on the methodological problems of measuring divorce (Barnes, 1949).

49

arrange it as soon as possible while the wife is still young and can be remarried. But the ability of the first husband to reclaim her many years after the divorce and after she had had children by her second husband is an anomalous cause of strain. On the other hand, it indirectly contributes to marriage stability. It gives an added gravity to arranging her first marriage and ensuring its success. A man's affines will be careful to pamper the marriage until the first pregnancy removes the danger of divorce. Only then are they in a position to exploit his herds with any degree of confidence. The total marriage payment then begins to mount up at a fast rate and there is no fear of having to return any of it. By contrast, a second marriage is an unhappy affair and no one can be certain how it will end. It is only when the eldest child is circumcised, perhaps 15 or more years after the marriage, that the husband and wife know that their future is secured. And it is only then that the affines can be sure that they will not have to surrender the marriage payments that have been in their herds for so long, multiplying under their care.

Recruitment into the Clan

The corporateness of the clan is not expressed by any belief in descent from a common ancestor. Most, if not all the major segments of any Samburu clan claim diverse origins, often from other tribes or other Samburu clans. Recruitment into a clan from elsewhere is common even today.

Thus, associated with every clan there are a few peripheral members who, though no longer distrusted as outsiders, have not yet associated with it long enough to enjoy all the privileges of clanship. It is unlikely, for instance, that the clan will help such a man obtain a wife by coercion: if he cannot acquire sufficient stock to marry, then he will remain a bachelor. If he behaves in an unworthy manner, then he will not be criticized openly and no sanctions will be imposed. Such behaviour will merely strengthen the view that he is still to some extent an outsider, and will serve to delay the time when he is implicitly accepted as a full member of the clan.

There is no custom which prevents such a man from marrying

into his adopted clan (unless they are his maternal kinsmen). But again such a marriage would delay his full incorporation into it by a generation or more. By creating this tie he is making himself a wife-receiver to the whole clan and hence an outsider. It does not help him to develop a relationship of true reciprocity and trust.

A detailed census of Pardopa clan revealed that among immigrants to it, there was no family which had been circumcised within it for two successive generations and yet still married into it. It is unlikely, for instance, that the sons of Kosoya (page 40) will marry girls of Pardopa clan. They will more probably extend their traditional exogamous obligations, which at present includes all Longieli clan, to include Pardopa clan and other segments associated with it. Similarly a newcomer will often oppose the marriage of his own sisters and daughters into this clan; this is less important from his point of view, however, since such a marriage concerns his own relationship with the man who marries her much more than his relationship with the whole clan.

In the course of a generation or more, a clan-associate either returns to his natal clan, or he becomes accepted as a full member of his new clan and obtains the benefits, the protection, and observes the exogamous restrictions of that clan. The tensions and ambivalent attitudes which accompany marriage among the Samburu are inconsistent with the unity which should prevail within the clan. The social barrier which surrounds each clan and cuts off outsiders is continually reinforced by new marriages which cut across it. Recruitment into the clan cannot be successfully achieved through marriage; it can only be gained through co-residence and all that that entails.

Summary

The exogamy of Samburu clans isolates the close bonds of clanship from the strains involved in a marriage. To a large extent these strains are correlated with the lack of any precise custom concerning the exact number of stock a man should give to his wife's kinsmen over the decades following his marriage, so that the conflicting interests of the two parties in the one herd can never be finally resolved. Instead of one bulk payment of bridewealth, a man's stock essentially remains with him inside his clan while his affines try to exploit him as much as possible short of ruining his marriage or their good name.

The strains of marriage are also correlated with the high degree of polygamy which implies a general scarcity of marriageable women, so that obtaining and retaining a wife may often be difficult. Clansmen help one another in these matters by avoiding competing for the same woman where possible, by assisting in building up one another's herds for marriage, and by lending moral and where necessary physical support in one another's claims.

But the clan also has a restraining influence. It is not in their interests that they should be known as mean, as bad husbands and greedy wife-givers. It is important that their daughters should be widely known as desirable wives, so that they can be married to the most worthy suitors. Clansmen will therefore interfere in the affairs of any member who shows signs of carelessness or greediness in any of these ways; for while it is he who stands to gain from belonging to a popular and worthy clan, it is they who lose prestige and general respect if too many of their fellow members are allowed to display mean traits. Not only will they all find it harder to marry into good lineages and clans in the general competition for wives, but they will also find that there is less competition for marriage with their own daughters and less chance of marrying them to desirable suitors. Thus minor tensions may arise within the clan as elders of a local clan group try to curb the excesses of their less worthy members.

Within the clan there is considerable unity of interests which accounts for its strongly corporate nature among the Samburu. This is a topic which is examined in greater detail in Chapter Seven. One aspect of this corporateness is the way in which clansmen can help each other to build up their herds for future marriages without hindering their own chances. This is considered in the next chapter.

Chapter Three

THE FAMILY AND THE HERD

THIS chapter is concerned with the complex set of rights which different members of a homestead have in the herd, and with the ways in which they can manipulate these rights to their own advantages. In order to appreciate these it is necessary first to outline the way in which a man's stock is divided among his various wives. After each marriage he allots a certain portion of his herd to his bride and he retains a portion himself for future marriages. The portion given to each wife is referred to here as her *allotted herd*, and the portion retained by the husband is referred to as his *residual herd*. The residual herd and all the various allotted herds of the homestead form the *total herd*.

The Wife's Allotted Herd

When negotiating for a marriage, a suitor does not tell his future affines how many cattle he has. But by the time they have decided to allow the suit, they will have formed a fairly precise estimate and will tell the girl how many cattle she should expect in her allotted herd; she will be warned that her husband may try to cheat her by concealing many of his cattle and persuade her to accept less.

On the day that she is allotted this herd, about one month after her marriage, the bride signifies that she finally accepts the portion given her by opening up her husband's gateway. Once she has done this, she cannot claim any right to further cattle from his residual herd ever again. If, therefore, she feels that he is still holding too many cattle in his residual herd and is not giving her as much as he can afford, then she has merely to refuse to open up the gateway. Invariably, or so it seems, the

53

initial allotment of perhaps 15, perhaps 30, perhaps even 50 cattle is followed by a considerable pause while the husband and elders of his local clan group urge the bride to open the gate; at first she refuses and the husband gives her several more cattle ranging from two to five or more. After she has opened the gate, one more female cow is added to her herd.

The husband cannot afford at this stage to treat his bride too unfairly in allotting her cattle, for such an act might induce her to run away to her parents' home where she would have their sympathy. This could lead to a quick divorce unless the husband agrees to allot her more cattle. In two recorded cases where the bride did run away for this reason, it was the husband's local clan elders who persuaded him to augment her herd. When, on the other hand, the husband has given his bride as many cattle as he can afford, she would not have the sympathy of anyone if she ran back to her parents.

In addition to this stock, a bride is generally offered a heifer by each of the other wives of the homestead, and where the desire to show good will is marked, she may be offered further gifts of cattle in the course of the first few months of her marriage. These animals are then transferred from the allotted herds of each of these wives to the allotted herd of the bride. Certain close kinsmen of the husband, including his adult sons, may each offer her a beast: the exact nature of this beast varies with the wealth and good will of the giver. Reciprocal terms of address between the bride and these donors are based on these initial gifts: they call each other by such terms as *patawo* (*ntawo* = heifer), *pamongo* (*lmongo* = ox), *paashe* (*lashe* = calf), *pakine* (*nkine* = goat), *pakuo* (*nkuo* = kid or lamb), and so on. Smaller gifts such as personal ornaments may be made and there are corresponding terms of address.

Sheep and goats also form a significant part of the allotted herd. As a source of food they are important, but as a form of property they are of minor importance compared with cattle. The death or the loss of small stock is a daily occurrence and critical competition over it would be too disruptive and too frequent for what it is worth. This chapter refers primarily to cattle and what is said of competition over cattle is only true to a far lesser extent of small stock.

The Wife's Allotted Herd

Each wife has certain rights in her allotted herd which the husband should respect if he wishes to keep domestic harmony. He has no acknowledged right to return a cow from a wife's allotted herd to his own residual herd or to give it to one of his other wives:

21. When Lomere's mother was newly married, his father had returned a heifer from her allotted herd to his own residual herd for some carelessness on her part. She did nothing about it, but told Lomere of the incident many years later. When his father died, Lomere's half brother automatically inherited the entire residual herd as the senior son of the family. At this point Lomere, acting on his mother's behalf, raised the matter of the cow wrongly taken from her and claimed all its offspring that still remained in the residual herd. As a moderate gesture, he waived his claim to those cattle which had been allotted to other wives. The local clan elders persuaded the half brother to accede to this highly reasonable claim.

Lomere could in theory have demanded all the offspring remaining in the total herd, but this would have caused bad feeling within the family and in moderating his claim, he earned the praise of the other elders.

Other cases where such cattle have been claimed on the death of the father have been recorded in which there has been no conciliatory gesture, and in two of them the size of the herd is said to have amounted to 40 head of cattle descended in each instance from one wrongly acquired cow.

A woman who has previously run away and then returns to her husband retains a right to all her original animals and their offspring:

22. Lunget's wife ran away and went to live with a man of another tribe. No one knew where she was and Lunget returned all the cattle he had previously allotted her to his residual herd. Several years later this woman was seen inside Samburu country and some of Lunget's clansmen seized her and took her by force back to him. She was still entitled to all the cattle of her previous herd which still remained inside the total herd, although a number of these had since been allotted to a more recent wife; but it was up to her to identify these cattle after all these years and to prove that other cattle which she had never seen were their offspring.

Lunget was quite unhelpful, and the wife was only able to claim with certainty about five animals in the total herd. Lunget told her that the remainder of her herd had died or had been given away and that there had been no calves. The matter might have rested there, but Lunget's father, realizing that the woman would be unlikely to remain with only a handful of cattle, told her exactly which beasts she was still entitled to. Lunget then admitted this and all the cattle of her allotted herd were returned to her. It is now generally accepted that Lunget's father was both correct and wise in interfering in the matter.

A man should not, then, take a cow allotted to a wife and give it to another wife or return it to his residual herd, but custom does allow him to take such a cow and give it away to someone outside the homestead (i.e. he may alienate it *from* the total herd, but he may not transfer it *within* the total herd). This right provides him with a means of exploiting his wives' allotted herds to his own advantage: he can draw on their herds to fulfil his obligation towards his wife-giving affines, his maternal kin and his stock friends without drawing on his residual herd. And then at other times he can augment his residual herd by begging cattle from his wife-receiving affines, stock friends, etc. By begging from each other and placing themselves under an obligation, stock friends are indirectly helping one another to exploit the herds allotted to their wives.

A woman rarely allows even a sheep to leave her herd without at least a show of indignation; but if the husband is skilful then he can avoid unnecessary friction by not seeming to exploit any of his wives unduly and where possible by playing them off against one another and even against their own predatory kinsmen. When, for instance, a kinsman of one of his wives comes to beg a cow from him, it is understood that the beast will be taken from her allotted herd. In so far as he does not wish to give away an animal and evades the requests with excuses or promises, the husband is siding with his wife; and in so far as he is willing to alienate an animal, he is doing this out of respect for *her* kinsman. In such circumstances the wife should only make a formal protest, as by saying that the loss will bring her hardship, but she should not start to bicker or threaten to run away as she might do at other times.

When his clansmen or maternal kinsmen come to ask him for a beast, then there are other ways in which he can play them off against one of his wives. The wife from whose herd an animal is taken will be far more moderate in her behaviour if she is on particularly cordial terms with the visitor who asks for the gift or if he is of the same age-set as her father and hence is a classificatory father. When he comes to make his request, he may make it easy for the husband to select a suitable allotted herd from which to take the animal by pointing out these various relationships.

An advantage of having several wives is that a man can alienate cattle from each of their herds at different times, and so long as he does not show unnecessary favouritism to any one of them, he can minimize general friction. When on one occasion he alienates an animal from the allotted herd of a particular wife then this wife may accuse him of favouring the others, but in doing so she does not gain their sympathy. So long as the husband *is* fair, each of his wives will appreciate this fairness, except at moments when her own cattle are implicated. A man with only one wife has less room to manipulate his rights and each animal he takes from her allotted herd may aggravate strained relations between them; if he avoids this by constantly taking animals from his residual herd then he also delays the time when he can take on a second wife.

Fairness to his wives includes taking into account their different degrees of luck. If one wife has borne him a large family and there has been no corresponding growth of her allotted herd or if her kinsmen have been excessive in their demands for stock, then the husband may take fewer animals from her herd in his gifts to his own clansmen and more from some other wife. He will also take into consideration the seniority of his different wives, their loyalty towards him, and the extent to which he needs to consolidate any particular marriage and avoid introducing new sources of strain.

The rights that women have in disposing of their allotted herds are limited: they can give stock away to any member of the homestead but not to anyone outside it (i.e. the stock must remain inside the total herd). It is no direct concern of the husband what they do with their allotted stock within these

57

limits. When the wives' kinsmen obtain stock, they acknowledge this custom by begging directly from the husband, who as the stock owner of the homestead is the only person who can alienate animals from the total herd. It is the husband who makes the final decision as to which beast should be given away, if any, without referring to her on the matter. A skilful man can foresee his wives' reactions to any action on his part and can assess accurately his most tactful course of behaviour. He has to choose between the herds of his various wives; he has to decide on the size and type of animal to give away; and he has to decide whether he should accede to the request, evade it, or even dismiss it. If he makes too generous a gift then there may be unnecessary bad feeling in his home, and if he makes too small a gift then he may damage his reputation and his relationship with his visitor. This is an inevitable and a recurrent dilemma which he should try to solve by maximizing his own personal satisfaction and not that of his wives or of his visitor.

Domestic harmony after alienating stock is not necessarily achieved more often by worthy men than by others. Damayon, a very popular worthy man, constantly has trouble with his wives, and this seems to be largely due to his over-zealous generosity with the stock he has previously allotted to them. It is said of Letuno, on the other hand, that he has a lot of trouble from his wives because he is not firm with them and is afraid to take away any of their stock: this is regarded as a mean trait. The general dissatisfaction in both homes tends to be directed against the husbands by the wives acting in collusion. A wise man can generally maintain a sort of domestic harmony by avoiding critical tension between any members of his homestead and yet be accepted as a worthy man. His clansmen clearly understand why Damayon has difficulty with his wives, but this in no way lessens his popularity.

Inheritance and Building up a Herd

When a man dies each of his sons can claim one heifer from his residual herd, and if this herd is large enough some of his brothers may also expect a heifer. Apart from these animals, however, the entire residual herd is inherited by the eldest son of his first wife, referred to here as the *senior son*. The Samburu say: 'When a man is old, it is his senior son who hands him milk to drink and lifts him onto a donkey when they have to move.' It is also this son who has been associated with the father and his herds for the longest time, handing on the skill in cattle management which he learnt from the old man to his younger brothers.

One other less tangible inheritance are the stock friendships formed by the father. As he grows old, he may give his sons a clear idea of the extent to which they now owe or are owed gifts and services. In this manner, stock friendships become another aspect of the tradition of mutual help which tends to be built up between families of a sub-clan where such ties are most commonly found.

But the main source to which a young man looks for cattle to build up a herd of his own is his mother's allotted herd. To some extent there is bound to be competition between full brothers for the cattle of this herd, a competition which does not concern their sisters or their paternal half brothers: the sisters as girls have no rights to cattle in their father's homestead and the paternal half brothers have mothers with allotted herds of their own.

Custom does not specify how the cattle of the mother's herd should be divided among brothers, and there is no obvious reason why competition within the elementary family should not be intense to the point of active hostility. But it seldom is. And it is evident from the table on page 15 that full brothers frequently live in the same settlement – a fact which suggests mutual dependence rather than competition when it is remembered that all stock owners are free to migrate as independently as they please. One is led to suspect that there are other less obvious factors which inhibit competition between brothers and encourage considerable co-operation.

Perhaps the most important factor is that competition between brothers is against the ethos of the society: it is criticized by the elders, and any man who pursues it to the point of open hostility is seen to be a mean man, a man who allows his own personal interests to have priority over his social obligations. A worthy man should discreetly move away from his brother before competition between them becomes intense. The Samburu approve of brothers who continually live together for this signifies that they are above competing with each other; but they also assert that all brothers should also live apart for much of the time so as to avoid friction which is always likely to arise between them.

A second factor, which is especially important during the time of their boyhood and youth when they are beginning to build up their future herds, is that there is normally a considerable age gap between successive brothers in an elementary family: this is partly due to restrictions on sexual intercourse during the 12- to 18-month period between birth and weaning, and also to the effect of a high child mortality; so that those children who survive to the age of, say, ten years are often rather older or younger than any of their siblings. During childhood even a small age difference of a few years between brothers is significant and care is taken by the Samburu to accentuate this difference, so that the younger of two brothers learns to respect the older who in theory will acquire a powerful curse over him. Their status difference encourages the unequal division of the mother's stock so as to favour the older and so as to discourage any active attempt at competition by the younger. When the father dies, the eldest son – once he has been circumcised – is in control of his mother's and his brother's herds: he cannot force them to transfer stock to one another or to him any more than their father could, but nor can they alienate stock without his permission and they remain under this restriction until their marriages: he is now the stock owner.

A third factor, which has already been noted, is the unpredictable quality of stock as a form of property which increases or decreases in size according to the skill, the energy and, in part, the luck of the stock owner. The example of Nakuru and Dorian (see page 25) is one of many instances confirming the general philosophy that every man who acts worthily and prudently can reverse his fortunes, no matter how great his initial disadvantage. The unequal apportioning of stock to different sons, then, may be of considerable importance at the time, but it is by no means final; and a man who adopts a philosophic attitude can argue that he has everything to gain.

Inheritance and Building up a Herd

Brothers obtain stock from their mother's allotted herd by asking her directly for one cow at a time and under pressure from them, she must decide how to divide the cattle among them. In so far as she is sensitive to the right of the older of two sons to a larger share of the herd and is firm with them all, competition may be avoided. It seems very likely, although informants never openly admitted this, that brothers also put considerable pressure on each other when they feel that they are being denied their rightful share or that one of them is asserting his own rights too boldly and is building up too large a herd. What appears to happen is that the oldest son asserts himself more than the others as he has no older brother to dispute his right to cattle from the mother's herd, and he starts to acquire stock of his own before they do. Each of the other sons stands in a similar relationship to his younger brothers, but the extent to which he can assert his rights is modified by the existence of his older brothers. Consequently, the herd of the eldest son tends to be rather larger than might appear to be strictly equitable and each succeeding son has a considerably smaller herd than any of his seniors.

The following table gives some idea of how the cattle of an allotted herd of 180 head of cattle might be distributed among four brothers after the death of the mother.[1]

Typical Distribution of a Mother's Allotted Herd among her Four Sons

Order of birth	Age	Number of cattle in herd
Eldest son	37 years	80 head of cattle
Second son	32 years	50 head of cattle
Third son	29 years	30 head of cattle
Fourth son	23 years	20 head of cattle

Each son in turn, as he marries at about the age of 30, expects no further gifts of cattle from his mother unless his need

[1] The Samburu do not readily divulge the exact sizes of their herds as this is thought to bring misfortune to the herd, and any attempt by another man at counting them could be regarded as a form of sorcery. Inevitably, then, these figures and those given below in the table on page 69 are typical of what I was able to collect when discussing the ideal division of cattle among brothers (and wives): they therefore represent an equitable division of stock as seen by various elders.

is very great: by this time his herd is generally large enough for him to cope by himself, thus giving his younger brothers a chance to build up their own herds. But the father always retains the ultimate ownership of all their herds for their cattle rightfully belong to his, the father's, total herd, and until his death or advanced senility, they should refer to him before alienating any cattle, Thus, by interfering in his sons' affairs (page 56), Lunget's father was well within his rights.

The father occasionally directs the mother to give one of her sons a heifer from her allotted herd, when for instance he is pleased with the boy's skill and initiative in managing the cattle in a difficult situation, or at the time of his birth or circumcision. Above and beyond these gifts it is the mother who gives away her cattle to her sons: so far as the father is concerned, these gifts still remain inside her allotted herd. He can only curtail any attempt by her at favouring one particular son in what he considers to be an unfair manner by indirect means:

> 23. Rianta had two wives. His senior wife was very fond of her second son and gave him more cattle from her allotted herd than the eldest son. Rianta disapproved of this, especially as he personally regarded the eldest son as a more worthy person. The only measures he could take to amend the situation were indirect: when a kinsman of this wife came to ask him for a cow, he would frequently take it from the herd accumulated by the second son as this herd was still a part of her allotted herd; and when his second wife died childless, Rianta took her entire allotted herd and gave it to his eldest son.

When a woman dies, her youngest son inherits the remainder of her allotted herd that has not been allocated to her other sons. The Samburu argue that these other sons have already had a chance to build up their own herds from hers and some of them may even have married with it; in her old age it is to her youngest son that she is expected to look for support. In certain circumstances, if she dies young before her various sons have divided the bulk of her herd among themselves, the elders may agree to the stock being divided among them so that the youngest is not left with an inordinate number compared with the others. If she dies leaving a son, then the elders would only agree to the father's reclaiming any of her allotted herd in exceptional circumstances. For instance, when Sopoitan married for the third time (page 43) after the death of his first and then his second wife, he had very few stock in his residual herd and those of his first wife belonged rightfully to her infant son. The elders of the local clan group agreed that he should use a substantial portion of this herd to marry with, arguing that it would be used to provide the boy with a foster mother. In theory, when he grows up, this boy should have substantial claims to her herd along with her true sons.

The continued absence of a wife from her husband's home provides both a reason for his wanting to exploit her herd more than that of any other wife and a means by which he can do it:

24. Parsakau's first wife was constantly running away from him and going to live with other men. During her absences he would unhesitatingly alienate cattle from her allotted herd in order to satisfy the requests of his stock friends and kinsmen. In this way he was indirectly helping his second wife and her sons to build up their allotted herd by not exploiting it for his own ends.

Meanwhile, his first wife gave birth to three sons by other men away from Parsakau's homestead; by custom they were his rightful heirs. When he was a very old man, Parsakau informed the elders of his local clan group that he wished the eldest son of his second wife to inherit his residual herd as this woman and her sons had been constantly loyal to him; he argued that the normal ties which bind father and son had never developed within his senior family and that normal rules of inheritance need not therefore apply. This was a dangerous suggestion, for the Samburu maintain that any change in custom, especially one associated with death, can lead to mystical misfortune; but it was not entirely without precedent, and the elders consented.

If possible, however, the elders of a local clan group will oppose the whims of an eccentric man who wishes to reverse custom. It is considered unnecessary to risk severe mystical misfortune.

25. On his death bed, Leparso accused his senior son, Malayon, of having poisoned him. He cursed him and disinherited him. After the death, the elders of the local clan group decided that Leparso had been almost delirious at the time and that his dying wish should be ignored. Malayon should inherit the residual herd.

They argued that there was no proof of his guilt and that it was most unlikely that he had tried to poison his father. As one elder pointed out to me, 'If Malayon did kill his father, then the dead man's curse will bring about his own death. God (*Nkai*) knows what is right. But to take away the cattle from Malayon when he is the eldest son is mystically dangerous (*kotolo*). God hates it.' It was felt that other people beside Malayon might suffer misfortune by such a change in custom.

26.* Seletu preferred the second son of his first wife to the eldest; he did not approve of the lavish generosity of the eldest, Modet, and asserted that it amounted to wastefulness. He said that if Modet inherited his residual herd then it would be rapidly dissipated, whereas if the second son inherited the herd instead then it would remain intact for this son was more prudent. When in 1959 he was very ill, Seletu insisted that the second son should inherit the herd. The elders of the local clan group disputed this decision after his death; prudence and meanness are matters of personal opinion, and they regarded Modet as a worthy man and Seletu and his second son as mean men whose 'prudence' prevented them from helping others in need. They therefore wanted Modet to inherit. Modet, however, said that as it was his father's wish that he should not inherit the residual herd, he had no desire to do so. He pointed out that he had already built up a considerable herd of his own from cattle allotted to his mother and that the irregularity in custom would only be really dangerous if he, the senior son, opposed it, which he did not.

By refusing to accept the elders' advice in the matter, Modet has strengthened his reputation as a worthy man. He has impressed them that he rates obedience to his father's wishes above immediate economic gain. The second son has a weaker claim to the cattle in his possession than Modet, and it is said that their maternal and agnatic kinsmen will come to him asking for gifts rather than to Modet. Altogether he is in a vulnerable position and in the last resort he may not benefit at all from his father's bequest, just as Modet may not lose.

Irregular inheritance, however, is comparatively rare, and every instance in which it is contemplated is a matter for careful discussion by the local clan group or groups involved. Public opinion will generally oppose it except in unusual circumstances. Any man with a grievance who feels that custom will support his case may raise the matter for discussion. If the elders see it as a clear case for restitution (as in example 21 page 55) then it is unlikely that anyone will effectively oppose their decision. Cases have been recorded of men, reared in their mothers' brothers' homes, who as adults came to reclaim large herds of cattle purloined by their paternal kinsmen and were unconditionally awarded them by the clan elders.

On the one hand, the inheritance of stock is defined by custom, and custom is controlled by the local clan elders who are prepared to intervene in any matter. On the other hand, the division of the mother's allotted herd, where custom does not determine the outcome, is primarily controlled by the mother and her sons among themselves: where they fail to arrive at a satisfactory solution, the father may indirectly affect the outcome by alienating cattle from the herd of one son and giving gifts from his residual herd to another, and more distant kinsmen may affect it by begging from one son and not from another.

The Husband's Residual Herd and Polygamy

Polygamy is popular among the Samburu and is eventually practised by a high proportion of them: the following table gives an estimate of the rates of polygamy at various ages:[1]

Proportion of Polygamists Associated with Age

Age-set and approximate age range of elders in sample		Sample size	Percentage with 2 or more wives	Percentage with 3 or more wives
Merisho	58–71 yrs.	372	60·8%	26·1%
Kiliako	43–58 yrs.	1,222	52·7%	12·1%
Mekuri	32–43 yrs.	1,278	30·3%	3·2%
Kimaniki	30–32 yrs.	2,863	1·4%	0·0%

In other words, a man who lives to the age of perhaps 50 has a good chance of marrying more than one wife. But he must be

[1] These figures are taken from the tax-book census collected in 1959. See the appendix for further details.

The age range of 30–32 years for the Kimaniki age-set refers only to those members who are likely to have married more than once and not to the age-set as a whole.

able to build up his residual herd considerably before he can contemplate a second marriage. The way in which he does this is now outlined.

At his first marriage a man divides his total herd, allotting the major portion to his wife and retaining the remainder. It is with this remainder, his residual herd, that he marries on subsequent occasions. After his first marriage he may have only five or ten head of cattle left in his residual herd and its natural increase will be too slow for his designs. He must therefore exploit his wife's allotted herd without antagonizing her unnecessarily and without openly contravening custom. He can protect his residual herd from those who beg from him by giving away cattle from his wife's allotted herd, but he is not obliged to give any further cattle to his wife after the initial allotment and any stock he acquires from stock friends and from his own classificatory sisters' husbands and sisters' sons are put into his residual herd.

In this way he is augmenting his residual herd at the expense of his wife's allotted herd, but only indirectly. If one man gives a stock friend a cow, a return gift is made only many years later; and when it is made, he may lie to his wife so that she cannot argue – even if she suspects – that it is, in effect, a return gift for the cow that he took from her some time ago and is rightfully hers. To ask for the return gift of a cow from a stock friend too soon would excite her suspicions that there is collusion between the two men to exploit her allotted herd and this could cause unnecessary bad feeling.

Within the homestead, so long as his sons are still too young to try to assert their own and their mother's rights, there is inevitably this competition between a man and his wife for stock, but it is not normally carried on to the point of being a constant sore in family relations. It is a point of conflicting interest about which both husband and wife normally appear to have a very clear understanding and a certain respect. The husband does not spend his time scheming to exploit the allotted herd, but when a clear opportunity presents itself to increase the obligation of a stock friend by making a gift without being unreasonable to his own wife, then he will probably take it.

The Husband's Residual Herd and Polygamy

In other respects, so far as stock are concerned, his wives' problems are his own problems. All the herds of the homestead are herded together and no one in the family wants any unnecessary losses. Each woman milks the cattle of her allotted herd and the husband allocates the milking of his residual herd to certain wives according to their present needs. The milk from these residual cattle is shared by everyone in the hut, but the husband retains full rights in the animals themselves.

It is evident from the table on page 65 that about 40% of the men who live to the age of 60 do not have second wives, and among these there are some who specifically maintain that they do not want further wives. The two reasons that they give for this choice are that co-wives tend to quarrel with each other and at times place the husband in an impossible position, and that in order to marry a second time a man must build up his residual herd which is only possible if he is prepared to estrange his own interests from those of his wife and family and face their mistrust. These men maintain that so long as the first wife bears them a number of sons, they prefer monogamy and domestic harmony.

Other men regard this as a strange attitude. Why, they ask, should a man prefer absolute peace with his first wife to the chance of having another wife and yet more sons? What does he do when his wife is old and all his sons are grown up? Polygamy creates new problems, but as was noted in Chapter One, it has many benefits for the Samburu.

It is sound policy for a man who wishes to marry a number of times to keep his residual herd fairly small, while at the same time increasing his stock friend's obligations towards him and obtaining promises for future gifts. If he were to augment his residual herd too rapidly then this would strengthen the claim of his wife that he should not alienate cattle from her herd when he has plenty in his own. It is only when his next marriage is imminent that he asks his stock friends, kinsmen and classificatory sisters' husbands and sisters' sons to fulfil their promises to give him stock. Even at this point, however, he may only build up his residual herd to a part of its effective size in order to conceal a number of cattle from his bride for future marriages. He may even drive some of his cattle to be

67

looked after by friends until after the marriage has been completed and the herd allotted; once she has no further claim to his residual herd he may drive back these concealed cattle without offering any explanation. Whatever she may think of his tactics, in the eyes of his own clansmen never could he show more prudence.

Begging cattle is infrequent and it is largely confined to the time when a man wishes to build up his residual herd in preparation for marriage. Up to this point he is the only person who knows the exact size that this herd could attain. At the same time as he is travelling about the country to get the consent of various close kinsmen of the girl he proposes to marry he may also be visiting his own kinsmen, stock friends and wife-receiving affines to ask them for stock. With the news that he is preparing for his own marriage, he has a strong case to ask their help.

Once he has started to build up his residual herd in this way, an elder is normally careful to refuse other people's requests for cattle. He does this in the first place because with a residual herd of a considerable size he has less justification in alienating cattle from his wives' allotted herds; and in the second place because there may be considerable anxiety among these wives concerning the future position of the new wife and he does not wish to aggravate their feelings.

The following table indicates how the total herd of an elder might be divided among his four wives in the course of his life from his first marriage to his death. The figures might be typical of an exceptionally fortunate man.[1]

By concealing a portion of his residual herd at each marriage a husband seems to give each successive wife a larger portion of his herd than in fact he does. By manipulating his rights in the various allotted herds, his residual herd has an average rate of increase which easily exceeds the average rate of increase of the allotted herds of his wives.

We are now in a position to appreciate why the Samburu, with such large herds, should be so concerned about the gift of a single animal. The size of an average herd may be about 80

---

[1] See footnote on page 61 above. In order to avoid complication, the stock given to the bride by each co-wife and the bridewealth payments made by the husband are ignored.

Summary

Typical Development of a Total Herd

Age of Elder (a) and other details	Residual Herd concealed	Residual Herd unconcealed	Allotted Herds 4th wife	3rd wife	2nd wife	1st wife	Total Herd
(a) 30 years old							40
(b) conceals 3 cattle	3 ↙ 40 ↘	37					
(c) marries 1st wife	3	2				35	
(a) 40 years old						50	90
(b) conceals 7 cattle	7 ↙ 40 ↘	33				50	
(c) marries 2nd wife	7	3			30	50	
(a) 50 years old					40	65	135
(b) conceals 5 cattle	5 ↙ 30 ↘	25			40	65	
(c) marries 3rd wife	5	5		20	40	65	
(a) 57 years old				30	50	90	205
(b) conceals 7 cattle	7 ↙ 35 ↘	28		30	50	90	
(c) marries 4th wife	7	3	25	30	50	90	
(a) 65 years old – dies	30*		30	35	65	110	270
Average annual rate of increase	15·1%		2·3%	3·8%	3·1%	3·3%	5·6%

* These 30 head of cattle are the residual herd inherited by the senior son.

head of cattle, but the size of a residual herd, to which a man looks for his future marriage, is much smaller and each beast in it has an enhanced value for him. Every animal which he begs from his classificatory sisters' husbands and sisters' sons, his kinsmen and stock friends may be put into this residual herd. The intense interest of a girl's kinsmen in the stability of her marriage becomes readily intelligible when it is appreciated that all the cattle they have received since her wedding have been placed in and are breeding in their residual herds and their value is increased. The power of the husband to demand a complete return of the stock plus increase plus replacement for any dead animals would make them seek to avoid divorce in all normal circumstances.

Summary

Bridewealth among the Samburu is low, amounting to six or

eight head of cattle only, and this is less than one-tenth of the average size estimated for Samburu herds. But wealth is nevertheless an important asset in marriage, not only because a man's affines stand to gain more if he is rich, but also because in order to marry he must be able to convince them that he can support a new wife and family adequately. Competition for his herds by the sons of various wives is avoided by allotting each wife a separate herd from which her sons can form herds of their own. But this does not altogether inhibit competition between brothers who share rights in their mother's allotted herd, and it creates a problem for the husband who wishes to build up yet another herd in order to marry a new wife. He achieves this by alienating cattle from his wives' allotted herds, a privilege which custom allows him, without necessarily returning cattle which he himself acquires to these wives: he puts such cattle in his own residual herd and as a result this herd grows rapidly at the expense of the allotted herds which are always being used to fulfil his social obligations. It is the importance to him of his residual herd for his future marriages which accounts for the concern that the Samburu have over gifts, especially gifts of female cattle: their total herds are quite large and a single cow is not particularly significant, but their residual herds are on average much smaller than this and each cow belonging to these herds has an enhanced value.

Thus another aspect of marital strain lies in the competition between a man and his wife for the cattle he allots her. Frequently, this does not correspond to the strain between him and her kinsmen for it is her kinsmen who ask him for cattle from her herd, and in complying he can avoid direct friction with her by playing her off against them. But at other times, the strain between husband and wife may correspond broadly to that which exists between him and her kinsmen, and if he exploits her herds too ruthlessly then she may be tempted to run away to her parents' home and have their sympathy. When this seems liable to occur, as on other occasions where there is a breach of custom, his clansmen will often interfere in his domestic affairs in order to ensure a satisfactory outcome.

Chapter Four

THE STRUCTURE OF SAMBURU SOCIETY

AT this point it is convenient to give a coherent outline of the social structure of Samburu society. Two institutions, the segmentary descent system and cutting across it the age-set system, stand out above all others in importance.

The Segmentary Descent System

The segmentary descent system has six distinguishable levels, each being characterized by certain beliefs and prescribed forms of behaviour which are summarized below. I refer to these in order of ascending size as: (*a*) the lineage group; (*b*) the hair-sharing group; (*c*) the sub-clan; (*d*) the clan; (*e*) the phratry; and (*f*) the moiety. Membership is automatically inherited through the father in normal circumstances. All the segments recorded for the upper four levels (*c* to *f*) are presented in the chart on pages 72–3.

(*a*) *The lineage group.* The lineage group is not always a strictly defined social unit, but it is useful to distinguish it here. When a girl is to be married it is understood that elders closely related to her should be consulted by the prospective suitor and that they have a joint claim to one of the heifers given in the bridewealth. Those men who are at any time included within this range may be thought to constitute a lineage group. The lineage group has typically between 10 and 20 male members dispersed over thousands of square miles and extending as a lineage to two or possibly three generations beyond the oldest living members. It is its size as well as its generation depth which determines the exact composition. If in the course of time it grows too large, then implicitly it divides into two or

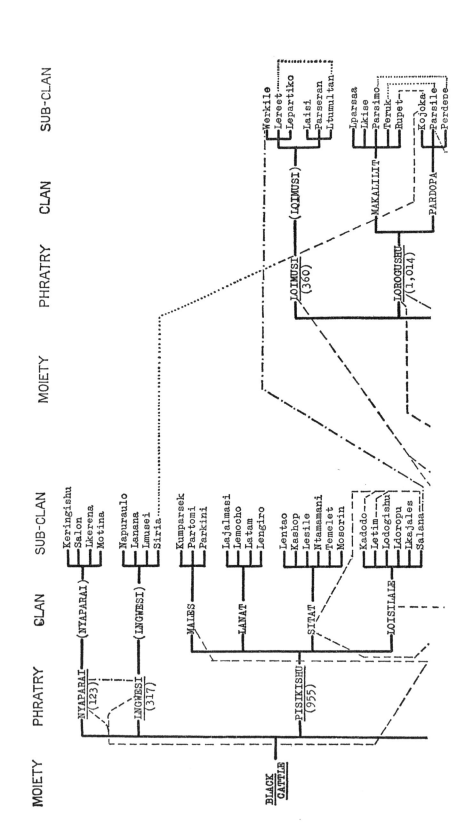

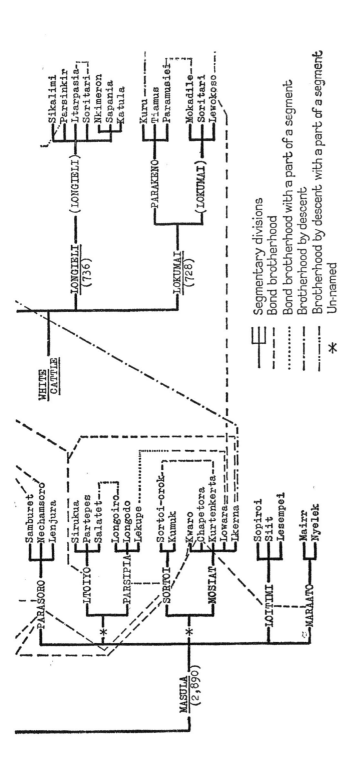

The Samburu Segmentary Descent System.

more lineage groups as the more distant kinsmen of some girl are not directly consulted on her marriage and can no longer claim the heifer of the bridewealth because there are always more closely related elders with stronger claims.

(*b*) *The hair-sharing group.* The hair-sharing group is more specifically defined. It is believed that when a man dies, the contamination of his death infects the hair of his age mates within a certain range of kinship, and in order to rid themselves of this contamination and avert misfortune, they must all shave off their hair soon after death: they are said to 'share their hair' (*kong'ar lpapit*). The 'hair-sharing group' may be defined as the range of kinsmen within which age mates share their hair, and would typically number about 60 men. There is generally a vague belief in a foundling ancestor, but only occasionally can a full lineage be remembered.

(*c*) *The sub-clan.* A sub-clan typically numbers between 100 and 200 men. There are two distinct customs associated with it. The first is that within an age-set only members of the same sub-clan normally address one another by their own personal names: other age mates may be addressed formally as age mates (*murata*), by some name referring to their family or lineage, or by a popular nickname: to address them by their own personal names would be a sign of gross disrespect. The second is that girls of the sub-clan are avoided sexually: this again is a matter of respect. The sub-clan is a group within which friendships tend to be cordial and lasting. Possibly more than three-quarters of a man's stock friends are members of his sub-clan.

(*d*) *The clan.* The clan emerges as a politically significant unit both among the elders (see Chapters Two and Seven) and among the moran (see Chapter Five). The moran of each clan, although dispersed over a wide area, form what is referred to here as a *Club* and they perform their age-set ceremonies together to the exclusion of all outsiders.

A common feature of the clan is that it is divided into three or more sub-clans (see the chart on page 72).[1] This is probably

---

[1] The one exception to this general rule is Maraato clan which has only two sub-clans. It is also atypical in other respects: it is the only clan which permits intermarriage between its sub-clans and it has close Dorobo associations in the north of the country around Mount Ngiro.

a significant factor in stabilizing the relationship between these sub-clans. In a dispute which involves two sub-clans of a clan, there is a third party (the other collateral sub-clans) that can mediate. Informants have actually pointed out to me that if a clan had only two segments then disputes would increase in intensity until there would be so little unity between them that they would become separate clans; where on the other hand, there are three or more segments, the disputes between them involve different segments at different times and this tends to be stabilizing. There is a general belief, for instance, that Lorogushu was at one time a clan with two sub-clans; but as these developed into opposed factions, there was an inevitable rupture and the two factions became what are today separate clans (Makalilit and Pardopa). Longieli clan, on the other hand, has seven sub-clans and there is a popular tradition that there has always been strife between them, although they have not so far aligned themselves into two distinct factions. These examples may well account for the fact that all other clans have between three and six sub-clans: less than three or more than six could be inherently unstable.

(*e*) *The phratry*. The Samburu have eight phratries which in theory are all exogamous and elect from each age-set of moran a *ritual leader* (*launoni*) with certain ceremonial duties and ritual powers. Members of the same age-set and phratry are referred to here as a *phratry age-set* (*olporror*): thus each phratry age-set has its own ritual leader and consists of the Clubs of each clan of that phratry. These are aspects of a model phratry as the Samburu themselves see it, but they are blurred in practice: one phratry (Masula) does not observe the rules of exogamy at all strictly, and another (Lokumai) has a variable number of ritual leaders in each age-set. Furthermore, the distinction between phratry and clan is not altogether a simple one, although it is useful. In the first place, four of the eight phratries are also single clans as they are not internally divided at this level of segmentation. And secondly, there is a certain local variation, especially within Masula phratry, in the way in which segments combine to form clans so that the segmentary structure of the clan sometimes varies with the area under consideration: commonly, when one clan is poorly represented in an area and

75

another clan of the same phratry is well represented, the two tend to become merged and the elders belong to the same local clan groups and the moran perform their ceremonies together and belong to the Club of the larger clan of that area. The chart on page 72 shows the generally accepted combination of sub-clans within each clan and of clans within each phratry, but for Masula in particular it is subject to considerable local variation, and to a minor extent this is true also of other phratries.

There is a marked difference between the information that a Samburu will give on the affairs and general structure of his own clan and those of another clan of his phratry: he can be precise and consistent on the former, but he is generally in-articulate, uninterested and even misleading on the latter. As a member of his own local clan group wherever he is, he is well informed on the affairs of his clan, but he is an outsider to other clans of his phratry and knows little about them.

(*f*) *The moiety.* There are two moieties, each consisting of four phratries. But apart from the fact that one of these, the Black Cattle (*ngishu narok*), is ritually senior, the division has no very great significance. There are so many exceptions to the general-izations which Samburu try to make about the tribal origins, the differences in customary practice, and the marital habits of the two moieties that these can only be accepted as state-ments which reflect the way the Samburu see themselves and not as statements of actual behaviour.

Of all these levels of segmentation, the only one which has a name regularly applied to it is the phratry, for which the term is *lmarei* (pl. *lmareita*). The closeness of this term to the word for rib (*lmarei*, pl. *lmarein*) could be significant: the ribs of a carcase are divided equally on both sides as are the phratries within each moiety. But the Samburu do not themselves point this out and nor do they associate the two moieties with the left hand and the right hand.

A common feature of these levels of segmentation, particularly between sub-clans and higher levels is the belief in diverse ancestry and often of immigrations from different tribes so that the Samburu tend to regard themselves as a mixed rather than a pure blooded society. Such beliefs do not correspond with any apparent lack of unity within the society: on the contrary, the Samburu maintain that the firm tradition of solidarity that has been maintained for several generations between segments is of greater importance than any myth of origin. It is not a fictional tie of blood which binds men together but the shared fortune and misfortune, the gift, service and repayment which are believed to make them one people; once an immigrant has entered into the life of the society economically and socially, he is a Samburu, and sooner or later this generally entails membership of a clan and sub-clan.

This essential unity of interests and loyalties is expressed in the terms of fictional kinship which clansmen and even phratrymen use with complete disregard for any conflicting beliefs in diverse ancestry: they refer to one another as brothers (*lalashe*, pl. *lalashera*) and address one another by terms which imply agnatic kinship. These include *arankaji* (*ara*=son of, *nkaji*= (lit.) a hut); *arankang* (*nkang*=a settlement, a home); *araang* (*ang*=our, used here as a pronoun); *arayieyo* (*yieyo*=mother), a term which marks exceptional cordiality as it is primarily used by full brothers who wish to draw attention to their uterine connection; and *aramenye* (*menye*=father), a term with a formal ring about it and certain coercive connotations, because it is primarily used by bond brothers (see below) when addressing one another. But whether cordial or formal, each of these terms is used to accentuate the close ties that bind them together and may be resorted to on occasions when the obligations of clanship are being invoked.

Inter-Segmentary Ties

The segmentary structure is cross-cut by a number of ties which link certain segments. These ties are of two kinds and they are referred to here as *brotherhood by descent* and *bond brotherhood*. In the chart on page 72 only those ties which implicate the larger segments are recorded.

In *brotherhood by descent* segments of different clans are linked by the belief that they are both descendants of one ancestor and this prevents them intermarrying. But the tie is a weak one, being no stronger than that which binds the clans of a phratry. Men tend to regard their brothers by descent as outsiders and do not commonly form close friendships with them.

In *bond brotherhood* there is not merely an acknowledgment of some putative agnatic tie, but there is also an exaggeration of the norms of behaviour between kinsmen: a man should normally comply with any reasonable request of a kinsman, but he is morally obliged to do so with the request of a bond brother, however unreasonable; peace and genteel behaviour are ideal between kinsmen, but they are absolutely essential between bond brothers if mystical misfortune is to be avoided. Any slight aggravation or disappointment, however involuntary, on the part of a man against his bond brother may have the effect of a potent curse; and as the relationship is completely symmetrical any bitterness which this in its turn engenders in the bond brother may have a reciprocal effect, and misfortune can be expected by both sides. Strained relations between them are to be avoided therefore at all cost. On the one hand a man is constrained to comply unconditionally with the request of a bond brother, and on the other hand he should avoid using his own powers of coercion, for though it is likely that he will be granted any request he makes, by making it he shows that he is prepared to initiate something which will not only cause some embarrassment, but could even lead to misfortune; he would be criticized by his own clansmen as well as by others if he used this power excessively. It is a relationship which engenders distrust amounting at times to hostility: every man would like to maintain that his clansmen do not exploit their bond brothers preferring to avoid them as much as possible. At the same time, many Samburu are prepared in private to criticize their bond brothers for not sharing these worthy sentiments for the relationship and for trying to exploit it unscrupulously. As one man put it, referring to a certain segment, 'We do not ask them for anything for they are our bond brothers and it would be bad to curse them. But they are mean; they are outsiders; they do not respect us in the same way.'

Other forms of behaviour expected of bond brothers are similar to those observed by members of a sub-clan. A man may call his bond brothers of his own age-set by their personal names and he should avoid their sisters, his bond sisters, and respect their requests. He may address the wives of a bond brother by the term *parsintan*, which implies a privileged familiarity and even a discreet sexual licence between them. But in point of fact it would normally stop short of this and be confined to jocular repartee verging on obscenity. To go further might excite the anger of the husband who should on the face of it accept the situation, but might harbour a secret resentment, and as he is a bond brother this above all things should be avoided.

Fortes has noted a similar relationship of privileged moral coercion between segments among the Tallensi, and at the same level of the political structure there are joking relationships.[1] The significance of the Samburu equivalent where a man has a power of moral coercion over his bond brothers and enjoys a mild form of joking relationship with their wives may be as follows: bond brotherhood involves an element of hostility; marriage also involves a certain hostility between man and wife (see Chapter 3); thus while a man may feel slightly hostile towards a woman because she is the wife of his bond brother, at the same time his mistrust of her husband is something he shares with her; the resultant of these opposed sentiments is a joking relationship in which the shared joke centres on their privileged familiarity with each other at the expense of the husband (i.e. expressing shared hostility towards the husband). In suggesting an explanation which relies on the sentiments of those involved, I would point out that there is no obligation to joke with a bond brother's wife and many Samburu do not do so: it is not a *prescribed*, but a *privileged* form of behaviour. But there are other men who show great delight in having an excuse to play in this way.

It is worth noting that only two instances (both quoted in Chapter Six) were recorded in which bond brothers had used their powers of coercion to settle disputes; and in each one they exerted their influence to control dissident moran after being 'invited' (i.e. coerced) to do so by the elders of that clan. My informants recognized these two cases as fully legitimate

[1] Fortes, 1945, pp. 95–6. It is perhaps worth noting that the Rendille do, in fact, have a joking relationship associated with certain of their bond brotherhoods. (See *The Survey*, Chapter Four.)

uses of coercion and no doubt there have been others; but generally it is the negative aspects of bond brotherhood which are most striking, and every effort will be made to solve disputes some other way before resorting to this method.

New ties of bond brotherhood between shallow lineages are formed from time to time after the seizure of blood-wealth following a homicide; in spite of the asymmetrical nature of a single homicide and reparation, such relationships are entirely symmetrical. This is not a topic which is discussed here,[1] but it is worth noting once again another element of hostility associated with the relationship. Some informants maintain that all ties of bond brotherhood must have originated with bloodshed, although the actual myths relating to the various ties, where myths exist, do not always stress homicide as the initial cause.

This way of forming a new bond brotherhood is a useful mechanism which manifestly inhibits the development of a feud between rival segments following some homicide: so long as the new bond brotherhood is acknowledged by both sides they tend to avoid each other and even small incidents which could lead to reprisals are avoided. The decision to form a bond brotherhood after a particular homicide appears to depend on the extent to which the elders expect further incidents after the initial conciliation.[2]

Of the two types of cross-cutting tie, that of bond brotherhood is the more striking and widespread.

The Age-set System

An *age-set* is quite different from an *age grade*. An *age-set* is composed of all the men who have been circumcised in youth during a specified period of time, and a new one is generally formed every 12 to 14 years. An *age grade*, on the other hand, is a stage through which each male passes at some period of his life (unless he dies first) together with others of his age-set. Thus

---

[1] Further details of bond brotherhood and its relation to homicide are given in *The Survey*, Chapter Three.

[2] cf. Simmel's comments on the mystically religious element of conciliation and the need for it to be lasting if it is not to be dragged down to the level of a frivolous game as every new breach is followed by a new conciliation (Simmel, trans. Wolff, 1955, pp. 117–21).

each man, although he belongs to only one age-set from his youth onwards, passes through a number of age grades.

There are three principal age grades among men. These are *boyhood* (from birth to adolescence) before they are members of an age-set, *moranhood* (from adolescence to early manhood) which corresponds to the period between their initiation into an age-set and their marriage, and *elderhood* (from early manhood until death).

At the beginning of 1960, living men belonged to six age-sets of which the members of five had previously entered the age grade of elderhood and a few members of the sixth were in the process of entering it as they married. The majority of the sixth age-set, however, did not contemplate marriage and were well within the age grade of moran. Later in 1960 the first initiates of a new age-set were circumcised and became moran. Normally there is only one age-set inside the age grade of moran, but during this transitional period of *change-over* when boys are becoming moran and moran are about to become elders, there are two age-sets.

These seven age-sets were as follows:

Dates of Initiation of Living Age-sets

Age-grade	Age-set	Date of initiation
Elders	Marikon	perhaps about 1880
	Terito	about 1893
	Merisho	about 1912
	Kiliako	probably 1921 (Masula) and 1922 (others)
	Mekuri	1936
Moran	Kimaniki	1948
	Kishili	1960 (Masula) and 1962 (others)

Women do not belong to age-sets, but they do have two age grades, *girlhood* and *womanhood*. A girl is circumcised at about the same age as a boy and is married as soon after this circumcision as possible.

The basic relationships which characterize the age-set system are equality between members of one age-set and inequality between members of different age-sets in which there is a moral

81

obligation to show respect for seniority. Members of one age-set, or *age mates*, are not merely equals, they are expected to observe certain norms of behaviour which derive from and express their joint membership of a corporate group. For example, no man should address an age mate related to his wife by the term which he would use for his other affines (*lautan*), as this essentially implies an asymmetrical relationship in which one of them – the wife-giver – has a superior claim to ask for gifts and favours: if he wishes to obtain help of some sort then he should ask him for this as an age mate and not as an affine. A man would never marry daughters of his age mates; he should avoid them throughout his life: by extension they are *his* daughters, just as their sons are *his* sons. When an elder stays overnight with an age mate, the latter should sleep in some other hut, leaving the visitor alone with his wife: this is an age-set obligation, and he should not pry into the sleeping arrangements that are made once his back is turned.

Members of adjacent age-sets are in a position of inequality, but the seniority of the older is not marked. If a member of the senior age-set is an elder when the junior age-set are still moran, then he should be respected as an elder because this is expected of all moran, but he has no power to curse by virtue of his seniority.

Members of alternate age-sets stand in a special relationship to each other in which the senior of the two has the power of a potent curse. This power is said to follow from the fact that it is members of the senior age-set who ceremonially bring the junior age-set into existence when it is first formed; they subsequently stand as moral guardians over the junior age-set and it is their duty to supervise its maturation, especially in its passage through the moran age grade. The particular act by which the new age-set is first formed and symbolically brought to life is the ceremonial kindling of a fire. Henceforth the relationship between the two age-sets is known as the *firestick relationship*, and so far as the junior age-set is concerned during its period in the moran age grade, the elders of the senior age-set are known as *firestick elders*. The term *firestick* (*olpiroi*) may be used to refer to these elders, or to the relationship between alternate age-sets, or as a reciprocal term of address

used between members of these age-sets when particular attention is being drawn to the relationship.

During the period of change-over when there are two age-sets
within the moran age grade, there are also two age-sets of firestick elders. Thus in 1960, when the Kishili age-set had been
initiated, the Mekuri age-set were their firestick elders and the
Kiliako age-set were firestick elders to the moran of the Kimaniki age-set. Previous firestick relationships which had existed
between the Mekuri and Merisho age-sets, the Kiliako and
Terito age-sets, and the Merisho and Marikon age-sets were
no longer of great importance as the junior of the two had in
each instance reached elderhood.

The feelings of affection between fathers and their sons
among the Samburu are held to be quite incompatible with the
firestick relationship: they point out that if a lot of firestick
elders have moran sons then their power as an age-set will be
weakened, for the fathers will be unwilling to curse their sons
and the curse will be less effective. For this reason, the Samburu
insist that no youths should be circumcised into less than three
age-sets below their fathers, even if a large number of them
must wait until they are well over twenty years old before they
can become moran. Exceptions to this rule are rare, and are
only made in special circumstances after the firestick elders
have carefully considered the merits of the case.

The age-set immediately senior to that of the firestick elders
are commonly known as the *fathers of the moran*. Thus the
Merisho, three age-sets senior to the Kimaniki, are their
'fathers', and the Kiliako are the 'fathers' of the Kishili. In
point of fact, only about one-half of the men recorded in
genealogies actually have fathers in this age-set; the remainder
are the sons of members of yet more senior age-sets. The
difference in seniority between men separated by two or more
age-sets is great and the senior of the two is held to have a potent
curse which is enhanced if he is actually an age mate of the
other's father. The power of the curse and the obligation to
show respect, however, are not stressed to the same extent as
they are in the firestick relationship: they are not a well defined
relationship between two age-sets, but follow logically from the
great difference in age.

83

Thus, the three principal age grades among males can be subdivided. In the age grade of boyhood there are *boys* and *initiates* about to become *moran*. In the moran age grade there are *junior moran* who have not performed a particular ceremony which gives them certain ritual and social privileges and the *senior moran* who have performed this ceremony: when there are two age-sets in the moran age grade, as there were later in 1960, then one of them are invariably senior moran and the others junior moran, and by the time the junior moran are promoted to senior moranhood, practically all the members of the senior age-set will have married and settled down to elderhood. In the age grade of elderhood, there are *junior elders* who have not yet become firestick elders to any age-set of moran, there are *firestick elders*, and there are *senior elders* who, while they still have a firestick relationship with the junior elders, are better known for the fact that they are fathers of the moran. The term *senior elders* may aptly be applied to elders of all the more senior age sets.

The distribution of the various age-sets in these age grades in 1957, 1960, and as it could conceivably be in 1966 is shown in the following chart:

The Development of Age-sets through the Age Grade System

Age grade	Sub-age grade	Age-sets 1957	1960	1966
Elders	senior elders	Marikon Terito Merisho	Marikon Terito Merisho	Terito Merisho Kiliako
	firestick elders	Kiliako	Kiliako Mekuri ⟋—	Mekuri
	junior elders	Mekuri	Mekuri	Kimaniki
Moran	senior moran	Kimaniki	Kimaniki	
	junior moran		Kishili ⟋	—⟋— Kishili
Boys	initiates		Kishili	
	boys	no formed age-set	no formed age-set	no formed age-set

In this chart, the years 1960 and 1966 are represented as years of transition for the Kishili age-set, and 1960 as a year of transition for the Mekuri age-set. For an indefinite period after 1960, the transition of the Kimaniki from senior moranhood to junior elderhood takes place as they marry and settle down, but there is no mass promotion as there is with age-sets when they are initiated or become senior moran. The years 1960 to 1966, therefore, represent a period in which the Kimaniki are both senior moran and junior elders, and the Kiliako are both firestick elders and senior elders. The process of change-over should be complete by 1966 when the Kishili may well perform the ceremony which promotes them to senior moranhood; and by this time the remaining one-third of their number who were not actually intiated at the very earliest opportunity because they were too young are likely to have been circumcised and incorporated as a recent addition to the age-set; it is uncommon for more boys to be initiated after this point has been reached. By 1966 the few remaining members of the Marikon age-set may well have died.

Age Grades and the Maturation of the Male

The modes of behaviour observed by males at different periods of their lives – at least those expected of them – and the attitudes and associated mystical beliefs are criteria by which the various age grades are clearly distinguished. The most striking of the privileges and avoidances are summarized in the chart on page 86 and an approximate time scale is indicated by the age of a fairly typical male. Shading indicates the expected behaviour and broken lines indicate possible, though rather unusual, extensions of behaviour. Considerable variation in the order of certain events associated with certain periods is possible and these are marked with an asterisk. The following notes amplify this chart.[1]

(*a*) Circumcision (approx. 15 years old).

About two-thirds of all the future members of an age-set are circumcised as soon as it is formed and become moran for a

---

[1] A systematic account of all the customs associated with these stages of a man's life is given in *The Survey* (Chapter Three). Here only a summary is given.

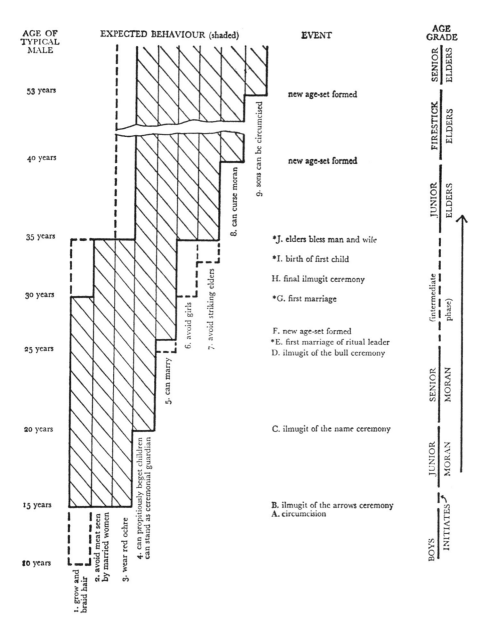

Modes of Behaviour Associated with Age.

86

period of perhaps 15 years. The remainder are circumcised several years later and are only moran for a part of this time. A boy does not become a *moran* immediately after circumcision. He is still an initiate under certain ritual prohibitions which govern his behaviour and diet. Both before and after their circumcision, initiates collect together in bands, singing their song, *lebarta*, and using it to coerce elders to give them food and to allow other potential members of their phratry age-set to join them and be circumcised among them.

These aspects of initiation are unique in the life of the male, but as they are only temporary, they have not been included in the chart.

(*b*) The *Ilmugit of the Arrows* Ceremony (one month later).

During their moranhood, youths perform a series of cere-monies known as *ilmugit*: at each of these they congregate in their clans present in one area and build a large settlement; every performer must provide an ox for slaughter or failing that a goat. The *ilmugit of the arrows* is the first of these cere-monies, and in the course of its performance all the initiates become junior moran. Each initiate has two ritual partners who slaughter his *ilmugit* ox (or goat) on his behalf and enter into a relationship with him similar to that of a bond brother-hood with the same privileges of moral coercion. These ritual partners lead him to his mother's hut where he vows to her that he will no longer eat meat seen by any married woman: such meat is *menong'*, despised food (*a-men* = 'to despise'). The avoidance of this food is the most characteristic restriction observed by Samburu moran, and they themselves see it as a determining criterion of moranhood. It is not surrounded by mystical beliefs, but only by social sentiments of pride: a youth who does not observe this restriction is something less than a moran – he is behaving like a child. A second prohibition associated with this one is on any moran drinking milk by himself inside a settlement – there should always be an age mate present, and if the milk comes from cattle belonging to any member of his mistress's hair-sharing group, he should abstain altogether. Having made this vow to his mother, the initiate is now a moran and he can put red ochre on his head and body for the first time in his life as a decoration (see 3 in the chart). Moran would consider it impertinent of a boy to wear red ochre before this time and they might beat him up. It is also said that if he has an older uncircumcised brother, then the latter might be in some mystical danger from the act: just as full brothers should be circumcised in strict order of birth, so they should only wear red ochre for the first time in this order.

(*c*) The *Ilmugit of the Name* Ceremony (approx. 20 years old).

The *ilmugit* ceremony whereby junior moran are promoted to senior moranhood is the *ilmugit of the name*. It is the most important of the *ilmugit* ceremonies, a fact which is emphasized by the performance of a second ceremony identically named one month later. At the first of these two ceremonies, a *ritual leader* (*launoni*) is chosen from among the moran for each phratry age-set and he is installed in office by seizure. He has a potent curse over other members of his phratry age-set which he should threaten to use only in the interests of their peace and well-being, and to a lesser extent they have a reciprocal power over him which they can only use collectively, but not individually. A name is also chosen for the phratry age-set at this time. If the ritual leader dies before his first marriage, then all his phratry age mates shave their hair, and a new *ilmugit* of the name ceremony is performed, a new ritual leader and a new name are chosen. In order to protect themselves from the dire misfortune which might follow his death, members of a phratry age-set should actively prevent their ritual leader from joining in any affray or raid. The deputy ritual leader who is chosen at the same time is far less important, and his early death would not cause alarm.

On becoming a senior moran, a man's ritual status changes in two respects (4): first, it is no longer considered dangerous for a woman and her family if she bears a child by him provided that she is circumcised and that the union is not an incestuous one; and secondly, if he is his mother's eldest living son and his father is dead, then he acts as the ceremonial guardian to his younger brothers and sisters at their circumcisions, and the local clan elders come to bless him. When in later years these younger brothers and sisters show a marked respect for him, they may explain this simply by saying: 'He had butter put on his head when we were circumcised.' In other respects his

88

position is unchanged: he still may not marry and he still has no acknowledged power to influence the elders in choosing husbands for his younger sisters.

(*d*) The *Ilmugit of the Bull* Ceremony (approx. 26 years old).

After the performance of this ceremony, there should be no further initiations into this age-set, and it is unlikely that there have been any for a number of years prior to it. No moran should marry (5) until he has killed his ox for this ceremony, and today those who are away at work or in prison still do not marry until they have returned to their homes and have ceremonially slaughtered an ox *in lieu* of the one they failed to slaughter at the correct time.

The ritual leader should be the first of his phratry age-set to marry and he accomplishes this by a special form of marriage by coercion. Any moran who wishes to marry before him must first obtain his consent and should pay him a heifer; it was formerly rare for this to occur, but is more common today.

From this moment there is no precise point at which moran retire to elderhood. Various events which occur after the *ilmugit* of the bull ceremony are all stages in the gradual process: (*e*) the marriage of the ritual leader (approx 27 years old); (*f*) the initiation of a new age-set (approx. 28 years old); (*g*) the man's own first marriage (approx. 30 years old); (*h*) the final *ilmugit* ceremony, the *ilmugit of the milk and shrubs* (approx. 31 years old); (*i*) the first pregnancy or child bearing of his wife (approx. 32 years old); and (*j*) the blessing which he and his wife are given by the local clan elders (approx. 34 years old). The relative order of certain of these events (*e, g, i* and *j*) varies considerably from individual to individual, from phratry to phratry, and from age-set to age-set. For the phratry as a whole, the most significant event in this process is the performance by each of its clans of the final *ilmugit* ceremony, which occurs when the majority of moran have married, and this is said to be the point at which they all settle down to elderhood. For the individual male, however, the blessing of his wife and himself by the elders is more significant, since at this point he ceases to observe the food restrictions applied to moran, and there can no longer be any doubt that he is an elder.

In this period of transition from moranhood to elderhood, different moran behave differently according to the extent to which they are prepared to settle down: those who wish to become elders as soon as possible generally try to marry early and start to acquire the dignity of elders; and those who prefer still to remain as moran retain the accoutrements and behaviour of moranhood.

Growing long hair and braiding it (1) is popular among moran and certain styles may be worn by older boys; but once a man marries, it becomes increasingly likely that he will shave it off and keep it short, and it is almost certain that he will do this before the elders come to bless him and his wife. Allowing hair to grow long and braiding it is a matter of personal pride in moranhood and it has no religious significance (unlike shaving it at the death of a kinsman).

As he marries and behaves more maturely, a man should stop having sexual relations with uncircumcised girls (6): this is a matter of having the developed sense of shame and respect of an elder. But individuals may interpret this restriction liberally and may only abstain after the elders have come to bless them and release them from their food prohibitions. Similarly, no elder should strike another elder (7); this is partly a matter of respect and partly one of mystical danger to their children. But again, junior elders may find it hard to rid themselves of the impetuosity of moranhood and may only observe this restriction when their wives have become pregnant for the first time or when the food prohibitions are relaxed. Red ochre (3), the principal adornment of moranhood, can also be worn by elders, but as they grow older they use it less and less except on prescribed ceremonial occasions.

The curse which a man first acquires over the junior moran (8) when he becomes a firestick elder (approx. 40 years old) and his right to have his sons circumcised (9) when he becomes a senior elder (approx. 53 years old) have both been discussed in the previous section.

Broadly, it may be said that the behaviour discussed belongs to two categories: first that associated primarily with moranhood (1-3), and secondly that associated in an increasing degree with age (4-9).

Three Types of Seniority

In interpersonal relations, three types of seniority are discernible. These are age-set seniority, segmental seniority and generational seniority.

Age-set seniority has been discussed in the previous section and the term is self explanatory. Each age-set is internally divided into three or four parts, *sub-age-sets*, which follows logically from the circumcision of batches of initiates into one age-set at different times. Sub-age-sets are discussed more fully in the next two chapters.

Segmental seniority might alternatively be called ceremonial seniority. In all major age-set ceremonies, there is a prescribed order in which initiates should be circumcised, huts be built or oxen be slaughtered, and this depends on the segmental seniority of the initiates, the senior males of the huts or the owners of the oxen. Segmental seniority refers to an individual's segmental position within his clan. Within his lineage group he has a recognized position which places him as senior or junior to all other members irrespective of generational differences (apart from father and son relationships). Similarly the lineage group has an undisputed position with respect to all other lineage groups of the hair-sharing group, and the hair-sharing group within the sub-clan, and the sub-clan within the clan. The inconsistencies between different accounts of genealogies concern the manner in which collateral lineages are linked, but not their relative positions of segmental seniority: this seniority is undisputed and is implicitly acknowledged in behaviour at each major age-set ceremony. Thus the Samburu segmentary descent system is not supported by a consistent, or even by a vaguely defined myth of unilineal descent incorporating the major segments of the tribe, but by prescribed ritual behaviour carefully followed under the keen guidance of the elders.

The maps on page 92 show two of the five settlements built by Pardopa clan for an *ilmugit* of the bull ceremony in 1958. They lay 60 miles apart, and the consistency with which segmental seniority determined the layout of huts may be judged by comparing the maps with the accompanying genealogy of all those who were present. The genealogy itself is drawn up

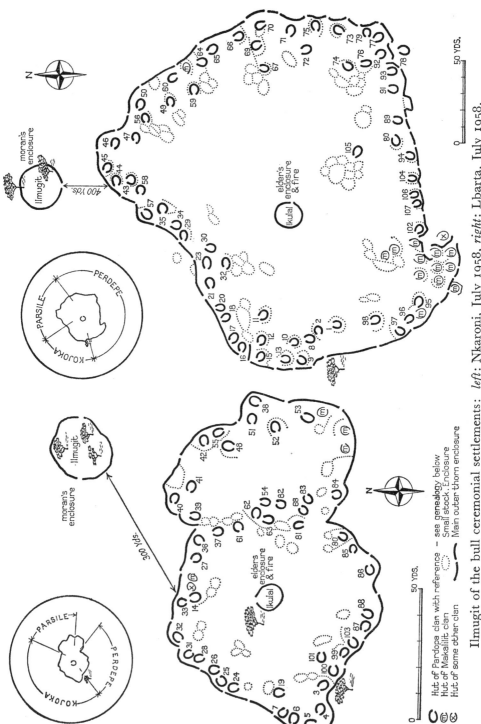

Ilmugit of the bull ceremonial settlements: *left*: Nkaroni, July 1958, *right*: Lbarta, July 1958.

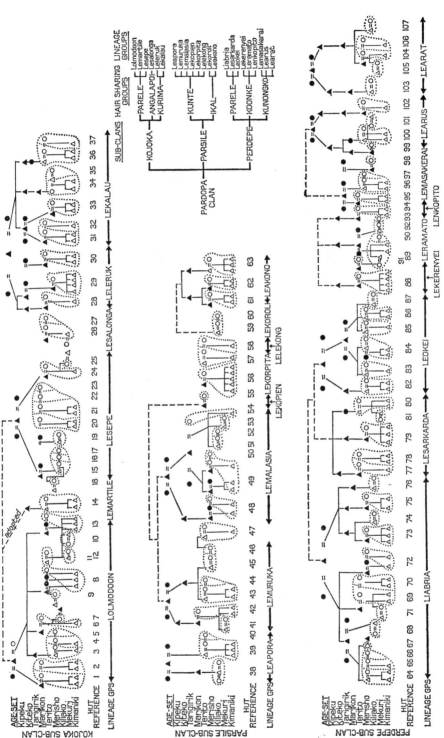

Plan and Genealogy of Two Ceremonial Settlements.

according to segmental seniority (from left to right) and age-set seniority (vertically). The ideal order of huts in each settlement should have been in a clockwise direction: i.e. the classifying number attached to each family and hence hut in the diagrams should have increased in order in this direction. The irregularities observed were all explained in terms of lateness of arrival at the settlement, inability to find space in the correct position (accounting for the confusion in the middle of the settlement at Nkaroni) or the wish to build close to a friend by some of those who did not regard themselves as playing an active role in the ceremony. Certain persons performing in the ceremony, particularly at Lbarta, belonged to the other Lorogushu clan, Makalilit. They had no prescribed position in the settlement, but their huts tended to be clustered together.

The genealogy represents just 25 % of Pardopa clan, nearly all the remaining 182 moran of this clan performed the ceremony at one of three other settlements. But by no means all the elders were present – this was not necessary. Moran who are full brothers are free to perform the ceremony in whichever of the *ilmugit* settlements they or their father may prefer, but they cannot split up to perform it in different places.

Generational seniority, as the term suggests, depends on the number of generations which men are removed from a common ancestor. In certain lineages it is of special importance where it concerns the relationship between a man and another's wife. If he is of the same generation as the husband or of an alternate generation, then he can enter into a relationship of privileged familiarity with her: they call each other by the term *parsintan* which implies that they can have discreet sexual relations and that the husband, though he is not expected to condone the affair openly, should at least be grateful if this leads to his wife's pregnancy. If, on the other hand, they belong to adjacent generations then the junior man and his wife stand as classificatory son and daughter-in-law to the senior and his wife even if their contempories in age. This implies avoidance, especially between the senior man and the other's wife and also respect by the junior and his wife for the other two. But the extent to which individual Samburu acknowledge these customs depends on the cordiality of their friendship, the for-

94

mality of the occasion, and the way in which they interpret such customs and are sensitive to public opinion: there is a distinct tendency among coevals to ignore generational differences on informal occasions and to lapse into reciprocal forms of behaviour. The system is well expressed by the term *alternations*[1] in which each man automatically belongs to the opposite alternation (*ltalepa*) to his father and sons, and to the same alternation as his brothers, his grandfather and grandsons.

In many lineages, this custom is extended and a set of alternations may be shared by all the members of a sub-clan or several collateral sub-clans, even though they do not share any belief in common descent. Every man in these segments knows which alternation he and all other members belong to.

An inverse correlation between these forms of seniority is occasionally to be seen among closely related kinsmen where a man's eldest son's eldest sons (segmentally senior) are contemporaries (age-set equal) of his youngest sons by a more recent wife (generationally senior). Thus in the chart on page 93, the moran of hut 54 is generationally senior to his age mates of huts 48 and 49, although he is segmentally junior to them: they respect him as a member of their father's generation, but they perform in ceremonies before he does.

The Structural Implications of Polygamy[2]

A high incidence of polygamy (i.e. polygyny), as occurs in this society, implies either an unbalance of numbers between the sexes or a large number of unmarried men. If in earlier times many men were killed in war but relatively few women, then this could have produced the necessary unbalance to make the first explanation possible, and it is commonly assumed that this is what used to occur. But it is open to question whether this explanation is entirely satisfactory: official documents and accounts of family histories refer to local massacres at the hands of raiders, and at such times it was the active males who had a better chance of survival: as recently as 1952 in a raid by Ethiopians on a Rendille settlement, among the 76 persons

---

[1] Following Gulliver, 1951, p. 127.
[2] Details of the censuses referred to in this section are given in the appendix.

killed there were 5 men, 20 women and 51 children, and it is probable that the latter included girls of all ages but only the smaller boys who were not away at a camel camp. Moreover, census figures make it quite clear that today there are equal numbers of males and females of all ages and that the high incidence of polygamy can only be explained by reference to the large number of unmarried men, that is, of course, the moran.

It is not perhaps immediately evident that by raising the age of marriage for men by, say, 15 years beyond that for women, the older men can practise polygamy on a wide scale.[1] At first sight, it would seem that by creating a large unmarried age grade among the younger men (i.e. the moran) one is indirectly creating a large number of widows among the older women, women who are prevented from remarrying by custom. In point of fact, census figures collected in 1958 indicated that there were approximately *two* married men (elders) and *two* unmarried men (moran) to every *three* wives and *one* widow: in other words, the numbers of widows in the society was considerable, but only one-half the number of unmarried men. To this exact balance between adults of each sex there corresponded a balance among uncircumcised children of nearly five boys to nearly five girls. This balance follows logically from the Samburu custom of circumcising all the children of one woman in strict order of birth regardless of sex: had the girls been circumcised at a later age than the boys then the census would have shown more girls than boys and fewer adult women than adult men.

This may be expressed diagrammatically. The figure on opposite page represents the general distribution of the population between the two sexes and the various age grades. A B C is a horizontal line representing the average age at which boys and girls are circumcised (say, about the age of 15) and D E is a horizontal line representing the average age at which moran may marry for the first time (say, about the age of 30). The areas A B F D A and B C F B represent the adult males (moran and elders) and the adult females (wives and widows) respectively.

[1] This has been pointed out by Monica Wilson (Wilson, 1951, p. 14).

96

The Structural Implications of Polygamy

If one accepts as given: (*a*) the age and sex distribution of the society; (*b*) that girls can most profitably be married soon after puberty; (*c*) that widows cannot remarry; (*d*) a system whereby young men are prevented from marrying in order to allow the older men to practise polygamy; and (*e*) a certain rate of polygamy which is partly determined by economic factors – then the exact position of the line D E is fixed: any variation in the age at which men first marry would interfere either with the rate of polygamy or with the age at which girls are first married, both of which are fixed according to the above premises.

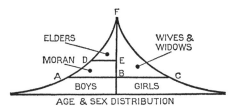

The Distribution of Age Grades by Age and Sex.

A second way in which polygamy can be viewed in this diagram is to consider lines D E and B C, which represent respectively the number of moran in the process of marrying for the first time and the number of girls being married. The two lines are of unequal length and the difference B C minus D E represents the number of girls who may become wives to men who already have one wife. In an 'aging society' such as our own, where there is no marked decrease in population with age between the ages of 15 and 30 (i.e. the line D E is approximately equal in length to the line B C), polygamy could not be achieved on a large scale by applying these marriage rules; but in a society with an age distribution as shown in the above diagram it can be achieved. The shape of this distribution seems to be due to a high incidence of mortality especially among small children, and a steady increase in numbers due to the general absence of warfare and the control of epidemic diseases by hospital services in the area. This situation is somewhat complicated in practice by the fact that

97

moran do not marry individually when they reach a certain age, but they are given permission to marry as an age-set. At this time there is an inevitable shortage of marriageable girls and it may be five or more years after the age-set has been given permission before the majority of its members have achieved their first marriage. During these years, there is considerable competition for all available girls, not only among moran, but also with elders who wish to marry their second or third wives.

It is the elders, in particular the relevant age-set of firestick elders, who decide when to hold the ceremonies which will precipitate the change-over of age-sets and foster in the moran a willingness to marry and settle down: the *ilmugit* of the bull ceremony and the circumcision of the next age-set are the most striking of these. In making such decisions, the elders are precipitating competition between themselves and the moran for wives. It is therefore to some extent in their interests to delay the change-over for as long as possible in order that they can benefit from the monopoly they hold in having the sole right to marry.

In due course, however, it becomes increasingly apparent that a change-over will have to take place. Pressures exerted on the elders by the senior moran who wish to marry and by boys who wish to be circumcised are not of overriding importance when this decision has to be made. But there is also a growing body of opinion among the elders who want the change-over to come about: junior elders want to become firestick elders, firestick elders want their sons to be circumcised and senior elders want their younger sons to be circumcised and their older moran sons to marry. In addition to these pressures, the shortage of marriagable girls becomes a problem: there is an increasing number of nubile girls who are the younger sisters of boys waiting for circumcision, and according to custom such girls cannot be circumcised before their elder brothers. Some of them may actually be betrothed to certain elders who are anxious to marry them before they are promised elsewhere.

Thus it is that the periodic interval between the initiation of successive age-sets, a period of from 12 to 14 years, and the customs associated with the age-sets systems are correlated with the degree of polygamy which is practised in the society. In so far as the degree of polygamy is partly determined by economic and partly by social factors, the periodic interval between successive age-sets too is indirectly determined by the same factors.

A very interesting confirmation of this general hypothesis is by comparison with the Rendille tribe who are mostly mono-gamists and whose age-set system is in many ways different from the Samburu. This is discussed in detail in Chapter Ten.

The Moran and the Bush

References to the position of the moran in this chapter have not taken into account their traditional role as the principal war-riors of the society. Apart from minor incidents, this role has no contemporary significance. But it remains a Samburu ideal of moranhood, and the set of values held by the moran today can only be understood by reference to their traditional military activities and to the supreme importance of these activities within the living memory of the older members of the tribe. Moreover, the Samburu do not regard this as entirely a thing of the past: when I last visited them in 1962, they saw the forth-coming departure of the British administration as heralding a return to their former way of life, and this gave a further reason for keeping their traditional attitudes towards the moran.

Moran are associated in their ceremonial and in much of their non-ceremonial behaviour with the bush, the areas away from the settlements. The *ilmugit* of their *ilmugit* ceremonies is a special enclosure some distance from the settlement in which they spend much of their time; in order to avoid married women when they have meat to eat, they must go into the bush; and it would be unpropitious for a moran to die inside the settlement: when he becomes seriously ill, he is taken by some age mates into the bush and they stay with him and look after him until he either recovers or dies. The Samburu explain this historically by referring to earlier conditions when the moran spent so much of their time in the bush, managing camps, keeping watch for signs of trouble and occasionally going on raids of their own. The camps with the surplus herds were often close to the

99

ungrazed no-man's land that separated the Samburu from hostile tribes, and these herds, containing some of their best cattle, required specially close guarding. Older people remember the settlements in those days as having been larger and built closer together than today in order to afford themselves better protection against raiders. They were surrounded by a scattered ring of moran whose duty it was to occupy this peripheral yet strategic position in the society.

But a structural explanation to this association between moran and the bush is also possible in terms of their present position. The moran are the odd men out in the society. Physiologically they are of an age to marry, but they may not do so for many years. They are in a limbo between boyhood and elderhood, and the elders like to keep them there outside the competition in marriage and outside the decision making of the local clan groups. From the point of view of these aspects of the society they are outsiders and this is consistent with their association with the bush.

There is also a more practical reason for discouraging the moran from coming to their settlements: the elders want to keep them away from their wives. Socially, the moran are immature and lack the dignity and wisdom of the elders, but sexually they are their rivals: the elders may have a monopoly in marriage, but the moran have youth and a greater attraction for the women. The amount of adultery that takes place between moran and wives is a daily topic of conversation, anxiety and joking. Jealousy and distrust is just one more strain engendered by polygamy. So long as the moran can be kept at bay in the bush and the wives can be confined to the settlements, adultery can be prevented; but this needs constant vigilance by the elders.

A Samburu once pointed out to me two herds of gazelle. The first herd, he said, was the herd of an elder and his wives and the second herd, in which two gazelle were fighting, was that of the moran who were not allowed to mix with the females by the elder who was stronger than they were. In giving me this lesson in nature study, he had described a social situation which was familiar to him in his own society and had used the appropriate social statuses in his description. The crucial difference between the herd of gazelle and the Samburu, apart from the degree of polygamy practised, was that the gazelle elder retained his position by his physical superiority, whereas the Samburu elders are physically weaker than the moran and maintain their position by asserting their moral ascendancy based ultimately on the general belief in their power of the curse.

The notion of a separate herd of young males, fighting among themselves and forming a society of their own because they have been extruded from their parent herd, is an apt one with which to turn to a closer consideration of the moran.

Summary

The segmentary descent system and the age-set system of the Samburu have been outlined together with certain customs and beliefs associated with them. The importance of the clan in the segmentary descent system, a topic which was discussed in Chapter Two, is also discernible in the age-set system: the moran of one age-set and clan form a Club and exclude outsiders from sharing in their activities.

The moran as a whole are in another sense outsiders. They lie outside the political manipulations and debatings of the elders and to some extent outside the family. It is a device which enables the elders to retain power in the society and to practise polygamy on a large scale. Today, the moran have lost their traditional role as warriors but they remain the most striking, the most characteristic, and the most controversial feature of the society. It is the position in which they find themselves today and their reaction to it which is the subject of the next two chapters.

Chapter Five

THE MORAN

I N many ways the moran are conspicuously different from the remainder of the society. This is so, for instance, in the ways in which they clothe and decorate themselves: their long braided hair covered in red ochre, their decorative bead ornaments, and their colourful loin cloths are a sharp contrast to the relatively drab and unobtrusive apparel of boys and elders. General attention is constantly converging in their direction, and the ostentatiousness of much of their behaviour appears to result from as well as result in this attention. They are the potential warriors of a warrior-oriented society: they are conscious of their position and of what is expected of them, and this gives an added importance to their actions. Standards of achievement are enhanced: anything less than complete success becomes failure, slights or insinuations become insults, and certain ideals of behaviour tend to be regarded as rigid obligations. This compulsive element in their behaviour is frequently referred to by Samburu elders as childish and irresponsible. But it must be emphasized that these youths *are* socially still only children and many of them have no responsibilities thrust on their shoulders.

A number of cases which are discussed in this chapter refer to the Clubs of the moran. It is emphasized at the outset that the Club is not a localized group with a high degree of social activity at all times: it is dispersed throughout the tribe in precisely the same way that its parent clan is dispersed. In so far as it is possible to speak of Club activities, then, these do not refer to collective action by all or even the majority of moran of one Club, but only to any number that happen to be gathered together at one time, whether this is about a dozen at some evening dance, 30 at some afternoon dance held at a girl's circumcision, or 50 or more performing in an *ilmugit* ceremony. Over the years their nomadic habits bring most of the moran of a Club into face-to-face contact with each other, but it is very unlikely that they would ever all be in one place at one time.

Honour and the Family

The Samburu have no word for *honour* other than *nkanyit*, which refers rather to the *respect* which other people have for a person or a group than to the *honour* which earns this respect. Honour is, nevertheless, a useful concept which is quite intelligible to the Samburu, especially the moran. The honour of a man is closely associated with that of his family, lineage and clan. It may be implicated in various ways, either with reference to his ancestry, or to his worthiness, or, among moran, to his courage.

The association of honour with courage is particularly evident at the time when initiates are circumcised shortly before they become moran. An important feature of this ceremony is that each initiate should remain absolutely motionless during the period of the operation which may last four minutes or more. Even an involuntary twitch would be interpreted as a sign that he wants to run away from it, and the word for such a slight movement in this context also means 'to run' (*a-kwet*, translated here as 'to flinch'). Actual instances of persons having flinched during circumcision appear to be rare, but as may be seen from the following example, kinsmen of the initiates do not always argue that it is a rare event: they treat it as a very real possibility. The honour of each initiate, of his family, his close agnatic kinsmen, and in the last analysis of the whole circumcision settlement and clan are implicated in his behaviour during the operation. If he flinches then they will all be shamed: no other initiate will want to form a ceremonial friendship with him (a feature of the period following circumcision) and no initiate from a neighbouring circumcision settlement of another clan will want to form such relations with *any* initiate of this settlement; his parents will put ash on their heads, and others will deliberately turn their backs towards his mother's hut and abuse it and they will drive his father's

cattle through the thorn fence of the settlement instead of allowing them to go out through the gateway: they 'eat their respect'
(*kenya nkanyit*) for the initiate and his family. The honour of the
family is tainted and this is a stigma which in theory can never
be entirely eradicated. For this reason it is unlikely that any
boy would be circumcised before he reaches the age of at least
12; and if he is timid by nature, he might be made to wait
until he is considerably older.

The following example illustrates the extent to which kinsmen of initiates showed anxiety during a circumcision
ceremony:

27.** Events leading up to the initiation of the *Kishili* age-set had
taken their normal course and all the necessary ceremonial
preparations had been completed in order to hold the first
circumcisions in July 1960. Excitement ran high in the circumcision settlement where I was staying: a new age-set of moran
would shortly be brought into being. On the evening of 6th
July, the elders of the Mekuri age-set, the new firestick elders,
agreed that two of the initiates should be circumcised on the
evening of the next day and the remainder on the morning of
the 8th.

Throughout the next day a major topic of conversation was
whether or not any of the initiates would flinch. More and more
elders and moran (of the Kimaniki age-set) gathered with pliant
sticks up to ten feet in length; these, they said, were to discourage
any initiate who had thoughts of running away to hide himself
in the bush before the operation. The initiates themselves stood
around in small groups, apparently nervous at the prospect of
the operation and aware of the general lack of confidence which
the moran and elders had in them. The previous evening their
singing had been pointed out to me as distinctly unsteady, and
now they were silent. They afterwards told me that it was the fear
of flinching rather than of pain which had worried them most; the
ordeal of the ceremony was not so much one of physical endurance
during the operation itself as of maintaining confidence beforehand in the face of unknown pain.

One elder saw them standing around in dejection and shouted
at them. 'Sing your circumcision song (*lebarta*)', he demanded.
'Show us that you are not afraid. . . . Or don't you want to be
circumcised?' One or two of the boys started to sing; and then
another elder, the father of one of them, ran towards them and

ordered them to stop singing. This, I was told, was because he was quite certain that his own son would flinch and he considered it less ignominious for him to be silent than for him to sing and boast and then afterwards to flinch.

This general anxiety came to a head just before the two circumcisions of that evening were to take place. The two initiates had to drive their fathers' cattle into the settlement, and one of them started to sing:

'Surua lai   impurronieki! Na mapik   nyileti.'
'My light brown bull – roar! For I will not bring dishonour.'

This boast caused some consternation and the boy's eldest brother, a Mekuri age-set elder, at first raised his whip to strike him and then checked himself. His gesture, coming as it did at a moment when nerves were frayed, sparked off a general release of tension. One moran ran up to strike the initiate himself and was seized by another Mekuri elder and thrown to the ground. Other men, both elders and moran, seized any person who showed signs of wanting to strike the initiate or to start an affray, and in some cases were themselves seized on this assumption. At least five moran broke down and had to be held firmly while they shook insensibly. The first two circumcisions were then carried out in a confusion of babbling and shouting, mostly aimed at the initiates undergoing the operation and the circumciser performing it, although the latter seemed to be the one man present who had a clear notion of what should be done. Once these two circumcisions had been performed, there was less anxiety, and the ceremony was completed the following morning still in an atmosphere of confusion and shouting, but without any signs of flinching from the initiates or fighting from the adult males.

Especially interesting in this incident was the reaction to the initiate's boasting to the bull of his family herd: his elder brother nearly struck him and his father, a very old man, seemed to be on the point of having a stroke. The boast itself was made to the bull of the family herd, and it was the same herd of cattle to which previous members of the lineage had boasted when they had been circumcised. If he had flinched then the herd itself would have been driven through the thorn fence and so long as the event was remembered no future member of this lineage would dare to make a boast of this sort. This is the one context in Samburu life where there is a

105

recognized way of openly shaming a person and his family, and a specific word for dishonour, *nyilet(i)*.[1] In retrospect, the elders did not criticize the initiate for showing too much confidence in himself before the operation: this boast was expected of him if he had any spirit, and as he kept his word and did not flinch he brought credit to his family for his boldness. But they did criticize the father and the elder brother who had shown too little confidence in him, thus publicly betraying that they regarded it as quite possible that a member of their family and lineage might flinch during circumcision. Other persons in private admitted that they too had felt the same way about the circumcision of their own kinsmen, but would not want to betray this in public. The news that reached the circumcision settlements of other clans in the area was not that someone had actually flinched in this particular settlement, but that the elders had expected someone to flinch. The incident was a minor humiliation which dampened the general elation once the ceremony was over. The shaking and shivering exhibited on this occasion is quite common among Samburu moran. More is written on this form of behaviour in Chapter Nine where it is examined as a hysterical type of breakdown associated with the strains of moranhood.

The initiate boasting to his bull has a clear parallel with accounts of organized raids in the past. Any moran who wished to boast of his own courage would call out his father's personal name before going on a raid and would repeat it on first sighting the enemy. At no other time would he ever utter this name. An elder is said to have hated his son's behaving in this way until it became known that he had lived up to his boast and had enhanced the family honour by fighting bravely and associating his own deeds with those of his father and close kinsmen.

Calling on the name of the bull at circumcision or of the father in a raid did not imply any mystical relationship between the boaster and his family's herd or his father's name. Rather

---

[1] At other times the initiates sing: 'The bulls roared loudly to tell of the boy who flinched' (*eipurro naleng laingok pee limu laiyeni okwet*); and 'I will not bring our cattle dishonour' (*mapik ngishu ang nyilet*). An initiate who flinches is also known as a *nyilet*.

they were accepted ways in which vows could be made in certain contexts. Family honour and not mystical beliefs was involved.

Honour and Prestige

The terms *honour* and *prestige* are used here to refer to different aspects of the same general notion. Honour implies a continuous attainment of certain standards of behaviour; it links the individual to the group, whether lineage, clan, Club or age-set, for his honour and the honour of the group are closely associated. Prestige, on the other hand, does not imply a general attainment of some standard by individuals or groups, but rather it implies a difference in the extent to which standards are attained. The two are not synonymous. For instance, in a whipping contest between two moran where they agree to fight each other with pliant sticks until one has clearly beaten the other, the loser loses prestige, but he may retain his honour. If, however, he runs away from the contest or refuses to accept the challenge, he loses both prestige and honour, and, incidentally, he brings dishonour to his close kinsmen.

The distinction is an important one in a description of the moran. Prestige implies inequality and competition, and as such it conflicts with the ideals of equality and solidarity within the age-set. It is in his efforts to gain or retain prestige that the individual may contravene the norms of the age-set and incur general criticism. Whereas honour implies only behaviour which satisfies the ideals of the group and does not necessarily lead to competition. Honour is initially ascribed to the individual and the group and any incident which taints that honour is a stigma that is not easily forgotten; prestige is something which is attained and which may also be lost. In order to distinguish clearly between them in the examples which are discussed below, a moran who acts in a certain way because it is generally expected of him is understood to satisfy his honour; if, on the other hand, there is no specific demand on him, any assertiveness on his part is understood to concern his prestige.

In the previous section, an association between honour and

courage was discussed. Any direct or implied challenge to a moran's courage is an affront to his honour and must be answered if he is to retain it. Outstanding courage, however, gains prestige in addition to honour. It is explicitly associated with warfare in the past when a courageous man was an asset to his side. He was willing to take more than his share of the risks in order to ensure success and by his example he inspired confidence and a will to win among his fellows. A brave man was to the moran as warriors what a worthy man was to the elders, and the term *lee* (worthy man) was one that could aptly be applied to him. Another word for a brave moran was *laingoni*, which also means a dead moran (who in a traditional context had died because he was in the forefront of the battle) and a bull (who is fearless and assertive when faced with a rival). The initiate in the above example who boasted to his bull was to some extent associating himself with it in a similar way.

A coward is known as *laroi*, the term used for a mean man among the elders. It also has a third meaning: at one time an assertive moran might bully another into becoming his personal servant or client, and this client was known as *laroi* with all the contempt that goes with that word.

28. Kisiemet, a courageous and forceful moran, bullied a younger and more timid age mate, Parais, into becoming his client. Parais accompanied him wherever he went, carrying his wooden water flask when they went on long journeys, supervising the cooking of his meat in the bush, and carrying out small errands for him. In return Kisiemet protected Parais from any other moran who might try to bully him. Kisiemet was ignoring any age-set obligations to treat Parais as an equal, but as Parais had made no attempt to assert his own rights to equality and freedom their age mates did not object to this. They despised him for the inferior position he accepted.

One day, when Parais had grown to his full height and was beginning to acquire some confidence in himself, he took the opportunity of freeing himself from Kisiemet's patronage. On this occasion there were a number of other moran of their Club with them and Kisiemet ordered him to pick up the water flask and to follow him on some errand. Parais picked up the flask and then flung it to the ground and smashed it.

Kisiemet could easily have beaten Parais in a fight with knobkerries, but according to the ideals of the age-set Parais was quite justified in asserting his independence and any attempt at punishing him for his audacity would have been criticized by their age mates. Parais, for once, had earned their approval and moral support by his action. Kisiemet submitted to the indignity gracefully and walked off alone. He knew that none of the others doubted that he could have beaten Parais soundly if he had wanted to, but he also knew that they would have a much lower opinion of him if he had tried to do so. Any such behaviour could have been interpreted by the others as a sign of weakness that he doubted the grandeur of his own prestige among them, and also it would show them that he was willing to put his own selfish interests above the behaviour expected of him by his age mates. Parais had gained in prestige, but Kisiemet had hardly lost any.

Parais performed the final act expected of him if he was to assert his prestige among his age mates: he went on a raid with them and distinguished himself with conspicuous bravery. Once he had done this, there could be no further question concerning his new status. But even today, he is remembered as the client of Kisiemet, and this is a slight stigma against his honour and the honour of his sons. It is ineradicable.

The subordination of a client to an age mate appears to have been fairly infrequent. No self-respecting moran would tolerate such humiliation and he would firmly oppose any age mate who tried to force one of his close kinsmen to become a client; similarly no Club would allow one of its members to become the client of a moran of some other Club. Occasional cases of clientship which have been recorded are of relatively young moran who had no close kinsmen in their own age-set and who for a time became clients to rather older and more forceful moran.

The practice of clientship was for some reason discontinued once large scale warfare had been abolished in the area. Today, many of the onerous tasks once carried out by clients are done by boys of any age between about 9 and 15. They are usually younger brothers of some of the moran whom they accompany in the camps or in the bush when there is meat to be eaten. Older boys, especially initiates and those who have already been circumcised into a new age-set, are to some extent respected by the moran and are not expected to undertake tasks which could be regarded as humiliating.

A more serious challenge to the ideal of equality within an age-set is seen in the following example:

29. After a raid in which some of the Pardopa moran of the Marikon age-set had captured a lot of small stock, Kipirashi, the strongest and bravest among them, divided the spoil in a very autocratic and unfair manner, keeping an unnecessarily large portion for himself. Only one other moran, Molite, challenged this division, and on their journey home he attacked Kipirashi several times, first with his spear and then, when Kipirashi had disarmed him, with stones. During each attack Kipirashi seized Molite and threw him to the ground, but he did not hit him as he was aware that he had acted unwisely and contrary to the principle of age-set equality; if he had retaliated more forcibly then the other moran might have intervened; but it is perhaps significant that they did not try to restrain Molite. After the fourth attack by Molite, Kipirashi called all the other moran and in their presence he divided his share of the spoil evenly between himself and Molite. It was a gesture of conciliation in which no one could accuse him of cowardice, although previously they might have disapproved of his autocratic method of dividing the stock.

In this, as in the previous example, a forceful moran was faced with a situation in which his prestige was involved. Both Kisiemet and Kipirashi had asserted themselves in a manner which was contrary to age-set equality, but both were shrewd enough to act with dignity when the propriety of their behaviour was openly challenged. Weaker men might have tried to assert themselves beyond this point 'and suffered considerable loss of prestige as a result. It is worth noting that a certain amount of assertiveness by a stronger moran went unchecked so long as those directly affected by his behaviour did not object. Thus in the first example, no one challenged Kisiemet's right to bully Parais so long as Parais did not attempt to assert his own rights to equality; and in the second example, Kipirashi divided his share of the spoil with Molite, but he did not offer any extra share to his other fellow raiders who had not objected to his autocratic methods.

Today, honour and prestige are still treasured values of the moran, and account for much of their behaviour. A moran who has been slighted in some way – perhaps he has been taunted or his mistress has been seduced – is expected to retaliate against the offender, and hence it is his *honour* which is involved. But when he exceeds these expectations in some way, asserting himself more than is necessary, it becomes also a matter of personal prestige.

A moran who wants to settle some affair of honour finally and to his credit may challenge his adversary and a whipping contest will be arranged by the other moran. The outcome of such a contest is likely to be in favour of the stronger of the two and a weaker man may prefer to make more certain of success by attacking the other unexpectedly with his knob-kerrie; this is a less creditable way of satisfying honour, but it is the more usual. There are no rules of fair play in this: he may lurk in ambush for his adversary and then attack him from behind, knocking him unconscious with one blow, or he may club him while he is asleep. He may wait for months or even years before doing this. The longer he delays, however, the more convinced others will be that he lacks sufficient courage to make the attack; and if he bungles it by hitting too gently at first or on a less vulnerable spot than his head then this also will be interpreted as a sign of weakness. If the attack is generally accepted as justified, then the elders and other moran will try to persuade the adversary to let the matter rest without any loss of honour. If, however, he chooses to take this as a matter of prestige, then it is fairly certain that he will still want to retaliate. It is then possible that other moran will intervene, either by arranging a whipping contest between them, or, if circumstances encourage them to take sides, by joining in a general affray.

Moran and Their Mistresses

As previously noted, the moran of one age-set within each clan form a Club, and the unmarried girls of this clan, who share in many of the activities and secrets of the Club, may be regarded as associated members.

Within a Club, moran and girls may pair off as lovers, unless the parents of any girl have forbidden her. As they are also usually members of the same clan, lovers cannot normally marry: from the very outset their relationship is doomed to end in separation at the girl's marriage.

A lover-mistress relationship is commonly formed as follows. A moran of sub-clan A wishes to ask a girl of sub-clan B to be his mistress; he therefore asks another moran of his Club of sub-clan C to approach the girl on his behalf. At first she will refuse: this is not only a desirable indication of her modesty, but also she does not wish to throw away the initiative she holds at this point. On being pressed, however, she may accept the offer and as a token of their relationship her new lover gives her a long string of beads to wear in coils round her neck; over the years this necklace grows larger and larger until it covers her entire shoulders and reaches to her chin – to the envy of less fortunate girls. The moran of sub-clan C is asked to liaise in the affair as a matter of tact: he is neither a member of sub-clan A who might be tempted to put too much pressure on the girl to accept the offer of his kinsman when in point of fact she does not want him; nor is he a member of her sub-clan who must avoid her sexually and therefore should not be implicated too directly in her love affair (lovers would never belong to the same sub-clan). As a third member of the Club only distantly related to the other two he is in an ideal position.

The two lovers may have discreet sexual relations, but they should make sure to avoid any pregnancy. If the girl does conceive before her marriage then the child would be aborted or killed at birth: it would be mystically dangerous to allow it to live.

The personal honour of a moran is implicated in his relationship with his mistress. He is expected to attack any other person who makes advances to her, seduces her, strikes her or rapes her; and once she agrees to accept him as her sweetheart, he becomes her lover, her protector and her master. In addition to honour, the possession of a mistress is also a matter of prestige, especially as there are rather more moran than girls of a suitable age and therefore grounds for competition. The ways in which some moran speak of their mistresses gives one the impression at times that it is as much a matter of prestige as of sexual satisfaction, and that genuine affection hardly enters into the relationship; but this is by no means invariably so. Time and again in matters where moran have taken up an affair of honour and converted it into a battle for prestige, it involves their relationships with girls or their relationships to each other through girls. A small incident which brings them into rivalry over girls may build up into a serious conflict. It is rather the way in which they choose to regard the situation than any direct incitement from the girls that leads to fighting.

Affrays Between Clubs

It is the possessiveness of the moran of a Club over their girls which prevents an outsider from having one of these as his mistress; and it is the same possessiveness which may lead two Clubs into an affray when a moran of one Club seduces a girl of the other. In the following example the two Clubs of Lorogushu phratry came into conflict after such a seduction:

30.* Doika, a Kimaniki moran of Makalilit clan, seduced a girl of Pardopa clan. Kipepial, the girl's lover, found out about this and a close kinsman, Maru, suggested that they went to beat up Doika. They were joined by a third member of the same lineage group, Moitan. Moitan's senior half brother, Lunget, heard of their plans and interceded before they had actually achieved their purpose. As an elder and a man closely related to each of them he was able to assert enough authority over them to avert their immediate aim, but not before they had made intimidating threats to Doika through the doorway of his mother's hut where he was resting.

Shortly after this incident, six members of Makalilit Club came across Maru and another moran of his Club, Kimiti, and at the instigation of one of them, Pasanga, they beat them up. This incensed all members of Pardopa Club who were in the area, and they collected together to fight Makalilit Club. The general affray which ensued was eventually stopped by the police who had been warned of the imminent danger of an affray by some informant and had hurried to the spot.

At a conciliatory ceremony arranged by the elders, Maru's senior brother, Kamatia, an elder of Mekuri age-set, provided an ox to be eaten by the Makalilit moran, and all moran involved in the affray were expected to be present. Maru and Kimiti, however, stayed away from the ceremony, indicating that so far as they were concerned, the matter was not at an end. Several months later, these two moran and a third member of their Club ambushed Pasanga and beat him up. During the scuffle, Pasanga managed to knock Kimiti down, but one of the other two seized hold of him and Kimiti was allowed to beat him soundly. After this final incident Maru and Kimiti said that they were satisfied and would not pursue the matter any further.

This feud is a clear example of the way in which an affray built up between structurally distinct groups, illustrating their corporate nature: an incident which involved the honour primarily of one moran, Kipepial, provoked *three* moran of his Club, including himself, to pursue the matter, and this in turn provoked *six* members of the other Club to retaliate, leading to a general affray between members of the two Clubs who were present in that area at the time.

A closer analysis of this whole affair can only be made with reference to the mistresses of the protagonists. As shown in the diagram below, Maru's mistress was a half sister of Kipepial's mistress, the girl who was seduced; Kimiti's mistress was Maru's half sister; and Pasanga's mistress was Doika's sister. It was more than coincidence that the protagonists of

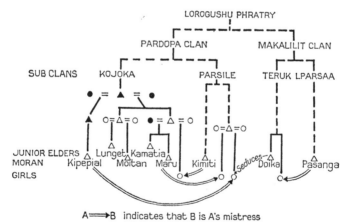

A⟹B indicates that B is A's mistress

Kinship Diagram: the Seduction of Kipepial's Mistress.

the affair were linked through their mistresses: it was one of the principal causes which converted a single seduction into a serious affray between Clubs.

Thus, Kipepial was expected by members of his Club to make some of form of retaliation against Doika who had seduced his mistress: this concerned his honour. Maru had initiated the attempt to beat up Doika, not merely because he was a close kinsman of Kipepial, but also because his own mistress was a half sister of Kipepial's mistress and might even have connived in the seduction: so far as Maru was concerned there was no general expectation that he should involve himself in the affair, but he was sensitive to this double link and chose to associate his own honour with that of Kipepial. In doing so he also introduced an element of prestige, for he was exceeding general expectations.

The threat against Doika by three Pardopa moran was an audacious one as it took place in full daylight inside a Makalilit settlement. This could have been taken as a sign of contempt against all Makalilit as well as an insult to Doika, and it provoked the attack by six Makalilit moran against Maru, the ring-leader. The instigator of this attack was Pasanga who was related to Doika through his mistress. To other Samburu, the knowledge of this relationship was sufficient to account for Pasanga's behaviour: he was his mistress's protector and by extension he chose to be her brother Doika's protector also. He was not obliged to take on this role and he also was responding to the incident as a matter of prestige – both his own and that of his Club.

Apparently by coincidence rather than design, the attack on Maru also implicated Kimiti who was the lover of Maru's half sister. Had it not been for this relationship or had Maru been willing to submit to the demands of the elders that the affair should end, Kimiti could have accepted their ruling without loss of honour. But as he and Maru *were* linked through his mistress and Maru was *not* prepared to allow the matter to end in an indecisive affray, Kimiti was expected by his Club to follow suit for he was now too deeply involved in the affair to let the matter rest: it was his honour and not just his prestige that was involved. It was for this reason that the Pardopa moran in retrospect considered that it was right that he, and not Maru, should have been allowed to deal the blows in the final attack on Pasanga.

It is interesting to note that an affair which had initially implicated Kipepial and Doika in an affair of honour, finally hinged on the conflict between Maru and Pasanga in a battle of prestige. Both of these were assertive and quarrelsome moran, and they had been mainly responsible for the incidents which had built a minor affair into a serious affray. The Makalilit moran maintained that Maru (Pardopa) was principally to blame, the Pardopa moran maintained that Pasanga (Makalilit) was principally to blame, and the elders blamed them both.

In retrospect, however, a number of Pardopa moran criticized Maru for behaving rashly in the whole affair. He had taken the matter of his prestige to such an extreme that he had not altogether enhanced it. It may have been because he was aware of these criticisms and disgusted with the affair that he decided to leave on a protracted journey to Rendille country shortly after this.

So far as the general relations between the two Clubs were concerned it is worth noting that moran who were hurt in affray did not have private accounts to settle as it had involved the two Clubs in a matter of prestige rather than individuals. At no point had spears been used: the custom that Samburu should not fight each other with anything more dangerous than knobkerries had been respected. After the fracas, the local clan groups of Pardopa and Makalilit in that area lived and migrated rather more carefully apart than they had done previously.

It is interesting to note that Maru's senior brother, Kamatia, who provided the ox for the Makalilit moran to eat at the conciliatory ceremony, had been largely responsible for a previous affray between Makalilit and Pardopa when his own age-set, the Mekuri, had been moran. In this earlier incident it had been the Lorogushu ritual leader of the Mekuri age-set who had used his powers of coercion over *both* Clubs to prohibit further fighting. In the present incident Kamatia was personally involved in the peace-making proceedings which brought antagonistic Clubs of a subsequent age-set together. As a moran he had actively participated in a similar affray; as an elder he was now expected to assert himself, if necessary, to maintain peace among the moran. When he offered the ox to the Makalilit moran, this was a voluntary gesture of good will which might have been made by any Pardopa elder; but the fact that it was he, Kamatia, who gave it suggested that he wanted to emphasize his present role as an elder and peace-maker in order to absolve himself from any suggestion that he in any way approved of the present fight between Makalilit and Pardopa or of his brother Maru's intention of continuing the affair.

> 30. (cont.) After the affray, three protagonists from each side were sentenced to four months' imprisonment. As matters had gone so far, there was no longer any age-set obligation for Kipepial to settle his account with Doika, but his relationship with his mistress could not continue on the same footing as before. On being released from prison for his part in the affray, he went immediately to her home and tore the beads he had given her as a token of their relationship from her neck: this was the accepted way of ending the relationship and shaming the girl as a slut. He then left his home and the district and found work as a policeman. No one has any doubt that he, at least, did this out of sheer disgust.

Other examples of minor incidents between Clubs building up into general affrays have been recorded, and in extreme cases the various Clubs of a phratry have united in a fight against those of some other phratry. A classic example of this, which is still vividly retold by the Samburu, occurred among the moran of the Kiliako age-set, an age-set which, incidentally, was the first to really encounter the strains of living under the British administration and changed political conditions. It built up over a number of years from an accusation by some Pisikishu moran that two Lorogushu moran had stolen a goat, to a major affray in 1929. Altogether five members of each phratry were killed. One of the main factors which apparently united the two Clubs of Lorogushu (Pardopa and Makalilit) was that in their initial reprisals the Pisikishu moran did not discriminate between Pardopa and Makalilit moran. And an important factor which may have united the various Clubs of Pisikishu was that their ritual leader was wounded and his deputy killed by Lorogushu moran in one of the earlier encounters.

Strains Between Sub-age-sets

In an age-set there may be considerable difference in age between the older moran who were circumcised when it was first formed and those who were circumcised subsequently. This difference is frequently more than 10 years, and where there is rivalry for the favours of girls, any suggestion that they prefer the younger moran who are still little more than boys is bound to incense the older ones. Younger girls between, say, the ages of 10 and 14 are to some extent enthralled with the notion that moran should be manly in every way, and it is said that they are attracted to the older moran who have the greater experience and stronger personalities. On the other hand, older girls, who are of an age to become mistresses and have closer relations with the moran in general, are less moran-struck. Their future marriages are likely to be with much older men, and, as the Samburu themselves point out, a number of them are repelled by this notion and prefer to become the mistresses of younger moran of their own age with whom they have more in common.

Adolescent girls do not invariably prefer younger moran to older ones, but incidents in which they transfer their affections from the older to the younger may occur often enough to create a strain between the moran of different ages, and this naturally tends to follow the cleavage between sub-age-sets.

31. Kasiata's mistress returned the beads he had given her and so ended the relationship between them. When she later became Dumal's mistress it was generally assumed that she preferred him because he was much younger than Kasiata. This was one of several similar incidents which had occurred within their Club.

Later, four older moran, including Kalawe who was a close kinsman of Kasiata and a member of his sub-age-set, met Dumal and two other younger moran in the bush. Kalawe openly challenged Dumal to a fight, and Dumal had to agree. A whipping contest was arranged at once: all the moran present cut and trimmed a number of sticks for the two opponents and then watched them fight it out. Kalawe soundly beat Dumal and had to be held by the others from hurting him further once he had clearly won the contest.

118

The Pardopa elders later heard of this contest and they forbade the two moran to fight again and ordered the girl not to have any more lovers. She was married shortly afterwards.

It is significant that in this example Kalawe brought the matter to a head in public. He did not want the girl as a mistress for himself and there was no direct matter of prestige between him and Dumal. When he challenged Dumal, both of them were in the presence of their coevals, and he was clearly asserting himself as a representative of his own sub-age-set and not just as a kinsman of Kasiata. His action did not merely implicate the prestige of Kasiata and Dumal over the possession of a single girl: it was an outcome of the rivalry between moran of different ages over success with girls in general. Had he challenged Dumal in any other context, the challenge might not have had quite the same implications. (Both he and Dumal were, incidentally, members of the same sub-clan, and this may have helped to accentuate the fact that this fight was essentially on an issue which brought sub-age-sets into opposition with each other and not the segments of a clan.)

It is also important to note that the strain resulted in a whipping contest between two moran and not in an affray between many. Affrays within a Club implicating a number of persons on both sides are very rare, and this particular strain between sub-age-sets had to be kept within bounds if possible. The contest was an effective way in which tension within the Club could be released. Once it was clearly over, the onlookers prevented further fighting.

In this example, as in the previous one, competition within the age-set arising from relationships with girls led to fighting, and the protagonists were unusually assertive moran, who were very conscious of prestige. Both instances were occasions when the ideal solidarity within the age-set broke down because smaller groups within it temporarily came into conflict demonstrating a greater solidarity; in one example these groups were of different Clubs and in the other they were of different sub-age-sets.

Singing and Dancing

The discussion in the earlier part of this chapter has drawn attention to the relationships between moran and their mistresses. The present section concerns moran and girls in general. That their relationship should often be a source of conflict among the moran does not require an elaborate explanation, except to point out that there are many more moran than adolescent girls and this implies either continence among the moran – an unfamiliar notion to them – or competition which is familiar enough, although it does conflict with their ideal norms of behaviour.

Girls are closely associated with the activities of the Club of their closest kinsmen and learn much of its gossip, especially from their lovers. A moran who loses or gains prestige does so not only in the eyes of the moran of his Club, but also in the eyes of the girls; and anyone who slights him in the presence of these girls is being particularly provocative.

The relationship between the two sexes is typified by some of their songs, such as *nshupa*. They themselves describe *nshupa* as an auction in which each sex tries to vie with the other in a game of one-up-manship. The moran who are rather older than the girls and travel more widely try to baffle them with their worldly knowledge. They allude in their verses to such innovations as typewriters and pistols, and until the girls can invent a verse which makes it clear that they now know what these are, the moran hold the advantage in the game. Underlying these riddles are hidden sexual insinuations inviting the girls to some tryst, and the rejoinders of the girls should have an equally smart double meaning. Each sex tries to outshine the other and avoid being left without an answer. It is a song which is quite similar to their chatter where the moran tease the girls for their lack of worldliness and flirt with them, and the girls try to hold their own and flirt back.

Another song in which the girls are on a stronger footing is *sesiei*. In this, a soloist of either sex gives a narrative account of stock thefts by members of the Club. There is little personal boasting in this song, but those that have stolen cattle can still enjoy an enhanced prestige when their deeds have become established in the repertoire of the Club. When the girls take over the lead they taunt those moran that have never been on a stock raid. It is, in effect, another game in which the roles are reversed and the girls hold the initiative by demanding more stock raids, while the moran are to some extent on the defensive. One popular verse of *sesiei* is: 'The way of a cowardly moran is to search for places full of girls and sing with them' – implying that he has not joined the other moran on a stock raid or (traditionally) has not been guarding against enemy raiders. In another verse, the coward is referred to as having a 'braided cloth' – again implying that he has never seen the wear and tear of bush life and is, in fact, a fop.

These songs do not only indicate a rivalry between the sexes: they also express the values they share in common, such as the allusion to sexual play between them in *nshupa* and the prestige a moran can acquire through stock theft in *sesiei*.

These songs are normally sung as music in their dances. Any occasion when the moran and girls come together in public is likely to turn into a dance if it is not actually a dance which brought them together in the first place. They have hardly any other type of communication and casual familiarity between the two sexes only seems to occur during and after a dance. The dance, then, is of major importance in considering the relations between moran and girls, and the various forms which it may take can best be analysed with due regard to this fact.

A typical evening dance may occur when a number of moran decide to go to some settlement where there are girls of their Club, especially attractive girls who are good singers. *Sesiei* and similar songs tend to be sung at first. Each sex forms a close group facing the other. Occasionally, a moran will break away to flirt some girl with his hair and then return to his group. I refer to dances of this sort as *Club dances*: they typify the dancing between the moran and girls of a Club, and each Club develops its own songs, based largely on the exploits of its members.

Once the atmosphere has warmed up, the two groups of moran and girls may break up and new dances are performed in which they jump together in a mixed circle, beat time, and sing a wordless, meaningless tune, while others chatter together outside the dance. These dances are sometimes called *boys'* *dances* by the Samburu because the participants sang them when they were boys (or very young girls). Occasionally, after several hours of lively dancing, the boisterousness increases even further, and some ambitious members try to introduce unfamiliar songs normally sung by elders or songs picked up recently from other parts of the country, while less ambitious members attempt to lead the dance for the first time in the evening. The result is nearly always a disorganized cacophony which does little to dampen the high spirits of the dancers. They try out new steps, and the moran make flirtatious advances to the girls that could hardly have been made in the earlier phases of the dance. Their singing, their dancing and their play at this stage bear a certain resemblance to the behaviour of much younger children. The latter can occasionally be seen earlier in the evening when they also uninhibitedly try to mimic dances that they do not really know and mix it in with their play.

The evolution of an evening dance of a Club, then, appears to be a progression through a series of phases, starting with the Club dances in which the two sexes remain apart as they express their shared values and their rivalry, continuing with the boys' dances remembered from their younger days in which the sexes intermingle, and sometimes ending with play reminiscent of young children. The exact sequence is not invariable, but it is extremely common. Rather than progression, it might almost be called regression.

There is always a real or at least a potential friction between Clubs, and when moran of various Clubs come together at a dance, there is naturally a certain amount of tension, and the dance usually takes a different form to the one described above.

The circumcision and marriage of a girl is the most common occasion when moran gather together in their Clubs to dance with girls of other Clubs. Particularly prominent in such dances are the moran of the Club of the girl who is being married and those of the bridegroom's clan. The dances take place in the afternoon and this gives moran from over a wide area an opportunity to collect together. It also allows an element of display that is not possible in the darkness of the evening dances. The following example is fairly typical of the dance at any marriage ceremony.

32.** A girl of Pardopa clan was to be circumcised and married to a moran of Longieli clan. At the ceremony, 20 splendidly embellished moran of Longieli Club came to dance and support the bridegroom, and about 15 moran from two other Clubs also came. The girls present were nearly all of Pardopa Club and the Pardopa moran were disconcerted by the prospect of the dance: they only numbered about 10 and could not hope to compete with the Longieli moran who would parade themselves and boast volubly to the girls.

The first dances to be performed on such occasions are always *dances of display* in which the girls are only spectators. The moran of all Clubs dance together in a close group, taking no apparent notice of the girls. Those who wish to display themselves come to the space in front of the other dancers and hop away from them to leap into the air; these are naturally the most prominent participants of the dance. The songs sung in accompaniment are individual boasts of achievements in stock thieving or vows to steal stock in the future.

On this occasion, the Longieli moran, with several assertive singers ably supported by their Club in chorus, dominated the dance. The Pardopa moran had neither adequate numbers nor skilful and assertive singers to compete with them. Earlier some of them had been anxious about this; now some of them started to shiver and eventually one was taken from the dance shaking insensibly. Within a few minutes three more Pardopa moran started to shake and were also led from the dance. The Longieli moran continued to retain the initiative.

No other moran shook during the afternoon and the four who had been led from the dance eventually returned, apparently quite recovered from their bouts. After perhaps two hours of dancing, there was a lull and the moran started to perform Club dances, at which point the girls joined them. The Pardopa moran now appeared to have no hesitation about leading the dance, and one of the most prominent among them was the moran who had shaken first of all. The girls took over the solo part at times and the songs they sang were invariably those of Pardopa Club as they knew no other. Leadership in the dance was no longer of the same importance as it had been earlier. Much later in the afternoon, the moran and girls started to perform boys' dances, but by this time many had left the dance to return to their homes, and others soon lost interest.

The presence of several Clubs in this dance prolonged the initial phase when moran tried to outvie one another in their dances of display. When this had worn itself out, the dancing turned to Club dances and to some extent the Pardopa moran managed to wrest control from the Longieli moran; but by this stage the dance had acquired a different character and dominance was less important. Towards the very end of the dance, tension had been relaxed so completely that moran and girls of all Clubs were able to perform some of their boys' dances. In other words, this dance had evolved in a similar direction to that of the evening dance previously described, but it had started with a greater tension and had not developed as far.

The boasting by the moran in the initial phase of such dances is also described by Samburu as an auction in which each singer tries to outvie the last. They are dances in which the moran are said to be angry and in which they frequently break down into insensible shaking. Occasionally their excitement leads to fighting: one of the incidents which occurred during the feud between Lorogushu and Pisikishu moran in Kiliako times (page 117) was an affray which took place when rival Clubs of the two phratries met at a marriage dance.

On some occasions when many dancers are present, the Clubs may be divided into two separate but simultaneous dances: the success of one dance (i.e. Club) over another is even more apparent as the girl spectators flock from one to the other. On other less spectacular occasions, the dancers may mostly be members of one Club, shaking may occur, but it is less usual and any fighting would be between particular adversaries rather than between groups. Inevitably, tension is soon eased and the initial dances of display soon are replaced by Club dances and the girls join in.

Thus, dancing among the moran focuses attention on their relationship with girls and all that this may entail, including tension between Clubs, jealousy between individual moran, honour, prestige and, above all, differences in sex, age and social status. The way in which their behaviour becomes progressively juvenile as the dance proceeds draws attention to the nature of the tensions they experience: these tensions are a product of the type of society in which they live and derive largely from instilled modes of behaviour which inhibit any tendency to give way to natural impulses. What beer-drinking may do in other societies, dancing does for the Samburu moran (who, incidentally, are forbidden by the elders to touch any form of alcohol). In the course of the dance, either the tensions and inhibitions are reduced allowing a release of pent up energies in a harmless way (i.e. juvenile behaviour), or the tensions build up and are released in shaking and even fighting. It is never quite certain which course a dance will take.

In a sense it may be said that the evolution of the dance is one in which the shackles of upbringing are progressively shaken off. The diagram on page 126 compares a moran dance with an individual's development as two reverse processes in relationships between the sexes: the dance leads ultimately towards a fusion of the two, while social development leads to a complete and inevitable estrangement after circumcision between moran and wives. This topic is developed further in Chapter Nine.

One of their activities for which the moran are notorious to both Samburu and Europeans alike is stock theft. Over the years the prestige-giving activities of the moran have been considerably modified, but the basic idea has remained and the song has always been the idiom in which it is expressed. As recently as the 1930s, the Kiliako moran would kill people of other tribes and steal their stock for prestige, without any political justification. The administration and elders effectively made the Mekuri moran give up these ideas; and the Mekuri age-set responded by trying to impress the girls at their dances with songs of their experiences as soldiers during the second world war, arguing that the wages they brought back with them were gained through fighting and replaced the cattle they used to bring back. The girls remained unimpressed and today they still demand that a moran should have stolen at least one cow if they are to sing of his deeds. Spear-blooding is no longer required.

In the Club dances it does not matter if the soloist himself has

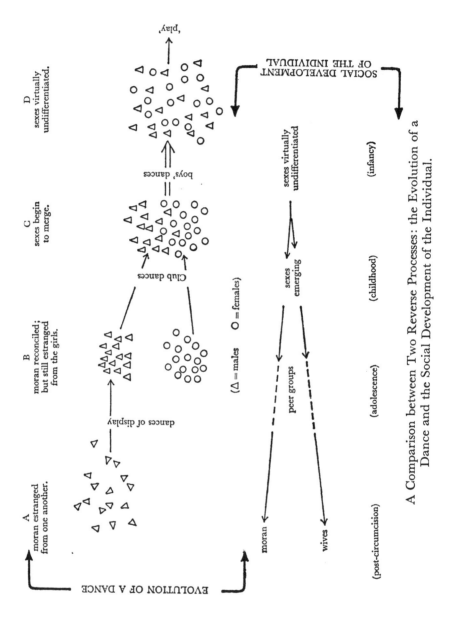

A Comparison between Two Reverse Processes: the Evolution of a
Dance and the Social Development of the Individual.

126

not been on a stock raid and many of the moran enjoying the dance have not been and have no intention of going on one. But still, stock theft, preferably from some other tribe, remains an ideal of moranhood today, and many are tempted to try it. That the taunts of the girls help to maintain this ideal and induce the moran to steal may be judged from this description by one moran. 'You are standing there in the dance, and a girl starts to sing. She raises her chin high and you see her throat. And then you want to go and steal some cattle for yourself. You start to shiver. You leave the dance and stride into the night, afraid of nothing and only conscious of the fact that you are going to steal a cow.' Needless to say, the girl had been singing of the stock thefts of some other moran. It is said that moran sometimes leave the dance and go to some other part of the country, tormented by the desire to steal stock and never quite being able to do it. No one knows whether they will come back having been on a pilfering excursion, or merely on a purposeless journey, haunted by the taunts of the girls at every dance and filled with a sense of inadequacy.

The week following full moon is the most active time for dancing: wedding ceremonies only take place during this week, and at night it is possible to see one's way clearly to a neighbouring settlement to join in a dance. The conditions are also ideal for stock theft: of 37 stock thefts reported to the police by Europeans in the area to the south between May and December 1959, 20 took place during the third quarter of the moon. Thus, for three weeks of the month the moran may not be particularly prominent in the society, and then during the fourth week they are to be seen splendidly embellished for wedding dances, heard singing in the evenings and suspected of the stock thefts which are being rumoured everywhere at that time.

Internal Control Among the Moran

This chapter concludes with an outline of some of the ways in which moran settle their affairs.

The powerful curse which the ritual leader can hold over members of his phratry age-set may effectively curb high spirited moran, as occurred when the Lorogushu-Mekuri ritual leader intervened in an affray between Makalilit and Pardopa clans (page 116). But he does not always act in this way: the Lorogushu-Kimaniki ritual leader did not even try to prevent the affair of Kipepial's mistress (page 113) from building up into an affray between the two clans. Instead, he chose to support his close kinsman, Pasanga, and joined in on the side of Makalilit. This action could have led to severe mystical misfortune for the whole phratry age-set. The Pardopa moran wanted to curse him collectively, and were only dissuaded from doing so by the Pardopa elders who were trying to bring the whole affair to a close. This incident makes it quite clear that the ritual leader cannot be relied on to interfere directly in the internal affairs of his phratry age-set; and he is certainly not simply a prefect over them, for collectively they have a reciprocal power to curse him. He does not, in fact, effectively use his powers of coercion to maintain peace within his phratry age-set on every possible occasion, and the dispersed nature of all phratries would, in any case, make this an impossible task for one man.

A further example makes it quite clear that although the ritual leader retains his power to curse his phratry age mates after they have become elders, he is still reluctant to use it. In example 20 (page 49), Dupua and Leperin belonged to the same phratry age-set, and moreover their ritual leader was living only a few miles from Dupua's homestead when the latter was harbouring Leperin's wife. Yet he took no part in persuading Dupua to return his wife; he preferred the course expected of all ritual leaders in normal circumstances: to dissociate himself from such affairs unless forced to intervene by the turn of events.

Internal control over their affairs, then, is predominantly in the hands of the moran themselves, or, when situations get out of their control, in the hands of the elders. It is unlikely that a deliberate breach of the accepted code of behaviour among the moran would tempt others to support the wrongdoer. It is more likely that they will take direct action to punish him, and a particularly obnoxious offence could lead to immediate physical reprisals:

33. Sakaine raped the wife of an elder when he and several other moran of Pardopa Club were visiting Mount Ngiro where the people were almost entirely of Masula phratry. This placed them all in a precarious position and if they were found by the Masula moran they would be attacked and beaten up. The offence was worsened by the fact that they were still junior moran and any pregnancy resulting from the rape could bring mystical misfortune to the woman and her husband.

They hurried from the vicinity, and once safely away from it, the other Pardopa moran cut themselves whips and beat Sakaine soundly. They included two of his close kinsmen who were not inclined to take his side in the matter on any grounds of family honour.

In this example, it was the danger which they all faced as a result of Sakaine's behaviour which infuriated the others and not simply their disapproval at his way of behaving.

Moran are encouraged by the elders to settle their disputes peacefully and to avoid violence where possible. They only approve of whipping contests and collective beatings when it is quite apparent to them that a peaceful settlement will not be accepted by all those implicated.

34.** (follows from example 27 page 104). Late in the evening after the first two circumcisions of the Kishili age-set in one particular clan, those initiates who were to be circumcised on the following morning were given an ox to eat. They slaughtered it and left one hind leg for the elders and one for the moran of the Kimaniki age-set. Four moran took this second leg and ate it without telling any other members of their Club.

This was discovered by the other moran, and after the circumcisions had been completed the next morning they held a discussion on this breach of age-set etiquette: meat given to an age-set should have been shared with the age-set no matter how little there was. At the very least, the offenders should have informed one or two other age mates, but as it was, they had deliberately concealed the meat from them. It showed, they argued, how little they respected their age-set obligations. They were all senior moran and soon to become elders; they had all developed a sense of respect during their moranhood. How, then, were they to interpret this unjustified greed? The moran at first demanded that each offender should provide a heifer-in-calf for slaughter to teach them a lesson, and if they tried to evade this then all those present would take the cattle by force. To this pronouncement, the four guilty moran agreed that they would comply with any punishment imposed on them and admitted that they had acted selfishly; but at the same time they implored the others to reduce the penalty as a gesture of good will. The matter was debated further and it was agreed that as the culprits had shown great respect for the decisions of their Club, the penalty would be reduced to one large goat apiece.

After the discussion, the other moran insisted to me that they had had every intention of carrying out their original threat, but it was the respectful attitude of the culprits that had mollified them.

It is perhaps significant that both the incident and the discussion occurred at the time when a new age-set was being initiated. It was a dispiriting time for the Kimaniki age-set as a whole, as they were about to be displaced as moran. Earlier a number of them had been involved in an incident which had nearly led to an affray (page 105) and now others were involved in a breach of age-set etiquette: the first incident betrayed a certain hostility towards the newly initiated age-set and the second betrayed a certain apathy towards their own. The four guilty moran had not been motivated by only greed, but also, it seemed, by a weakened sense of responsibility towards their age-set as a direct result of the earlier circumcisions. Their selfish behaviour at this juncture could only weaken age-set solidarity yet further unless strong sanctions were imposed on them as an expression of renewed solidarity.

In dealing with this breach of etiquette, the moran showed considerable maturity. In the first place, they settled it by discussion as the elders would have done; secondly, they modified their demands once it became evident that the culprits had accepted the wrongfulness of their behaviour and had shown humility and respect: and thirdly, it seemed to me that they also showed considerable tact in the way that they handled the offenders. They criticized the breach of etiquette as immature and lacking in respect: such behaviour might be expected of boys or very young moran, but not of really mature moran. The criticism of the culprits in referring to their childlike behaviour seemed to be aimed at *humiliating* them by drawing attention to what they had not achieved (a matter of their prestige), but it avoided *shaming* them by not suggesting that they were in any way inferior to other moran (a matter of their honour). This made it possible for the offenders to accept the judgment with a certain dignity and respect which did them credit, and harmony was restored.

The arguments used in this debate may also have had a less direct implication. This criticism of childlike behaviour could have been a self-conscious allusion to the standards they now expected of themselves in contrast to those they might expect of the new initiates of the Kishili age-set; this point may even have been raised in the discussion. This would draw attention to the vast difference which existed between the two age-sets: the Kimaniki age-set could not maintain a monopoly of the privileges of moranhood for very much longer and they could not remain the general focus of interest in the society once the Kishili were well established, but they could at least show how very much more mature they were than the new age-set, and in doing so they were preparing themselves for acceptance in the age grade of elderhood.

Summary

The moran of the society are forced to share one another's company to a very large extent by the restrictions placed on them: they share the hard life of the cattle camps, the hunger in times of scarcity and the feasting in times of plenty; they accompany each other in long and short journeys and cannot normally eat or drink except in each other's company. It is a situation in which relationships between them are inevitably intense ranging from the extremes of loyal friendship to bitter enmity. These are clearly expressed in their notions of honour and prestige and the ways in which small incidents may build up into serious affrays. The intensity of these relationships between them may to some extent be correlated with the relative distance of their relationships with girls which tend to be confined to bantering and sexual play. Their songs and dances are the most developed idiom of communication between the two sexes. Nevertheless, their relationships with girls provide the moran with an important aspect of their games of prestige and honour among themselves. For the moran these are not games, but matters of very real importance. For the elders, however, they are to be regarded as games which they must grow out of sooner or later.

Chapter Six

THE MORAN AND THE TOTAL SOCIETY

THE moran are in their late twenties or early thirties before they are allowed to marry, and this is a possible cause of strain among young men, many of whom may not altogether accept their prolonged bachelorhood without some resentment. The system continues because the older men are jealous of the monopoly they hold of political power and marriage, and they enforce the restrictions on the moran, even at the risk of increasing tension between the two age grades.

In other societies, a high rate of polygamy may create considerable tension between the males of a family. Among the Turkana to the north-west of Samburu, for instance, a man in search of stock from the family's herd for his first marriage, is brought into competition with his brothers, and with his father who may also wish to marry for the second or third time. This competition leads to a tension within the family and resentment, but it does not normally amount to open hostility. The theme of secession by young people with stock belonging to the old is a common one among the Turkana and related tribes of the Karamojong cluster in their myths of descent.[1]

The Samburu manage the same problem rather differently. In the first place, all their young men are initiated into an age-set at adolescence and they are not allowed to marry until their age-set has reached a certain seniority. Restrictions on their first marriages, then, are imposed on all members of one age-set by the age-set system itself under the control of the elders and not directly by the father or elder brothers of each moran. And

[1] Gulliver, 1951, p. 102; pp. 127–38; and Gulliver, 1955, pp. 133–4.

133

secondly marriage does not involve intense competition for stock as the initial bridewealth payment is comparatively small. The relationship of young men with their fathers and elder brothers is inevitably less fraught with tension than among the Turkana. But the strain among young unmarried men still exists and resentment is directed not towards kinsmen but towards the elders in general, particularly those who impose the restrictions on the moran, the firestick elders. *The most significant function of the Samburu age-set system is, I believe, that it diverts forces which could be disruptive to the family and places them under the direct control of the elders.* The Turkana age organization is less constricting than the Samburu one: it does not in any way delay the age of marriage of males or effectively control irresponsible behaviour among young men, and hence the family is exposed to considerable strain.

A Sense of Respect: Nkanyit

The Samburu are aware of the tension between successive generations among the Turkana and they have their own version of the myth of descent of this tribe. According to this version, the Turkana were once Samburu. Some uncircumcised Samburu boys and their sisters were living at a cattle camp, and in order to get better grazing for their stock they moved farther and farther away from their tribal territory, ignoring all the messages from their fathers that they should return to their homes. Eventually they were entirely cut off, and being only young and knowing no Samburu customs they grew up as children: they had no sense of respect (*nkanyit*); boys married their own sisters, for they knew no better; clan and age-set obligations were of no significance to them; and they paid no attention to such Samburu customs as circumcision. In fact they behaved in a very similar way to the Turkana today, as seen through Samburu eyes.

This myth is interesting, not merely because it echoes the theme of secession of the young from their parents with their stock, but also because it draws attention to the Samburu attitude towards the Turkana – that in their behaviour they show absolutely no sense of respect and are consequently similar to children.

A sense of respect is an attitude which is inculcated into persons of both sexes from a fairly early age. It is a virtue which is constantly referred to by the elders in many contexts, and it is the keystone of Samburu morality. All social obligations which form a part of the Samburu moral code may be expressed with reference to it. Certain of these obligations may be odious and apparently unfair, and other persons may sympathize with a man who expresses his personal feelings in private and may appreciate his attempts to evade the demands of his affines or maternal kinsmen; but they will criticize him if he tries to flout these liabilities openly for this shows that he has no sense of respect.

'*Nkanyit* is a wonderful thing,' said one elder. 'When the other elders see that a man has *nkanyit*, they all respect him (*keanyit*), for his heart and his stomach are good. . . . He may not be rich. He may not be a skilled debater. But he is a worthy man, and no one will curse him. God (*Nkai*) likes *nkanyit*.'

On the whole, moran have a less developed sense of respect than the elders, although a greater sense of respect than boys. Moranhood is a period when the elders, particularly the fire-stick elders, try to inculcate a sense of respect into young men. Before their circumcisions, their moral education was a casual restraint imposed by their fathers and senior kinsmen. Now, as moran, it is the subject of many public harangues. A recently circumcised moran may show an outward respect for elders – this much at least has been instilled into him ever since he was a fairly young boy – but he may be less able to do so when faced with an unexpected situation, because he cannot conceal his own personal feelings. If, for instance, he is hungry and has only a small portion of meat – what will he do when an elder comes and asks him for some meat? Or if he wishes to water his own cattle and then finds that some elder is using his water hole without permission – how should he react? Or if he is tired in the evening and a man whom he hardly knows asks him for help in looking for some stray cattle – can he refuse? In each of these instances a senior moran who has a strongly developed sense of respect would accept the situation placidly:

he would offer a larger part of the meat to the other; he would wait until the other has finished watering his cattle; and he would readily help in looking for the missing cattle. A younger moran might react more impulsively: he might give away only a smaller piece of meat; he might lose his temper on finding the other using his water hole; and he might find some excuse for not being able to join in the search for the missing cattle.

The very real difference between mature senior moran and newly circumcised junior moran was quite apparent in 1960 after the first initiations of the Kishili age-set had been completed. Technically the initiates were now moran, but in everything that they did, in their manner of speech and behaviour, they were still essentially like boys. The way in which the senior moran of the Kimaniki age-set seemed to draw attention to their own comparative maturity at this time was mentioned in the last chapter.

The Developing Strains of Moranhood

The strains which young men encounter as moran vary in intensity and character as their age-set progresses through the various stages of moranhood. There is, in addition, a considerable difference in the ways in which individual members react to these strains.

Shortly before the initiation of a new age-set, there may be a certain restlessness among the older uncircumcised boys who are steadily increasing in number, and this behaviour indicates to the elders that the new age-set should be initiated fairly soon; it is only when they are aware of the large number of boys waiting for circumcision that they give their consent. The senior moran of the preceding age-set are likely to be the only people to resent the initiation of the new moran, regarding them as intruders who are challenging their exclusively held privileges. In particular, they dislike the increasing attention which the new age-set is gaining at their expense, not only from the girls, but also from the remainder of the society. Time is against the senior moran. Older girls who have been closely associated with them and have remained loyal to them are taken away in marriage. But the younger girls now regard them as elders and prefer to associate with the junior moran. In time, as more and more senior moran marry and settle down to elderhood, the remaining bachelors become inclined to follow suit and the competition between senior and junior moran for general attention dwindles. For the junior moran this is, perhaps, the most jubilant period of their lives.

After four or five years of moranhood, however, a new source of tension appears. Young girls, who at the age of 12 or 13 were the oldest to associate themselves with the new age-set on its initiation, are now of a suitable age to be married and, for the first time, the moran experience the frustration of losing these girls to the elders and being absolutely powerless to prevent it. This is about the time that they are promoted to senior moranhood. At about this time, also, antagonisms within the age-set, which may have been moderate at first, begin to develop into more serious proportions: Clubs come into a more marked opposition against one another, the older moran and younger moran within each Club find themselves as rivals for the same girls; their increasing boldness leads to threats and warnings from the elders who are no longer as well disposed towards them as they were at first. The elders now expect them to have acquired a greater sense of respect, and they show less tolerance for their shortcomings. It is tempting to regard the period of junior moranhood as a preparation for senior moranhood, in which the elders assert their control over the moran before the period of critical tension between them is reached.

The antipathy between the moran and the preceding age-set does not necessarily diminish as the latter settle down to junior elderhood. It is sustained by new sources of competition; it is the junior elders who marry many of the girls associated with the moran, and it is these wives that the moran tend to have secret affairs with.[1] The moran show more respect for the fire-stick elders and senior elders who marry such girls as their second and third wives and they are more careful in their dealings with them. But they do not sincerely respect the junior elders, many of whom may be marrying for the first time, and there is a certain resentment. An example of this disrespect is the singing

[1] Table E of the appendix suggests that of the marriages between girls and elders, 70% are with junior elders, and only 30% with more senior men.

of a song, *ntira*, when a girl is taken away from them in marriage. The song amounts to a curse on the bridegroom and implicates to a lesser extent all those who have conspired in arranging the marriage. But out of respect for the bridegroom the moran would never sing this song if he is a senior elder or an age mate and they would not normally sing it when he is a firestick elder. In other words, it is primarily sung at the marriages of junior elders. This song is understood by the Samburu to be an expression of disrespect and animosity rather than an effective curse.

After the moran have been promoted to senior moranhood at the *ilmugit* of the name ceremony, they remain for about six years in this vulnerable state where they constantly lose girls to the elders without being able to become elders themselves. Even after the *ilmugit* of the bull ceremony which entitles them to marry at the end of this period, they should wait a further year or two for their ritual leader to marry first. By this time, many of them are over thirty years old. It was these older youths who, as boys, were the protagonists in agitating for the initiation of their age-set, and who later on were the more assertive and experienced moran of the age-set. And it is also they who are likely to be the first wanting to marry and settle down. They are among the first to acquire a developed sense of respect and their behaviour towards the end of their period as moran is comparatively restrained, especially if they have lost mistresses in marriage and have not formed new attachments. By behaving in a mature manner they convince the elders – particularly their own kinsmen and those of the girls they propose to marry – that they have all the necessary qualities to make a successful marriage. 'When a moran has acquired a sense of respect,' said one man, 'then what is he but an elder?'

But at this point the younger moran of the age-set, who have so far been overshadowed by the more assertive senior members, are still attracted by the privileges and the freedom of moranhood and they show no intention of settling down to elderhood. In so far as an age-set shows any hostility towards the initiation of a new age-set, it is these younger moran and not the older ones who are likely to be the protagonists. More or less at the point at which the senior members of an age-set begin to

138

behave with less assertiveness, the junior members begin to become assertive.

Thus during the final years of moranhood, the moran are pulling in two directions: the older ones are restraining themselves in an effort to be acceptable as elders which is the first stage towards marriage, and the younger ones are showing every intention of remaining moran for many years. In 1957 and 1958 when the Kimaniki performed their *ilmugit* of the bull ceremonies, very few moran expressed any immediate desire to marry and settle down; in 1960, when a considerable number of them had married and the new Kishili age-set was initiated, many of them had modified their ambitions of remaining moran indefinitely; and by the beginning of 1962 most of them had shaved off their hair although the majority were still bachelors without immediate plans for marriage and the age-set as a whole was still suspected of the stock theft in the area which continued unabated. This was 10 years after they had been promoted to senior moranhood.

The strains of moranhood are considerable, but they do not affect the age-set uniformly; they affect moran of different ages and different dispositions in a variety of ways, and they change in the course of development of the age-set. Moreover, it would be misleading to imply that they are not outweighed by the attractions of moranhood. A fundamental characteristic of the Samburu age-set system which is in part responsible for its effectiveness in delaying the age at which men first marry is this attraction; and without it there would be far more tension between the moran and the elders.

The Attitude of the Elders Towards the Moran

The Samburu do not have any clear notion that if they were to shortern the period between successive age-sets and allow the moran to marry earlier then this would effectively decrease the amount of polygamy in the society, but it is obvious, even to them, that the immediate effect of allowing the moran to marry and settle down to elderhood is to increase the number of elders and the competition for wives. If, therefore, the elders wish to limit the monopoly of power and rights in marriage to a small number of persons, it is in their interests to hold up the advancement of the moran for as long as possible. Whether this is a basic motive in their behaviour towards the moran or not must remain a matter of conjecture; but it is at least evident that their various ways of encouraging and restricting the moran have the effect of impeding their advancement towards elderhood, even if this is not the expressed intention. The elders justify their own policies by pointing out that the moran are as yet too immature for marriage and elderhood; they say that they want to maintain the traditions of the society and that this can only be done by instilling a strong sense of respect into the moran over a long period. Their reasoning is circular, however, for without close association with the elders, the moran have only a narrow idea of how they should behave, but until they behave in a mature way, the elders will not associate with them at all closely. The result is that for a number of years the moran are in a state of social suspension when their rate of advancement to elderhood is slowed up considerably.

So it is that the various ceremonies that mark stages in their advancement to elderhood, and the ceremonies which herald the initiations of a new age-set which will displace them as the moran of the society, are delayed under various pretexts – that the moran have too little sense of respect, that the boys are too few, that drought conditions prevent the gathering of large numbers of people – an argument which alone may be sufficient to put off a ceremony for several months if not a year or more. The marriages of certain ritual leaders may be deliberately forbidden until the initiation of the new age-set and this will delay the marriages of many other moran belonging to their phratry age-sets.

Apart from impeding ceremonial activity, there are two other ways in which the elders effectively influence the moran to remain as moran for an extended period: the first is to persuade them that they are still immature and have no right to expect more than they have, and the second is to encourage them to cling to the privileges of moranhood.

The moran of one Club are persuaded of their immaturity by the elders of their clan in public harangues, and on many informal occasions. The harangues are particularly important;

perhaps 10 or 20 elders and twice as many moran meet by arrangement, and one after another the elders, in particular the firestick elders, address the moran, give them moral advice, rant at them, accuse them of irresponsibility and a lack of real respect; they make allusions to the adulterous and thieving habits of the moran, they remind them of their power to curse them and to bless them. These orators are sometimes reduced to repeating one word, *nkanyit* (a sense of respect), four or five times successively in an almost speechless fury. They pick on any defaulters among the moran and shame them before the others. They single out the most prominent moran to act as spokesmen for the others, and they expect them to agree with all that is being said against them. In reply, these spokesmen admit that they, the moran, lack a sense of respect; they assure the elders that they want to gain this, and they promise them that they will try to behave with greater respect in future. The harangue may last several hours before the moran are blessed and sent away.

A typical speech by an elder during one of these harangues might run as follows. 'What do you want? . . . What do you want? . . . Don't you want the advice of the elders? . . . Don't you want to gain respect? . . . Do you want our curse? . . . You know what things you ought to do. . . . We have told you many times. . . . Why do you lurk near the settlements?' (This is an allusion to those moran who wait for any opportunity to seduce some elder's wife.) 'Get out to where you belong! . . . To your cattle camps. . . . To your herds . . . So that you may become rich elders. . . . Why do you go looking for cattle to steal (*reiya*)? . . . Forget your songs and listen to the elders. . . . Why go away stealing, when your own herds are hungry and thirsty? . . . Listen to us now. . . .' etc., etc.

The elders admit that in order to impress the moran on these occasions, they grossly exaggerate the gravity of the situation, and they justify this by claiming that this has always been the custom. The accusation against moran that they are worse than all their predecessors is admitted to be a well worn cliché and is sometimes denied in private. But there is little doubt that much of the behaviour of the moran, especially adultery with the wives of the elders, is irritating and is sufficient to induce in the elders a sincere desire to vent their furies against them during these harangues.

Harangues inevitably take place after local disturbances when the elders call the moran together to settle the issue; they are also an indispensable feature of any ceremony when the moran and elders are conveniently gathered together in one place for some time.

My own impression was that on these occasions, the moran were being given a form of brain-washing. In many harangues the emphasis was not so much on the fact that moran should acquire a sense of respect and behave in a manner consistent with this, as that they were a thoroughly bad and irresponsible lot and almost incapable of improvement. Manifestly the elders professed to be helping the moran to acquire the necessary sense of respect so that they could eventually become elders, but in effect they were impeding their progress by convincing them that they had only deteriorated since becoming moran and were exceptionally backward in their development. The moran do not maintain among themselves that the elders are insincere or are overstating the issue. On the contrary, they say that all that the elders accuse them of is quite true and they maintain that the only way to gain a sense of respect is to attend these harangues, and, if necessary, to ask for more harangues – which they sometimes do. It is only possible for a considerable number of moran and elders of one clan to come together on infrequent occasions, but in spite of the intermittency of these meetings there is no doubt that the moran accept the general truth of the accusations levelled against them.

Of the two Samburu words for 'to harangue', *a-itarian* and *a-ikok*, the second is particularly apt as it also can mean 'to hit a person in a sore place' (such as a bruise or an open wound). The relentless ways in which the elders attack the moral standards of the moran and keep hammering away at the same point in their harangues may well be thought of as hitting them in a sore place.

The gravest breaches of etiquette are generally perpetrated by the younger moran. But the elders treat the whole age-set as an undifferentiated mob in their criticisms. Thus, so long as new initiates are circumcised into the age-set their childish beha-

142

viour can be taken as evidence of the immaturity of the age-set as a whole. This is another possible source of strain between the senior and junior sub-age-sets of moran (see page 118). Similarly, unusually assertive moran who are often prominent in affrays may be taken by the elders as examples of the truculence of the whole age-set. In their reasoning, the elders tend to ignore the fact that individual moran, according to their personal dispositions and ages, may have acquired more than an average sense of respect: the age-set is treated as though advancing in its standards at the pace of the slowest and most recent members, and the more sophisticated members are held back.

There is, at the same time, a clear realization that the age-set must be allowed to mature eventually and that all males should be moran for a number of years before retiring to elderhood; and elders therefore do not generally allow further circumcisions to take place once the age-set has been founded for six or seven years. Custom allows circumcisions to occur at any time before the *ilmugit* of the bull ceremony, but an age-set of moran are unlikely to recruit further members four or five years before this time in order to give all moran some chance of maturing before they are ritually in a position to marry.

There is another side of moranhood which the elders try to encourage. They all remember with horrified affection their own years spent as moran and they tend to talk of it as if it were the zenith of their careers. Fathers, elder brothers, close kinsmen, and others tell the moran about their own adventures in more dangerous days with pride. Moranhood is understood by everyone to be a period of health, vitality, close fellowship, freedom and fearlessness, and the elders admire the moran as much as anyone else. It is the prime of life before the cares of building up a family and a herd take their toll of a man's health. With elderhood, men lose their fine looks, their close fellowship and their freedom. They regard their physical decline with sorrow. They dress plainly and shave their heads; by the side of the dashing moran with red ochre, bright loincloths beaded ornaments, and long braided hair, they look quite plain. Once when I asked an elder in his late forties if I could take his photograph, he replied: 'Do not photograph me. I am dead! Go and take a photograph of the moran.' And there was seldom much difficulty in doing that.

The glamour of moranhood is superficial. It is the plain broken elders, whose wives are so frequently unfaithful to them, who are the political rulers of the society; and by not interfering too closely with the lives led by the moran, they lessen the tension between them. In allowing them freedom and encouraging them to pursue their affairs of honour within limits, they indirectly subscribe to a situation which easily leads to violence and disorder. At harangues, they express disgust and urge the moran to keep away from married women, not to steal stock and not to take matters of honour and prestige so far that they fight one another. Yet they still insist that the moran shall associate closely with one another and they organize their ceremonies on a clan basis, both of which succeed in upholding the Club system. They make no attempt to prohibit songs which encourage stock theft or fighting, as they maintain that these are a part of the heritage of the moran to which they have a full right. They continue to take girls away in marriage and thereby increase the temptation for the moran to commit adultery. All that the demands of the elders at harangues appear to amount to is that the moran should at least show an overt respect for them.

The elders do *not* like the thought of the moran seducing their youngest and most attractive wives, they do *not* like the collective levies imposed by the administration for lawlessness and stock theft by the moran, and they do *not* like to see their own sons and brothers dangerously involved in affrays arising from excesses of pride and enthusiasm. But nor do they want to see the moran system discontinued, and these unseemly aspects of their behaviour are accepted as an integral part of that system: a part which, incidentally, can be used by the elders as a justification to impede the progress of the moran to elderhood.

The Attitude of the Moran Towards the Elders

The attitude of the moran towards the elders is also an ambivalent one. They appear to accept without question the merit of gaining a marked sense of respect, and as they mature, their behaviour towards the elders and towards one another tends to become more restrained. They recognize that it is from the elders that they acquire this quality and they associate it with many of the modes of behaviour expected of them as moran. Thus, when they are first circumcised, they avoid calling their age mates by name and observe the food prohibitions of moran-hood because this is expected of them and not to do so would humiliate them in the eyes of others for it would suggest that they were something less than moran: they would be behaving like children. But later, in the course of their development, observing the correct modes of behaviour is also understood to be a token of the respect that they should have for one another and for the society as a whole: non-conformity would be an affront to others as well as the sign of immaturity, and it would only be tolerated from a feeble minded moran incapable of knowing better.

This development of attitudes towards their behaviour was apparent in 1960, when members of the new Kishili age-set understood that certain things were required of them, but in their general bewilderment and excitement they could only say that this was the way of all moran: the elders had told them what they should do and they did not try to explain at this stage why they should do it. Senior moran of the Kimaniki age-set, however, understood only too well that not to follow these norms indicated a lack of respect as they pointed out quite explicitly in the discussion that followed the incident in which four moran tried to conceal meat from their age mates (page 129). Moran-hood is a period during which young men gain a sense of respect, and in gaining it they acknowledge that they are emulating the elders.

On the other hand, in addition to this sincere attitude of respect, there remains the tension between the two age grades; and this appears to express itself in much of the dissident behaviour of the moran. It must be emphasized at once that to say that much of the behaviour of the moran reflects their hostility towards the elders is a conjecture: a few younger moran do admit that they dislike as well as fear the elders, but most of them maintain a respectful silence, and are far more ready, especially in their songs, to admit a revulsion for the imposed administration for interfering in their lives and traditional ways of behaving. But the moran make no secret of disliking many of the restrictions and frustrations which the elders impose on them, even if they do not normally admit to disliking the elders themselves. Very occasionally, this hostility leads to fighting and affrays with elders, but it is rare that their intimidating methods are insufficient to maintain control.

The hostility of the moran for the elders is more usually expressed indirectly as in stories they tell of the physical incapacity of the elders or their greed and selfishness – weaknesses which the moran despise. The best example of their concealed hostility is perhaps in their attitude towards adultery with the wives of elders. Among the elders it is a topic which is a continual source of irritation, gossip and rueful speculating; a man with two wives in different settlements is said always to be worrying about the fidelity of whichever one he is not actually staying with at the time. Among the moran, however, and I suspect among the younger wives, it is a topic which arouses considerable amusement as well as anxiety. A moran who commits adultery is ashamed when his parents hear of it; he is personally harangued in front of the other moran by the elders, and he is despised by the girls who are jealous of moran who satisfy their lusts elsewhere. But among the moran themselves, he has achieved a certain distinction which is not a together despised: and if his secret is not known to anyone save the moran, then this distinction is enhanced. When discussing this topic with moran, I constantly had the impression that for my benefit they were overstressing the fact that this was an activity detested by the elders with a certain element of danger involved if it was discovered, and that quite apart from the satisfaction of lust there was a certain prestige among moran to be gained from the act; it seemed quite likely that many of the moran who hinted that they had just come from an adulterous liaison were lying deliberately to impress their audience. Among senior moran there need be no apprehension of the consequences of impregnating a wife as there is with girls and this gave an added enjoyment to adultery.

As in other contexts one can examine the attitudes of the moran by looking more closely at their songs. It is not so much the content of these songs which suggests their hostility towards the elders as the fact that they deliberately baffle the elders by introducing new words and giving new meanings and implications to familiar words. The elders can guess broadly what these songs are about – stock theft and flirtatious advances to the girls – but prefer to ignore them as topics which they disapprove of than to probe their inner meanings. They dislike *sesiei* because it is a song which encourages moran to steal cattle and this leads to repercussions from the surrounding tribes and from the administration. But the song they dislike even more than that is *nshupa* (see page 120). Before it was introduced in about 1956, there was another song, *ntoo*, with a similar idiom. At first *ntoo* seemed to be a harmless game among the moran and girls in which they vied with one another in riddles. These often introduced allusions to sex and the elders took no notice of them, especially as they were obliged to avoid girls and anything remotely connected with their sexuality. But later, when some of these girls had been circumcised and married, the elders had a shrewd suspicion that the moran were using this song to arrange secret meetings with these wives who knew the idiom even if their husbands did not. They therefore banned the song in 1956 and asked the administration to confirm this. The ban was successful, but at this point the new song, *nshupa*, with an identical idiom became popular among the moran. Is *nshupa* being used by the moran to call the young wives to meet them in the bush? Or are the moran just singing it out of gleeful defiance of the elders because of its dubious associations? The elders do not know and have tacitly allowed the song to continue. The Kimaniki had by this time reached a point where they would shortly settle down to elderhood and the elders thought it more dignified to ignore it.

Each Club has its own versions of these songs and they are secrets largely shared by the moran and their girls. But uncircumcised boys also know what these songs are about for they hover round the dances of the moran and overhear their conversations in the cattle camps. When in time a new age-set is formed and they become moran, they must develop a new idiom for their songs, since with the promotion of the old moran to elderhood, the secrets of the old songs are no longer hidden from the elders. And so a new set of games played by the moran and girls during their dances develops with each new age-set.

The Samburu say that this rift between moran and elders has only been marked since the Kiliako were moran, when the tribe came properly under British protection and inter-tribal fighting was no longer necessary for survival. The elders welcomed this and would have liked the moran to accept the fact that as warriors they were now redundant. But the Kiliako, largely encouraged by the taunts of the girls and by their own inherited notions of what moran should be, continued to blood their spears and make small raids for stock. These led to collective punishments on the tribe as a whole by the British, which in turn caused the elders to resent the behaviour of the moran, and the moran to resent the interference of both the elders and the British. Their lawlessness now involved not only raids on other tribes, but also stock thefts and affrays within the Samburu tribe on an unprecedented scale. One of the climaxes of this phase was the feud which built up between Lorogushu and Pisikishu moran referred to on page 117. The Kiliako were also the first age-set to devise songs which were unintelligible to the elders. The Mekuri were under great control and caused less trouble; but the Kimaniki have been troublesome, committing adultery as never before and persistently stealing stock.

This is the change within the society as the Samburu themselves see it. On the other hand, there is evidence in the writings of the early travellers to the area that the Samburu moran did not devote their entire energies to warrior activities in the past. The Rendille were firm allies of the Samburu, and yet it is reported by both Chanler (in 1893) and Arkell-Hardwick (in 1900) that the Samburu persistently stole stock from them, and Arkell-Hardwick even records that they 'looted' Rendille wives.[1] It is very unlikely that the two tribes would have remained on such friendly terms if the Samburu really had behaved like this; but it is worth noting that in Samburu, as in colloquial Swahili, the word 'to steal' (*a-purr*) can also mean 'to seduce' when applied to women, and this suggests that adultery and stock theft were not altogether unheard of in those golden days. Confronted with this evidence from the past, the

[1] Chanler, 1896, p. 290; Arkell-Hardwick, 1903, p. 241.

older men agree that they were unruly as moran even within their own tribe, but not, they say, to the flagrant extent that the Kimaniki are unruly today.

The impression gained from these informants is that up to the time when the British took over the administration of the area, the moran were thoroughly involved in being warriors in the fullest sense of the term with a definite role to play in the survival of the tribe, and that this overshadowed any frustrations they experienced at the hands of the elders and even provided an outlet for their resentment. But after the arrival of the British and the establishment of a new order of political stability in the area, the moran were deprived of their traditional role and were not offered any substitute. The antagonistic attitudes were no longer diverted away from the society in which they lived and they developed into a delinquent faction within it. With no institutionalized outlet for their animosity, they had, in effect, turned from warriors into angry young men.

The Firestick Relationship

The control which the elders have over the moran and the respect and fear which the moran have for the elders are most explicit in the firestick relationship. It was the firestick elders who ceremonially brought the age-set into existence, and it is they who arrange all its ceremonies and lead discussions concerning the maturation and discipline of the moran. Other elders may express their opinions, but the decisions of the firestick elders in these matters are final.

The firestick relationship is essentially between age-sets rather than between individuals. It is not the actual fathers of the moran who are responsible for supervising the progression of a new age-set through the moran age grade, but the firestick elders of this age-set who, by custom, are precluded from being their fathers. The firestick elders are the one age-set who are most likely to be disinterested in manipulating the advancement of the moran to suit their own personal ends.

The following figures illustrate the extent to which family relationships tend not to coincide with the firestick relationship between alternate age-sets. They are taken from the clan census of 1958.[1] Of the 294 moran in the clan, 2 had fathers, 9 had full brothers, and 23 had half brothers who were members of the Kiliako age-set (i.e. their firestick elders); the other 260 moran had no kinsmen of this order inside this age-set. The two moran whose fathers were firestock elders had only been circumcised by special permission of the Kiliako elders: one had lost both parents when a child and had no close kinsmen to help him look after the large herd of cattle he had inherited; and the father of the other was blind and very deaf, but as he was still alive it seemed preferable for the family to come under the direction of the son as soon as possible than to come under the guardianship of the father's brother. There were other orphans of the Kiliako age-set who were not allowed an early initiation because their circumstances did not demand special consideration. Thus of the 114 living members of the Kiliako age-set in this clan, only one, a blind and nearly deaf man, had a son who was a moran. This compared with 56 living senior elders of whom 50 had sons who were moran.

That the senior elders could hardly have been impartial in their judgments on moran is quite evident from these figures. The Samburu themselves recognize that both the family and the firestick relationship are strengthened if the father of any moran does not also stand as a firestick elder to him. 'Is there any man who would want to curse his own son?', they sometimes ask. Elders are expected to sympathize with the mischievous behaviour of the age-set of their own sons, and this attitude is incompatible with the disciplinary nature of the firestick relationship. When suitable punishment for unruly moran is debated by the elders, it is the firestick elders who demand severe measures and the senior elders, fathers of the moran, who plead for a degree of leniency. In so far as the moran are encouraged to continue to be what they always have been, it tends to be from the senior elders that they get this encouragement; and in so far as they are openly criticized, held in contempt, and urged to show a greater respect, it tends to be from the firestick elders that they get these rebukes.

But the ambivalence of the attitudes of the two age grades towards one another is not entirely to be explained as a differ-

[1] For details of this census, see the appendix.

ence between the indulgent senior elders and the stern firestick elders. In the first place, there are many firestick elders who in private express a genuine affection for the moran and succeed in breaking down the social barrier that separates them by showing a personal interest in their affairs and speaking candidly with them: such elders are both liked and respected by the moran. And secondly, the firestick relationship has a mystical as well as a social significance for the Samburu. It is not simply a relationship of fear by the moran and intimidation and contempt by the firestick elders; there is in addition a certain association between the two age-sets in the minds of all Samburu. This is most explicit in the ways in which they see similarities in the fortunes they have encountered during their period or moranhood: similarities which to an outside observer appear to be largely fortuitous, but to the Samburu are significant. Thus, among the most recent age-sets which have shared a firestick relationship, the Merisho and the Mekuri both gave little trouble to the British and fought with them in their wars (the Merisho in the 1914 punitive expedition against the Turkana and the Mekuri during the second world war), both were rather small age-sets and both obtained sufficient stock to settle down fairly quickly to elderhood. Whereas the Terito and Kiliako age-sets, also in a firestick relationship, did not openly consort with the British and they did not have sufficient stock to settle down quickly; and more recently, the Kiliako and the Kimaniki age-sets as moran have shown a certain defiance towards too close administration, have been unusually large in numbers, and during their moranhood the cattle have suffered severely from epidemics. The Samburu occasionally point to similarities in the fortunes of one age-set and the age-set of its 'fathers' (i.e. three age-sets senior to it), and suggest that these are significant, as, for instance, the fact that they lost cattle when the Marikon age-set were moran (i.e. during the Disaster) and again when their 'sons', the Kiliako, were moran. However, this second type of similarity is not often stressed.

The association between alternate age-sets is in the minds of the members of these age-sets themselves, especially of the junior of the two. The Kimaniki age-set today say that they respect and even fear the Kiliako age-set as their firestick elders; but in stressing the fact that it is the Kiliako, the truculent Kiliako who were so strong and assertive when they were moran, their fear is mixed with a certain admiration and even, perhaps, identification. In a similar way, the members of the Mekuri age-set proudly assert that the Merisho, the last age-set to fight in a large scale inter-tribal war, were severe firestick elders; and the Kiliako say similar things about their firestick elders, the Terito. It is the junior age-set of a firestick relationship who are most conscious of it. For them it is a unique link with the age grade of elderhood which draws them up into that age grade by instilling them with the values acceptable to the elders. For the senior of the two age-sets, it is an important relationship which in certain respects gives them more power than even the senior elders, but it is still only one of the many facets of elderhood and it does not have the same unique importance.

It is less easy, therefore, to obtain statements by firestick elders which indicate any personal feelings of identification with the moran. Their whole attitude towards the latter appears to change considerably as they mature. In 1960, when the Kishili age-set were first initiated, the Mekuri age-set were interested in the prospect of having a new duty to perform as firestick elders to this new age-set and had every confidence that they would accomplish this task to everyone's satisfaction. The Kiliako age-set, after having been firestick elders to the Kimaniki age-set for 12 years, in public expressed exasperation and disappointment; although in private particularly affable members of this age-set expressed some feeling of satisfaction at what they had achieved in instilling respect into the Kimaniki and they regarded their short-comings as inevitable. The Merisho age-set, previously firestick elders to the Mekuri, did not show any further interest in the relationship, but they did show considerable interest in the welfare of the Kimaniki among whom so many of them had sons. These attitudes, if they are all typical of the firestick elders at different phases of the relationship, suggest a logical development from enthusiasm and confidence, to disappointment, and ultimately disinterest as each successive age-set is initiated.

Of the various aspects of the firestick relationship, it is the curse which is most often stressed, and other aspects tend to be related to this in one way or another. This emphasis draws attention to the latent hostility which exists in the relationship. In common with other potent curses in the society, it is held that resentment alone is sufficient to cause misfortune even though no curse has been pronounced. From time to time following some disturbance, the senior elders have actually asked the firestick elders to pronounce their curse, not so much because they want their moran sons to meet with misfortune, as because they feel that this is a way of teaching them a sense of respect and of bringing the smouldering resentment of the firestick elders to a head; and then harmony can be restored through a blessing. This is preferable to keeping the moran in an uncertain state when the hidden resentment of the firestick elders could lead to misfortune at any time.

An offence by a few moran against the elders tends to be interpreted as a sign of the disrespect of the moran in general: they are all considered to be potential evil doers on the verge of lawlessness, and all in need of being taught respect. And the offence could inflame the resentment of the firestick elders against all of them. Therefore, on such occasions, the moran of the local clan group and often those of the same Club from further afield are called for a harangue and a blessing. If the offence is particularly noxious, then they may all be told to contribute towards a placatory gift in return for the blessing: once an elder accepts such a gift, there can be no mystical consequences even if he harbours a hidden resentment in his heart.

The extreme curse of the firestick elders is to break a firestick symbolizing the one with which they brought the age-set of moran into existence; it is said that this could lead to their utter extermination and that it could never be rescinded. There is no known instance of its ever having been used among the Samburu. By using less potent curses when they feel obliged to do so, the firestick elders are not altogether abandoning the moran to their fate, and conciliation through placatory gifts and blessing is always possible. The link joining the moran to the elders is never entirely severed.

153

Case Examples

The following examples have been chosen to illustrate various points made in this chapter, and each one is discussed briefly.

The age grade of moranhood is an institution which delays the age of marriage of young men and protects the family from strains which this would otherwise entail. It does not follow that by initiating a new age-set prematurely, the previous age-set will be able to settle down any more easily: it is more likely that there will be two age-sets of moran (senior and junior) coexisting for a longer period of time and the strain between them will be considerable.

> 35. In the early 1930's, the Kiliako age-set, then moran, showed considerable truculence towards attempts by the administration to subdue them, and it was officially decided to hasten their retirement to elderhood by ordering the initiation of a new age-set and forbidding the Kiliako to wear the accoutrements of moranhood any longer. This led to the initiation of the Mekuri age-set in 1936. The administration then ordered that the Mekuri age-set should perform *all* their ceremonies up to the *ilmugit* of the bull ceremony in 1936 and 1937, so that they could start marrying immediately, and another age-set could be initiated in three years time.

In other words, it was intended that the period of moran-hood should be cut down from about 13 years to 3, and that the number of moran in any one age-set should be drastically reduced so as to quench their lawlessness. The administration did in fact succeed in making the Mekuri age-set perform all their ceremonies up to the *ilmugit* of the bull ceremony, but they could not force them to marry and nor could they force the elders to give their daughters away to them in marriage. Those few moran of the Mekuri age-set who tried to marry at this stage were competing with older men who owned far more cattle and who had developed the sense of respect which any Samburu expects of his affines. Just as a Samburu will not wish his daughter to be married to a mean man who has no sense of his social responsibilities, so he will not wish her to be married to a man who has not yet had time to acquire this sense. Ceremonially, the Mekuri age-set had qualified for marriage by 1938, but economically and socially they could not compete successfully with the members of senior age-sets in obtaining wives. Had the administration continued in its policy for a number of years with new age-sets initiated every three years, then it is likely that instead of one, or sometimes two age-sets of moran in existence at one time, there would have been perhaps four or more; but many of the features of the previous system – the high rate of polygamy and the prolonged bachelorhood of young men – could have remained. As it was, the administration's policy was discontinued and the subsequent age-set was not circumcised until 1948 when the Mekuri had been moran for a full twelve years. This modification of policy was partly due to the outbreak of the second world war and partly to new troubles which appeared in 1939.

> 35 (cont.). In 1939, three years after the administration announced that the Kiliako age-set had been retired to elderhood and just one year after one optimist expressed the belief that the social organization of the Samburu had been destroyed, an attempt to count and cull Samburu stock on Leroghi led to a bloodless rising in which the Kiliako age-set again dressed themselves as moran and played a leading part in intimidating all the elders appointed to government offices. They were encouraged to do this by a number of influential non-government elders. The Mekuri moran appear to have played an insignificant part.
>
> The government elders retired to Maralal for protection, and it was six months before complete order was restored in the district, by which time the stock census and attempts to cull the stock had been abandoned.

This was a clear demonstration of the fact that moran do not cease to be moran as soon as a new age-set has been circumcised, but only when a large number of them have succeeded in marrying and settling down. The Kiliako did not succeed in settling down quickly and this is said to have been because they had too few cattle. This statement may be interpreted in two ways. In the first place, it may have been that after the severe cattle epidemics which the Samburu had suffered in recent years, their herds were badly depleted in number and those Kiliako wanting to marry could not depend on their closest kinsmen to help them build up their herds; this would automatically prejudice their chances when competing with older and richer men who did not have to rely to such an extent on kinsmen and stock friends. Secondly, it may have been that the Kiliako had not seriously prepared for marriage up to this point by concentrating on building up their herds prior to asking their kinsmen for help. When such a situation occurs, a long period of change-over is inevitable before the senior moran succeed in settling down to junior elderhood. It is evident that even in 1939, the Kiliako were still the dominant age-set of moran.

The fortunes of the Samburu had considerably altered by 1948 when the Kimaniki age-set were circumcised and the Mekuri age-set settled down very quickly.

The change-over period is inevitably one of strain between senior and junior moran. The incident immediately before the first circumcisions into the Kishili age-set (page 105) was generally accepted as a symptom of this strain. A clearer example is given below:

> 36. In 1936, shortly after the Mekuri age-set were circumcised, there was an affray inside Pardopa clan between the junior moran of this age-set and the senior moran of the Kiliako age-set. The Kiliako eventually drove the others away with their spears. At a subsequent meeting between the elders and moran to settle the issue, some elders of the Ltoiyo clan, bond brothers of the Pardopa, had been called and they threatened the moran of both age-sets that they would curse them if there was a recurrence of these hostilities. The matter went no further.

It was particularly suitable that it should have been the bond brothers of the two groups of moran who threatened to use their curse. In the first place, spears had been used and although no one had been hurt, it was a serious breach of custom which called for a serious remedy, and few people are more respected than bond brothers. In the second place, as two adjacent age-sets were involved, there was no one inside Pardopa clan who could threaten to use a curse which would have an equal effect on the antagonists. The Terito age-set, as firestick elders of the Kiliako, might threaten to curse them, but they would not want to use the same threat on their 'sons' of the Mekuri age-set; and the Merisho age-set, who might threaten to curse the Mekuri as their firestick elders had no power over the Kiliako age-set. At best, it would have been a joint agreement among the elders to make a collective threat about which each man would have had rather mixed feelings. The threat of the bond brothers was potent and it would affect both age-sets equally.

One other example in which a bond brother was invited to intercede in a clan affair is worth mentioning as it illustrates a number of other points:

37. One of the incidents which precipitated the return of Letore to his paternal clan (page 39) was when his moran son, Kingeyo, had a fierce quarrel with Keseker. As may be judged from examples on pages 45, 48, 193, 202 and 228, both men are rather aggressive and implacable, and it is hardly surprising that an initial slight should have developed into something far more serious.

When they were moran living at the same cattle camp, Kingeyo referred disparagingly to Keseker's age: the latter was among the oldest members of his age-set and strains between the sub-age-sets had begun to appear; Kingeyo was a petulant and much younger moran. Keseker at once hit Kingeyo with his herding staff. Some time later Kingeyo ambushed and clubbed him in return. At this, Keseker swore he would kill Kingeyo.

This was too much for the elders to ignore: they knew how dangerous Keseker could be: the leading part he had played in inciting the Lorogushu moran to fight in their affray with Pisikishu (page 117) left no doubt about that. A meeting of Pardopa clan elders and moran was held. First, the firestick elders tried to persuade Keseker to agree to hold his peace with Kingeyo: he refused. Then the ritual partner at his initiation was called to exercise his powers of moral coercion; and he had no better success. And finally, an elder of Ltoiyo clan, bond brothers to Pardopa, was asked to intercede. He called over Keseker and offered him a sprig of greenwood (life) or a dry stick (death). Keseker chose the first: he was in effect choosing the blessing of the bond brother and agreeing to forgo his revenge against Kingeyo.

Here, a bond brother succeeded in solving a dispute when other means had failed. This is not a course regularly chosen by Samburu, but it is recognized as one which they can resort to as a final measure. Few Samburu are as difficult to control as Keseker, and this was an unusual incident. As a moran, Keseker had been the spokesman (*laigwenan*) for his Club, a position he earned by his forcefulness. But on reaching elderhood, he failed to adapt himself to the more peaceable ways of elderhood and lost the influence he once enjoyed. In one sphere, however, he was without a rival: when his age-set became firestick elders to the Kimaniki, he had the bullying temperament ideally suited to such an elder, and during my field work he was the man most feared by all the moran of Pardopa Club. At harangues, he held the Kimaniki moran spellbound as he ranted at them, shouting and waving his staff. It was he who led the violent *ilmugit* blessing described later on page 267. In their debates, the other elders tend to ignore his wild suggestions and accusations, but they allow him to take on this major role in haranguing the moran: his is the type of personality required to intimidate them, and every age-set of firestick elders may well have a number of men of this calibre.

The strain between adjacent age-sets may continue after the change-over period to the point at which the senior of the two have settled down to elderhood. The source of strain is no longer rivalry over the privileges of moranhood, but adultery. The junior age-set who are still moran constantly lose girls in marriage to the elders, and they respect the junior elders less than others. They are, in consequence, less careful in the way in which they conduct their affairs with these men's wives than they are with the wives of more senior men. A junior elder is still young enough to be prepared to attack any moran who has seduced his wife.

38.* In 1958 there was considerable tension among the Masula at Ngelai between the moran of the Kimaniki age-set and the junior elders of the Mekuri age-set. This was evident from the constant accusations of these elders that the moran were seducing their wives; this enmity was more marked than elsewhere at the time. A minor incident occurred in which one rather foolish junior elder accused his younger brother, a moran, of trying to seduce his wife when he found him talking to her and he told him to keep away from the settlement and struck him. The incident incensed other Masula moran and a small group of them decided to beat up this elder. In the meantime, however, other junior elders, realizing what was about to take place, gathered to support their age mate. The proposed attack by the moran was then delayed while they collected together larger numbers. By the evening, elders of all age-sets had gathered together in order to avert an affray. At this point they were attacked by possibly more than 100 Masula moran with knobkerries. Their intention was to attack only the junior elders, but in the increasing darkness they could not at first distinguish the age-sets of the various elders and they clubbed any man who offered resistance. The fracas was over long before the next morning when an assertive and greatly feared firestick elder, whose unrivalled qualities had earned him appointment as a government chief, ordered the moran to disperse.

This affray had involved not only junior elders, but also firestick and possibly one or two senior elders who had come to maintain peace. This was a serious matter. It was quite sufficient to place the moran in danger of severe mystical misfortune without any curse being pronounced. Most informants assert that the firestick elders did lay a curse on the moran, although it is not absolutely certain that this was ever explicitly pronounced. The method of restoring the moran to a normal ritual condition would have been the same whether or not there had been a curse.

In the discussions which followed the incident, members of the Merisho age-set (senior elders) asked the Kiliako age-set (firestick elders) not to be too harsh in imposing penalties on the Kimaniki moran. They reminded the Kiliako that they themselves as moran had made a serious attack on the elders and that one man had been killed on that occasion. In this way, the Merisho age-set, although they too had been involved in the affray, were acting on behalf of their sons: an attitude frequently adopted by the senior elders on such occasions. But elders of other phratries had been involved in the incident and it was obvious that these outsiders and their clansmen were genuinely shocked by what had happened and were waiting to see how the Masula elders would handle the affair: a light penalty was out of the question.

In a series of ceremonies performed in the course of the next eight months, the moran gave gifts of blankets, sugar, tea and tobacco to certain elders involved in the affray and to one or two other influential men. They were then blessed and restored to a propitious ritual state. Other Masula moran who lived elsewhere and had not taken part in the affray were also made to contribute towards the collective fine and were included in the blessings. The Masula elders insisted on this because, they said, the incident had been so serious that it was sufficient to antagonize the firestick elders towards the Masula moran in general and so they were all in some danger of suffering from mystical misfortune; the incident had shown how little the moran respected the elders and had the others been present then they too would have taken part in the affray. In this way the elders evaded admitting that they were acting under the critical scrutiny of other clans, but preferred to draw attention to the latent hostility that existed between them and the moran. It was a counterpart of the attitude of some of these other moran who jubilantly told me the story of the affray and even tried to make out in confidence that they had taken part. If just one moran strikes an elder, it is considered a disgrace that he should lack self-control and respect, but when as many as 100 moran were involved then the matter assumed different proportions and it was almost a matter of personal prestige to have taken part.

This example also illustrates that even after its members have become elders, an age-set retains a certain solidarity: the junior elders rallied to support an age mate threatened by the moran. As elders they still have and make use of certain obligations of moral support and hospitality towards one another; and later, when they become firestick elders, they share the responsibility of maintaining control over the moran. In another instance Lotien has been cursed and two of his heifers-in-calf have been killed by his age mates because he raped two of their daughters – girls whom he should avoid above all others. In a third, Sutilai has been supported by some age mates in his recent threats to take back Peyon's wife (see page 203 below). And in a fourth, one man who tried to poison his father with a concoction prepared from the deadly desert rose could not be dis-

160

inherited as he was the only son of the family, but he could be cursed, and it was the father's age mates who collected together to do this.

In the first two of these four instances, the Ngelai affray and the case of Lotien's being cursed by his age mates, the elders concerned were of one age-set but various clans: the two incidents transcended clan loyalties. This is less likely to occur in any critical issue affecting the moran: their notions of clanship are more rigid and are maintained by the bitter inter-Club, and hence inter-clan, affrays. Moran do not have quite the same broad outlook on important issues as the elders. They think rather in terms of Club and clan than of the society in general.

This difference between the outlook of the elders and that of the moran appears to help the former in maintaining control. They are united in their opposition to any relaxation in the restrictions imposed on the moran, and the general tension between age grades cuts right across clan and phratry boundaries. But the moran are disunited among themselves by their constant inter-Club rivalry, and this places them in a weak position *vis-a-vis* the elders. This is perhaps fortunate from the point of view of the elders: those over whom they rule are already divided. In other words, one might say that among the moran there is always a potential state of gang warfare between the various Clubs; and that if the elders wish to retain ultimate control over the society in their hands, then it is not in their best interests to curtail these delinquent tendencies too effectively, unless at any time they constitute a revolt against the system itself. The seriousness of the Ngelai affray was that it did constitute such a revolt; and hence the elders mustered all the forces at their disposal to regain the moral ascendancy over the moran and prevent any recurrences.

The Social Condition of the Moran and Ilmugit Ceremonies

The foregoing sections should make it fairly clear why so much attention converges on the moran even though they are placed outside the remainder of the society to some extent. But why the moran should also be the focus of so much ritual activity, in particular the *ilmugit* ceremonies, has not yet been discussed.

It has previously been stated that moranhood is a period of considerable frustration for the moran and that for a number of years their rate of advancement to elderhood is slowed down considerably: this was referred to as a state of social suspension. The frustration which they experience is not oppressive, but it is persistent and relentless; it is, perhaps sufficient to explain the obstinate, unpredictable and sometimes fiery nature of their behaviour. I suggest that they are in a social condition which is similar to *anomie*, described by Durkheim in his work on suicide: there is the same lack of balance between means and needs (ambitions), traditional rules lose their authority, passions are less disciplined, and there is a state of exasperation and irritated weariness.[1] Among the moran, however, this condition is not demonstrated by a high incidence of suicide, but by impulsive and unpredictable behaviour. They have periods of restlessness and irresponsibility. They are prone to deep disgust after a violent fit of shaking, after losing a mistress, or after losing in some matter of prestige; when they are in this state, they are irritable and are likely to leave their homes without warning. This restlessness leads many of them to travel constantly to distant parts of the district and nowadays to search for work. The Samburu accept these eccentricities unquestioningly (except during harangues): 'Why ask why they do these things?', said one elder, 'They are moran, and moran have always behaved in that way.' My own presence among the Samburu as a young man far away from his own home who frequently travelled about the country on fruitless errands was interpreted by many Samburu in this light; and I was sometimes asked if my mistress had been taken away from me before I left England and if my kinsmen had the slightest idea where I was.

The extreme forms of behaviour of the moran are collective violence in a major affray on the one hand and utter purposelessness on the other. It is said that sometimes a group of moran behave like mad bleating goats. They jabber, they quarrel and they brood; no one takes any notice of what others are trying

[1] Durkheim, 1897, trans. Simpson, 1951. Especially chap. 5, pp. 246, 253 and 357. Durkheim notes also a relationship between anomie and crime.

to say; if one man tries to strike another then others may not intervene to prevent a fight. It is a condition of dysphoria known to the Samburu as *nshakera* or goat-madness. Two *ilmugit* ceremonies performed in recent times, one by the Kiliako age-set and one by the Mekuri, are both remembered as the *ilmugit of the goat-madness (ilmugit lenshakera)* because of the behaviour of the moran at this time.

This condition of dysphoria is perhaps as much of an indication of the social condition of the moran as the lawless effervescence exhibited when affrays break out. They are extreme aspects of the same exasperation and undisciplined passions produced by this state of suspension in which the moran are too little involved in the total society. They are forms of behaviour which do not occur among the elders. The elders admire the worthy man who is dependable and tolerant, the prudent man who takes the responsibilities of his herd and family seriously, and the wise man who gives good advice. Such men have ambitions well adapted to their means. Even in this hazardous environment when some catastrophe can disrupt their fortunes and deprive them of the means to achieve these ambitions, they are well insured through the close social ties they have developed with their clansmen and others. The moran are in a quite different situation which is altogether more brittle: if they have mistresses, they almost certainly must lose them; if they pursue their matters of prestige, they risk considerable humiliation and criticism and make it hard for themselves to settle down to elderhood. The goal which they are urged to achieve, the attainment of respect and ultimately of elderhood, is too remote to attract them sufficiently. As an age-set they are held back by the younger and the more irresponsible members, and this means a longer period of waiting for those who do wish to settle down.

It is in this vacuous situation that the moran cultivate the values and aims expected of them as moran and create a game of prestige and honour in the framework of the Club system. But it is a game which bears the seeds of its own destruction, for it is bound sooner or later to turn against the interests of the total society and at this point the elders will intervene and may impose further restrictions on them. Moreover, it is not a game which helps them to cultivate the necessary qualities of elderhood. A wise moran who seriously wishes to settle down successfully can best achieve this by not letting the game of honour and prestige interfere unnecessarily with his herding activities. By devoting himself to the welfare of the herd he learns better management and he gains the gratitude of his close kinsmen and the respect of others; such behaviour ultimately results in a larger herd and a wider range of social ties. There are many moran who are forced by firm fathers or elder brothers to follow this course, and many more who accept it voluntarily once the first pleasures of moranhood have lost their fascination. But there are also plenty of others who prefer to remain irresponsible and continue with their moran activities until they are on the verge of elderhood.

It is, I suggest, with reference to their social condition that the series of *ilmugit* ceremonies which young men perform during their moranhood becomes partially intelligible.

It is necessary first to emphasize that *ilmugit* ceremonies are more than just ceremonies performed only by the moran. Other people also take part. The elders, notably the firestick elders, are expected to participate indirectly in the ceremony by ensuring its correct performance and making it an opportunity to harangue the moran. Persons of all age grades and both sexes are present and are apportioned prescribed cuts of meat from the animals slaughtered in the course of the ceremony. It is a ceremony which indirectly involves all categories of persons and brings the moran into a specific relationship with the rest of the society. It is an occasion when their estrangement from the rest of the society is partially broken down. Symbolically, they are still associated with the bush and must eat their meat in an enclosure some distance from the ceremonial settlement: this enclosure, like the ceremony itself, is known as the *ilmugit*. But ceremonially, they have prescribed links with the settlement and with other categories of people, and the whole occasion is focused on them.

Broadly speaking, three types of *ilmugit* ceremony can be distinguished.

The first type is performed by every age-set of moran and it marks some step in the development of the age-set. To this category belong the *ilmugit of the arrows* when initiates become junior moran, the *ilmugit of the name*, when junior moran become senior moran, the *ilmugit of the bull* when the ritual leader and following him other moran may marry, and the *ilmugit of the milk and leaves* when in effect the whole age-set become elders and the series is brought to a close. They are, in fact, the 'rites of passage' of the age-set system, and it is the large numbers of moran involved which adds to their importance. The sheer magnitude of each successive age-set of moran in relation to the total society and the marked discontinuity between successive age-sets means that instead of a smooth flow of individuals through the various stages of maturation, there are mass promotions and the system progresses in a series of jerks. Each of these jerks is accompanied by one of this first type of *ilmugit* ceremonies.

There are only two ceremonies of the second type, and each of these is associated with one of the above. The *ilmugit of the roasting sticks* is performed shortly after the *ilmugit* of the arrows, and the *second ilmugit of the name* is performed shortly after the *ilmugit* of the name. These ceremonies are performed if possible only one month after the previous ceremonies and on the same site. The elders arrange the two ceremonies to run consecutively in order to have a chance to harangue the moran constantly and instil them with a marked sense of respect. It is felt that at times when initiates become moran and when junior moran become senior moran, there is considerable excitement and it is especially important that they should be brought under the firm control of the elders.

The third type of *ilmugit* ceremony may be performed at any time according to the directions of the elders. Often it is only performed by one Club or even by a portion of a Club living in one area. What information has been collected about them suggests that they are performed when the solidarity and the morale of the Club are low. The *ilmugit of the goat-madness* seems to belong to this category. Another one of this type is the *ilmugit of the smell of roasting meat (ilmugit lesekea)* which at one time was performed after any serious defeat in which a number of moran had been killed, and is still performed when there have been an alarming number of deaths in one Club in a short time, as occurred among the Pardopa moran in the Sonia area in 1958. It is believed that severe or persistent misfortune must be due to malignant mystical forces and the moran can only be brought out of danger from further misfortune in this way: the name of the ceremony has for the Samburu a propitious ring about it in contrast to the putrid smell of death. On a sociological level of analysis it may well be that the collective performance of this ceremony restores confidence and a feeling of well-being to the moran who have been demoralized by a succession of misfortunes.

An important function of the *ilmugit* ceremonies, then, may be to break down tendencies among the moran towards the extremes of lawless effervescence and demoralization (i.e. towards *anomie*) by temporarily bringing them into a closer contact with the remainder of the society. This would account for the emphasis in these ceremonies on the structural relationship between the participants, such as the plan of the settlement, the order in which animals are slaughtered, and the prescribed methods of dividing the carcase among the various age grades and sexes. The moran are placed out in the bush in their *ilmugit* enclosure, but they have at least a specific relationship with the remainder of the society in the settlement.

Important blessings of the moran, as occurred some time after the Masula affray at Ngelai (page 158), do not necessitate *ilmugit* ceremonies, but they have the essential feature of an *ilmugit* ceremony of bringing the moran and the elders together in one settlement for a short period of time and focusing attention specifically on the moran. The blessing itself, as occurs on a lesser scale at any harangue and on a greater scale at the *ilmugits* of the name, of the bull, and of the milk and leaves, is specifically a way in which the firestick elders, supported by others, evoke the protection of God (*Nkai*) on the moran and it is, in effect, a way of confirming the social relationship between them. It contrasts with the curse which places the moran further away from the protection of the society and abandons them to the mercy of mystical forces. It brings them back to a propitious ritual state.

I. A moran, acting as soloist in a Club dance, stands apart from the dancers and sings of the stock thieving exploits of his Club.

II. A firestick elder (extreme left) carefully watches a group of moran killing an ox at an *ilmugit of the bull* ceremony; after performing in this ceremony, they may marry.

Similarities Between Alternate Age-sets

To an outside observer the progressive tranquillization of the whole tribe with increasing external administration has on the whole affected each age-set more than the last, with perhaps certain temporary lapses. It has already been noted that the Samburu see some of these setbacks as significant, referring to similarities between the behaviour and the fortunes of alternate age-sets and to a lesser extent of every third age-set. Certain factors which may produce a very real resemblance between alternate age-sets are discussed below. In considering contemporary age-sets it is necessary to avoid those aspects of the society which have changed such as its size, political and economic conditions, or products of these changes.

The essence of the argument is as follows. In the absence of inter-tribal warfare, it is reasonable to assume a fairly equal balance between sexes at any age and census figures bear this out. During any period between the initiation of one age-set and the next, the number of boys being circumcised and becoming moran is almost exactly the same as the number of girls being circumcised and married (page 96). Thus, if one age-set is unusually large, then the number of girls that are married during the decade that follows its initiation will also be unusually large; and if many rather young boys are circumcised into it, then the average age at which girls are circumcised and married may also be lower than usual. But if, for some reason, an unusually large age-set is large because it has recruited many young males who might otherwise have belonged to the subsequent age-set, then there are a number of possible consequences. In the first place, the total age span of the members of the large age-set is likely to be wide; secondly, the initiation of the subsequent age-set may be delayed because it has lost many of its oldest potential members; thirdly, as the large age-set approaches elderhood its members may have some difficulty in marrying and settling down as there are fewer girls for them to marry, corresponding to the fewer members of the subsequent age-set and following logically from the large number of girls who have been married in recent years; and fourthly, there will be an unusually large number of families with *several* moran trying to settle down at the same time and competing with one another for cattle from their mother's allotted herd in order to do so. The period of change-over at this time will inevitably be prolonged and rivalry between the senior and the junior moran may be severe. Example 35 (page 155) is a good illustration of the strains of change-over when a small age-set (Mekuri) displaced a large one (Kiliako) and the latter found it difficult to settle down. The same factors are also likely to produce greater strains within the age-set during moranhood: a large age range indicates considerable physical and social differences between the older and the younger members of the age-set, and fewer unmarried girls implies greater rivalry for their favours. Similarly, tension is liable to be greater between the moran of a large age-set and the elders, since unmarried girls are relatively scarce and enhanced in value and there is more resentment when they are lost in marriage to the elders, and possibly more adultery. The longer period of moranhood implies also a longer period of strain. Example 38 above, illustrates the hostility existing between the Kimaniki (a large age-set) and the elders at a time when the moran of this phratry were just beginning to try to get married.

Conversely, a small age-set does not encounter these strains to such an extent: there is no shortage of girls, no prolonged period of moranhood, no wide age range among its members, no difficulty in settling down, and less resentment at the time of change-over when it is displaced by a new age-set.

One pattern which has emerged among the last five age-sets which is not altogether explained by the previous model is that these age-sets have been alternately large and small. For some reason, the three large age-sets, Terito, Kiliako and Kimaniki, appear to have attracted large numbers of males at the expense of the intermediate age-sets, Merisho and Mekuri. Thus, many men who might have been among the oldest members of the Mekuri age-set became the youngest members of the Kiliako age-set, and others who might have been among the youngest members of the Mekuri age-set became the oldest members of the Kimaniki age-set.

The Samburu attitude towards their age-set system is perhaps partly responsible for the emergence of this pattern. Ideally, a boy should be circumcised at the very first initiation of his age-set; this will give him a chance to be prominent as a moran and he will have plenty of time to acquire a sense of respect. But at this time there are many boys who are too young for circumcision, and the fathers or elder brothers of these boys may choose either to allow them to be circumcised into this age-set in, say, four years time, or make them wait another twelve or thirteen years for the initiation of a new age-set. Their choice is often determined by whether they wish to have another adult male in the family sooner or later: an old man with few sons may prefer an early circumcision in spite of its social disadvantages, whereas a poor man with a number of sons already in this age-set, all of whom will want to marry and settle down more or less at the same time may prefer to delay this circumcision. This choice may also be influenced by the prospect of an early or a late initiation of the subsequent age-set. If the present age-set is small and it is fairly evident that it will retire to elderhood quickly and quietly, then there is a general feeling among the elders that it would be unwise to circumcise young boys later into this age-set: they would only impede its progress. It is felt that it is better to wait for an early initiation of the subsequent age-set. This subsequent age-set, when it is initiated, is inevitably rather large with a large number of relatively old members. It is inevitably less docile and the time when it will retire to elderhood appears remote. It seems unlikely that a new age-set will be initiated for many years and men are therefore more willing to allow their sons to be circumcised late into the age-set.

Such preferences convert an already large age-set into a larger one, and deprive its successor of many potential members; and conversely, they allow an already small age-set to remain small and ensure that its successor will be a large one.

The following statistical data on the five age-sets of the present century collected from the clan census (Pardopa clan) indicate the extent to which the above model is substantiated by figures.

It will be seen that in each of these columns the figures are larger for Terito, Kiliako and Kimaniki age-sets than for the others. They are, however, liable to considerable error owing

169

The Moran and the Total Society

Statistical Similarities between Alternate Age-Sets

Age-set, and its reputed character	Column I Proportion of moran to total male population	Column II Standard deviation of ages in years	Column III Percentage of moran who did not settle down quickly	Column IV Period of moranhood in years
Terito (warlike)	23·5%	4·50	52·5%	app. 18
Merisho (undistinguished)	14·3%	3·76	35·5%	app. 10
Kiliako (truculent)	21·6%	4·58	53·0%	14
Mekuri (docile)	11·8%	3·42	21·0%	12
Kimaniki (troublesome)	23·6%	4·33	not yet available	14

to the methodological difficulties in their collection and assessment. The significance of the figures and possible sources or error in each column are discussed in the following notes.

Column I. The proportion of moran to the total male population is an estimate for each age-set ten years after its initiation when all the junior circumcisions should have been completed. A high proportion (shown in alternate age-sets) indicates the popularity of that age-set.[1]

Column II. This is a measurement of the age range of members of one age-set. Thus, the three large age-sets, as might be expected, also display a wider range of ages among their members. In order to determine the standard deviation of ages about a mean age, it was assumed that all males of one sub-age-set were of the same age, an age which had been independently estimated. The true standard deviation, if it could be determined without making these assumptions, would be different, but all figures would be affected in the same way and the alternation between large and small should remain.

Column III. The percentage of an age-set who did not settle down quickly was obtained from information concerning first marriages. If a man was remembered to have married a girl previously associated with his own age-set then it could be said

[1] The method used to arrive at this estimate is outlined in the appendix (page 323).

that he settled down quickly. Thus the Terito age-set and the Kiliako age-set were both large ones followed by smaller ones and they did not settle down as quickly as the other two, and hence their figures in this column are larger. Wives who have died childless or have been divorced tend to be forgotten or withheld when censuses are compiled and this would distort the true figures of this column. Moreover it would distort it to a greater extent for the older age-sets whose earlier marriages have had a longer period to have ended unsuccessfully and be forgotten than for the younger age-sets. Because of the inconsistency between informants on figures for this particular detail of the census, it became necessary to accept the information of one exceptionally reliable man *in toto* and to ignore the others.

Column IV. More strictly this column refers to the number of years between successive initiations as senior moran do not become elders as soon as a new age-set is formed. The column should be taken in conjunction with Column III: thus, the Mekuri age-set had been initiated a full 12 years before they were displaced by the Kimaniki, but the very low figure of 21·0 % in Column III also indicates that they settled down very quickly once this had happened. It is, I think, more significant that the Samburu, not altogether certain of the number of years between successive initiations, remember the Terito and the Kiliako as having remained moran for a very long period and the Mekuri and Merisho for only a short period. They do not realize that the period between initiations of the Kiliako and Mekuri age-sets is of the same order as that between the initiations of the Mekuri and the Kimaniki age-sets.

Suggestive as these figures are, it would need rather more accurate means of obtaining them, and also information on a far larger number of age-sets under politically and economically stable conditions in order to substantiate the present model adequately. Factors of chance, such as an epidemic of smallpox when the Terito were moran or a change in administrative policy when the Mekuri were first initiated, are all liable to produce inequalities between age-sets, and five is a very small number with which to establish a pattern.

It must, then, be admitted that fortuitous factors may have played the most significant part in establishing what appears at first sight to be a regular pattern. Nevertheless, a certain correlation between large age-sets, a wide span of ages, a long period of moranhood, difficulty in settling down, and a trouble-some disposition is reasonably well established by this chart. The strains of moranhood are magnified in a large age-set.

Summary

A society in which the marriage of young men is delayed per-mitting older men to practice polygamy on a wide scale and retain power in their own hands is inevitably prone to a certain resentment among these young men. The Samburu age-set system may be regarded as a mechanism which diverts forces resulting from this resentment away from the family and places them directly under the control of the elders. The forces re-appear as hostility between the moran and the elders.

It is the elders, notably the firestick elders, who hold the moran in their place by bullying them and encouraging them, and in effect they slow down their rate of maturation and keep them in a state of social suspension. It is the elders who are the most powerful section of the tribe, and the way in which this power is distributed among them is examined in Chapter Seven.

Chapter Seven

ELDERHOOD AND THE CURSE

The Transition from Moranhood to Elderhood

THERE is no exact moment at which a moran settles down. Sometime after the initiation of a new age-set and after he has started to behave in a more reserved manner acceptable to the other elders, he joins them – perhaps even at their suggestion – in their gossiping and discussions. As his moran adornments are begged from him or become tattered with age, he does not acquire new ones. Unobtrusively, he assumes the attire of an elder: at first he shaves off his long hair and replaces his ivory ear-rings with brass ones; and then he gets himself a larger cloth which can be worn over the right shoulder and reaches down to below his knees; at this point he may also begin to carry a longer heavier staff and stop decorating his head with red ochre, except on infrequent ceremonial occasions. He would not, however, carry a fly-whisk made of some animal's tail until his age-set are on the verge of becoming firestick elders. At no point does he assert himself in any of these ways, as this would show an essential lack of respect which he, as an elder, would be expected to have.

A married moran, if he is to be accepted as an elder, must now respect and to some extent avoid the unmarried girls of his Club, for they are his classificatory sisters and also they are uncircumcised. His wife in certain respects takes over the role of his mistress, joining with his age-set in their dances and being allotted certain portions of meat at the remaining *ilmugit* ceremonies which would otherwise have gone to his mistress. He is also expected to avoid using physical violence against any other elder; violence is the way of the moran, whereas discussion and ultimately the use of the curse are the ways of the elders. When one elder strikes another, all the other elders gather round to

173

curse them both, and each of the offenders – the man who struck the other and the other who provoked him to do so – should in theory kill a heifer-in-calf in order to secure their blessing. In practice this payment is frequently modified: if those involved are as yet little more than moran, if they fight each other somewhere well away from the settlement, or if it is only a minor skirmish among clansmen when no outsiders are present, then there may be no collective curse and a smaller payment may be accepted.

Resort to violence among the moran and their behaviour towards their uncircumcised clanswomen are both regarded by the elders as aspects of their general immaturity and lack of a sense of respect. But as in other ways they are neither effectively encouraged to show a greater maturity by solving their disputes peaceably nor expected to avoid these girls until they are on the threshold of elderhood.

In his first marriage a senior moran is at a disadvantage when competing with older men. He is as yet a nonentity, and what is known about him may concern his activities as a moran and may not be altogether to his credit. He is quite likely to be poor and has not had a chance to show that he will make a good husband and affine. Perhaps he will treat his wife roughly at first: such is the way of young men. For these reasons an older man may be preferred: older men are richer and more indulgent towards their young wives, combining the qualities of father and husband; they are personally known to more men of the girl's clan and have had a chance to show that they are desirable as affines. But for all its disadvantages, marriage with a younger man has the essential advantage that the girl will become his senior wife and her eldest son will be the senior son of the homestead. If the marriage is successful then the affines stand to gain considerably, and she has in addition a partner who is closer to her own age. It is a risk which many are prepared to take.

A young man marrying for the first time is frequently directed by his father or guardian to seek to marry a particular girl, and a father may even act on behalf of his son to make these proposals and help overcome any objections towards him. In associating himself with the marriage he makes it clear that the girl is not being taken away by an irresponsible young man who is not in a position to feed her properly and who may maltreat her; she is being taken away by a family which commands a certain respect, and the father may stress that he will act as a guardian over the couple to ensure that the marriage is a success.[1] If he happens to be of the same age-set as the girl's father then he is in a better position than ever to stress that she will continue to have a 'father' in her new home, and his proposal on behalf of his son takes on the character of a request from one age mate to another.

Junior elderhood is a time when a man settles down to the serious task of building up a herd and rearing a family. His energies are devoted to this end and his health may suffer in his efforts to see that his family is well cared for. Until he has dependents, preferably sons, who can help him in the upkeep of the herd, he can only associate with his fellow elders occasionally in their gossiping and discussions, and he is cut off from the principal means of gaining a real insight into his society and acquiring the knowledge and wisdom necessary to have influence among other elders. 'When I first became an elder,' said one man, 'I knew nothing. But I sat in the shade with the older men and listened to their gossiping and debates. And now I am beginning to know things.' A man is unlikely to be in a position to add materially to the elders' discussions before he has become a firestick elder.

The Discussion: Nkiguena

Before paying closer attention to the ways in which elders impinge on one another's affairs and muster public opinion to their side, more must be said of their method of arriving at collective decisions.

As previously stated, an elder is ideally free to migrate and manage his homestead as he pleases. In practice, however, his homestead may be economically interdependent with other neighbouring homesteads (Chapter One), and other elders of his local clan group may interfere in his domestic affairs

[1] The extent to which married men tend to live with their living fathers was noted on p. 17.

(Chapter Two). His autonomy is limited therefore by the extent to which his actions are compatible with the best interests of the society and in particular of his clan. Any issue which becomes a matter of controversy between the elders will be a subject for discussion.

A minor crisis, as occurred when Kimiri beat his junior wife (page 33) may lead to a discussion involving only a few elders. The resolution of this particular dispute was straight-forward: once he had pointed out that he had a certain justifica-tion in beating his wife, Kimiri was quite prepared to accept the contention of the other two that it was in his own interests that he should treat his wife more tolerantly in future. When Letuno beat his wife (page 33), however, it was less easy to persuade him to be moderate, more local clan elders attended the discussion and it was conducted in a more formal manner and lasted a longer time.

A major crisis, as for instance occurred when the Masula moran attacked the elders at Ngelai (page 158), leads to an even larger and more formal discussion or even to a series of discussions. Influential elders travel many miles (up to 50 in the above instance) to attend the discussion, and there may be 40 or more men present. The length in time of a discussion, the numbers that attend it, and the formality with which it is conducted are all indices of the seriousness of the topic that is discussed. The issue is decided by those present at the debate, and no notice is taken of the fact that any particular man, how-ever influential, is not present whether this is for reasons of health or freedom from domestic affairs. The matter is discussed and concluded in his absence.

These discussions provide excellent opportunities for men to air their grievances in public and gain a general sympathy. Even if the course of action which is eventually agreed upon does not give them entire satisfaction, they have at least given vent to their feelings and have the satisfaction of having done this. In the remainder of this section, this aspect of their discussions is taken for granted and the method by which the elders arrive at joint decisions is described in fuller detail.

The Samburu say that a discussion is like an acacia tree, which has many branches but only one trunk: every man comes with his own ideas, and through discussion all men are able to modify their ideas and arrive at a compromise solution. The debate continues until all are willing to accept a particular course of action.

These discussions are held without any chairman or acknowledged leadership, and the very fact that they often concern controversial issues would make for utter confusion unless a certain etiquette were observed by all those taking part. There must, in addition, be a general spirit of compromise which will make the arrival at a unanimous agreement possible.

The etiquette of procedure is quite straightforward and surprisingly effective. The elders sit, squat, lie and often doze in the shade of a tree at some convenient point, usually close to a settlement. The general gossiping turns to a discussion at the point at which one elder rises to his feet, always with a stick in his hand and addresses the others stating the nature of the problem and his own views on it. Others listen more or less attentively. At the end of each major point in his argument, he stops speaking and squats for a second or more as an invitation to any other man with views on this point to rise and express them. If no other person gets up immediately then the first speaker himself will do so and take up a new point. When finally he finishes what he has to say, he returns to his place and sits down.

One elder after another rises to his feet and talks, bringing forward his views on any matter which has so far been raised and raising new issues relevant to the subject, and each debater is expected to observe the same rules of etiquette. Ultimately, all the various views have been expressed and compromises are suggested. The discussion continues until one man, usually one of the more influential men present, sums up what has been said and suggests a course of action which will be acceptable to them all. If this is not disputed, a blessing is called for and is led, usually, by the oldest men present – and by the firestick elders when matters concerning the moran are being discussed. Very old men do not normally take an active part in these discussions and they tend to be only half aware of what is actually being discussed; often they are asleep. But it is they who are asked to lead the principal blessings, and they may be woken up for this purpose.

A number of totally different issues may be raised at one meeting of the elders and there is a blessing after each issue has been discussed and settled. At any time during his discourse, a debater may pronounce a blessing to which the others respond. These interlocutory blessings are apparently intended by the debater to evoke the benevolent influence of God (*Nkai*) so that the elders can arrive at a really wise and clear-sighted decision. And the final blessings, which are rather more formal, are intended to clinch the matter and make certain that the decision which was, it is hoped, reached by guidance from God will have happy consequences.

Apart from one or two invocations appropriate to the occasion, Samburu blessings tend to follow a fairly standardized form. The man leading it waves his staff with each invocation. 'May *Nkai* look after you. . . . May *Nkai* look after you. . . . May *Nkai* give you life. . . . May *Nkai* give you cattle. . . . Peace as the flatness on water. . . . As the *lokorosio* tree. . . . May *Nkai* give you children. . . . As (many as the fruit on) the *enparuei* tree. . . . May you live as long as the *nkusuman* tree. . . . May you be sweet. . . . As the *seiye* tree. . . . May *Nkai* look after you . . . .' etc. The other elders respond between invocations by chanting, '*Nkai*', and closing each hand or, especially on more important occasions, waving their own staffs.

Of course, there may be one or two rather assertive or excitable elders who prefer to flout the rules of etiquette in order to express their views, and it is here that the elders seated around call on them to sit down or be quiet. When, for instance, one speaker squats after making some point and in doing so invites any other person to take over the discussion, it is not altogether certain that he will in fact allow any other man who rises to his feet to interrupt the argument, and he may tell him to keep quiet for the time being and this may lead to a quick exchange of retorts between the two in which each tries to assert himself by resorting to a forceful tone of voice and using any terms of address which imply that the other should give way out of respect. The other elders are not slow in assessing the situation: they can see whether the first speaker has been too

controversial in his arguments to be allowed to continue to a
new point without immediate discussion, whether he has been
too long winded and should allow some other person to continue, or whether what he has said implicates some other man
who should be given a chance to speak for himself. In each of
these cases they will call on him to give way and allow the other
to make his own point. But if the argument of the first speaker
has been logically presented and is clearly about to lead on to
other closely related topics then this is a very good reason for
him to complete the argument without interruption and the
other elders will call on the interrupter to be silent. In every
such incident which I have seen there has always been a clear
majority among the other elders in favour of one speaker or the
other and the debate has continued after a break of only 5 or
10 seconds. It is clearly understood by all present that every
man who wishes to speak shall have a full opportunity of doing
so before the discussion is concluded and the immediate issue
is merely to decide who should be allowed to speak at this
particular moment.

Squatting after making a point when the speaker has no
intention of allowing any interruption appears to be a polite
convention and implicitly an invitation to the elders to support
him if someone does try to interrupt him. Less polite debaters
may not even bother to sit down after making each point and
they risk being interrupted by another elder at any point. Again
the situation arises in which there is a rapid altercation between
the two and the other elders shout out to one man or the other
to sit down and be quiet.

The most eloquent debaters and respected men do squat
constantly during their speeches and are allowed by the other
elders to say all that they have to say without interruption.
Their manner shows a respect for their audience and they gain
attentiveness by the logical constructions of their arguments
and the persuasive manner in which they deliver it. The elders
are less impressed by sheer assertiveness and a complete lack
of regard for etiquette. In a discussion, a well constructed
argument by a well-known and liked orator is sufficient to
persuade many elders of a useful way to approach the problem,
whereas a torrent of half-formed ideas delivered as if at a

harangue is not only unimpressive but often unintelligible – even to those Samburu who appear to be trying to listen most attentively! Sometimes it may even provoke laughter.

It has been shown, then, that the lack of a chairman to regulate proceedings and of a method of voting to arrive at a solution are effectively compensated for by an unlimited amount of time to discuss any issue, an etiquette, a consensus of opinion among the elders which leads them to shout down any man who tries to violate this etiquette or stubbornly refuses to give way on a point in which he is clearly without support, and finally a pervading faith that there is only one correct outcome to any issue and a willingness to compromise personal opinions in order to arrive at this. The correctness of the decision is then confirmed by pronouncing the blessing.

At any debate, the issues discussed may range from the choice of a suitable husband for some girl of the clan, to the control of a horde of rebellious moran or the course of action towards some government measure. They are, in fact, the sorts of matters which have been taken as suitable examples in this study; and similarly, just as I have arranged an assorted number of examples in order to present a model of the society as I see it, so each of these elders in gossip and discussion presents his own model to the others by giving his own interpretation of previous events and decisions, thereby substantiating his points as to the correct application of customary law to the present circumstances. It is assumed that any previous decisions arrived at by the elders – even a generation or more ago – were reached in a similar manner and that the happy consequences of this particular decision proved their wisdom. In this way knowledge of tradition is kept alive in the minds of the elders, and their decisions become further precedents in a society which they believe should change as little as possible.

Power and Social Values

It is through their discussions that the elders wield the power they hold over the remainder of the society. In this section, I consider the extent to which individual elders may be said to have power, and for that matter the extent to which the notion of power is a useful one when considering the society of elderhood.

Leach has written '. . . I consider it necessary and justifiable to assume that a conscious or unconscious wish to gain power is a very general motive in human affairs. Accordingly I assume that individuals faced with a choice of action will commonly use such choice so as to gain power, that is to say that they will seek recognition as social persons who have power; or, to use a different language, they will seek to gain access to office or the esteem of their fellows which may lead them to office.'[1] Before considering whether this is a necessary or a justifiable assumption when considering the Samburu, it must first be pointed out that the only two types of office in this society are the government appointments which do not concern the indigenous system discussed here and the office of ritual leader which is ascribed and not achieved. Any wish to gain power among the Samburu in their indigenous system, then, is not to be gained by seeking office. Nor is it a power which enables one elder to control directly the actions of another. The most that an individual can attain is influence among his fellows, and he is respected for this influence. The term *laiguenan*, derived from the same root as such words as *a-iguen* (to advise, give an opinion), *a-iguena* (to discuss), and *nkiguena* (a discussion, debate), may best be translated as 'an influential man' referring to his ability in debating and giving advice: it is a status he has achieved rather than an office. It is at first sight incongruous that the Samburu should often apply this term to government appointed elders who hold specific offices with definite powers attached, but it appears less incongruous when it is realized that they have no term of their own closer to 'chief' or 'headman' than this one, and that government elders cannot effectively interfere in the internal affairs of the people unless they assert themselves using traditional methods in debate and thereby subscribing to the traditional system.

Each man can ideally act as he pleases, but if he does defy the opinion of the majority he may impair his social relations with his friends and kinsmen. For this reason he may be willing

---

[1] Leach, 1954, p. 10. Firth also questions this assumption ibid., pp. vii–viii; and so does Parsons (1949, pp. 200 ff.).

to migrate to areas which he would not have chosen for himself, consent to marriages of which he disapproves, or support a locally adopted policy towards new grazing schemes introduced by the administration although he previously had no intention of doing so.

It was this inert quality about the Samburu which baffled many Europeans in the early days of administration. Some of these men made the following observations. 'The Samburu Chiefs and Headmen are a collection of the most useless and boneless and effete tribal rulers I have ever had to do with in my experience of 15 years of Native tribes. They can neither control or govern their villages.' 'The Samburu as a tribe are conservative, unenterprising and lacking in any kind of initiative.' 'The Samburu native is the laziest native that I have met in East Africa.' 'I have yet, after nearly twenty years in Africa, to discover a still more useless race than the Samburu.'[1]

These are admittedly extreme views on the Samburu, but they do reflect certain qualities which seem to contradict any assumption that a wish to gain power is a *general* motive in human behaviour: even the chiefs and headmen referred to in the first quotation apparently did not impress the writer as having some incentive to acquire power either by ingratiating themselves with the administration or by leading a popular opposition against it, and yet these men would normally be expected to be among the most influential elders who might conceivably have some slight wish to gain power.

Having expressed this caution it can now be admitted that the influence of a few really dominant men is, and appears to have been for many generations, considerable and in certain individual cases extends to distant areas of the tribe and transcends clan and phratry boundaries. On the whole, however, an influential man is only influential within his own clan and his presence is not normally felt outside his own local clan group. His influence is retained only so long as he consistently gives good advice and continues to persuade others.

Any ambition to gain power, like prestige, implies competition and this contradicts the Samburu ideal of conformity.

[1] The first two quotations appear in early records and the second two in the evidence before the Kenya Land Commission in 1933 (pp. 1547 and 1591).

III. A group of moran at a meeting; they shortly expect to become elders and a number of them have already shaved off their long hair.

IV. Elders give their blessing at a wedding, as the best man and groom finally lead the bride away from the mother's hut to begin a new life.

The man who conforms with general expectations is worthy and well suited to have influence among his fellows. Ideally the influential man has a placid temperament and has built up his reputation for worthiness by conducting his own affairs with wisdom. Such a man is capable of accepting compromises readily for he attaches a greater importance to an equable solution for all than to a satisfactory solution for only one party – even if he himself is personally implicated. His suggestions in discussion may reflect something of his placidness and compromising attitude, and they may eventually turn out to be the only views which are compatible with all interests. His whole approach to life is a model of the ideals of elderhood whether this concerns his own domestic affairs or the more general affairs of the community. As Homans has expressed it in discussing leadership in informal groups, the leader (i.e. influential man) 'gets his power only by conforming more closely than anyone else to the norms of the group. He is not the most but the least free person within it.'[1]

Outstanding influence over a large portion of the tribe, however, requires a degree of insight into novel situations and a certain degree of assertiveness to persuade other more conservatively minded elders, and this is a quality that a really placid worthy man may not have. But such outstandingly influential men must have at least some degree of worthiness. It would be inconceivable for a man who is generally accepted as mean to have influence. Any view he expresses in a discussion will generally be interpreted as having some ulterior motive, a wish that he, rather than the community or clan as a whole, should benefit. He may make himself ridiculous in the eyes of others by trying to justify quite inexcusable behaviour in order to obtain general approval. But in the terms he uses, the arguments he resorts to, and the act of publicly acknowledging that he cannot conduct his own affairs entirely without the general consent of the other elders he is still subscribing to the values of Samburu society. He merely seeks to interpret these values in a rather different way.

If one is to accept Leach's hypothesis in discussing the Samburu, one must, I think, use this term 'power' in a very broad

[1] Homans, 1951, p. 149.

sense. In a society where an individual can acquire an impressive reputation of having great foresight and understanding and can influence others by persuasive arguments, his ability amounts to power over the majority who are willing to allow themselves to be guided by his judgments. The majority of Samburu elders are far too sensitive of public opinion to assert themselves in order to gain power: the virtues of being a worthy man, a prudent man, and a wise man are all necessary to attain influence and they cannot be held by a man who shows any marked tendency towards competition with his fellow elders. The voiced ambitions of Samburu elders are to build up large herds, to marry several times and to have direct control over a large and growing family, to have cordial friendships with a large number of clansmen, age mates and others – these are prerequisites of worthiness. Influence may in a sense imply power, but it can only be attained by expressly denying the very ambitions it may satisfy. True power is only vested in each man over his family and in the elders over the remainder of the society – in particular the moran; within the age grade of elderhood structural and cultural features inhibit its growth.

Each elder has, however, one particular power which he may wield with terrible effect, and this is his curse. The power of the curse is so important when considering the behaviour of elders that it is the main topic of discussion for the remainder of this chapter.

The Belief in the Curse

The ultimate power which the elders have over the total society, and in particular over the moran, rests on the unshakable belief in the curse. During my field work I collected examples of people who were prepared to risk being cursed for flouting social conventions, but I met no one who even in private would express any doubt on the general efficacy of the curse. It is possible that there was a hidden scepticism among certain independently minded persons and that this accounted for some of the more flagrant violations of custom: but as I shall show later in this chapter, ultimately these violators were powerless to defy custom so long as the beliefs in question were held by the majority of Samburu. A brief introduction to these beliefs is given here in order to aid further discussion.[1]

Among the Samburu there is great consistency in the belief that certain actions will lead to misfortune through the agency of supernatural forces directed ultimately by God and that others will lead to good fortune. Those that lead to misfortune are referred to here as *unpropitious (kotolo)*: the omission or mishandling of certain prescribed details of a ceremony, the breaking of certain articles, or the throwing away of others are examples of this. The same word (*kotolo*) may be used of certain objects that are held to bring misfortune, or of people who bring misfortune to their closest kinsmen. The latter are generally first born twins, children of at least one uncircumcised parent, or of an incestuous union: they are normally killed at birth or aborted before then.

When the Samburu are asked why they perform their various ceremonies, the only answer they give is that these are their customs and not to do so would bring ill-fortune instead of good. Ceremony and unpropitious actions are related in the beliefs accompanying them which take it for granted that there is a certain interaction between human behaviour and supernatural forces; but in another sense they are opposites, the one bringing good fortune and being carefully observed, and the other bringing ill-fortune and being carefully avoided. Knowledge of these things is an important part of the wisdom of the elders.

An unscrupulous man may deliberately try to harm an enemy by performing some unpropitious action such as cutting short the tail of one of his cattle. Such a man is a sorcerer (*lairuponi* pl. *lairupok*). The Samburu profess a general ignorance of the techniques involved in sorcery and a man who wishes to harm an enemy in this way normally goes to the Dorobo or Tiamus tribes who know how to prepare suitable magic medicines (*setani*) for him to use. Sorcery is, in fact, deliberate and carefully directed unpropitious behaviour. In cases where individuals are accused of poisoning others, as for instance in example 25, informants are not always certain whether a natural poison

---

[1] I have given a fuller account of Samburu religious beliefs elsewhere (Spencer, 1959).

has been used or a sorcerer's medicine: whether a man is a poisoner or a sorcerer, his intention and the final result are identical.

Witchcraft is similar to sorcery in that it is considered to be unjustified and wicked. The Samburu maintain that among all the tribes in the area, only the Turkana have witches (*nkapelani*, pl. *nkapelak*); witchcraft is an inherited power and is stimulated by greed; it is most commonly practised when a witch sees another man eating food and feels jealous; it is transmitted through the eyes of the witch to the food or to the man eating the food, and the latter has a fit from which he may die. Among the Samburu themselves only a few men known to have Turkana ancestry are believed to be witches, and hence accusations of witchcraft within the tribe itself are infrequent.

The curse (*ldeket*, pl. *ldeketa*) is rather different from either sorcery or witchcraft in its moral implications and its operation: in situations of extreme provocation a man may be considered morally justified in pronouncing a curse.[1] The Samburu say that the curse is like poison from a poison arrow tree: if it enters a place where the skin is cut (i.e. a wrong has been done) then it will inevitably kill, but if the skin is whole (i.e. no wrong has been done) then it will have no effect. The curse, then, unlike sorcery, cannot harm an entirely innocent person. If it is morally justified however, it can lead to the most severe misfortune to the cursed man, his wives, his children or his cattle. God is the supreme arbiter who decides whether the curse is justified or not and who brings misfortune to the wrong doer. It is God who confers a potent curse on certain persons such as mother's brothers, firestick elders, bond brothers, etc. And it is God who makes the curse of a mean man who is always resorting to it progressively less effective.

There are many ways in which men can curse one another. Sometimes these curses are accompanied by unpropitious actions which relate them in a sense to sorcery, as when a firestick elder deliberately breaks a stick, symbolising the firestick, or when a man throws earth at another (invoking anthrax) or a piece of string (invoking a poisonous snake). But as curses, these would invariably be coupled with an oath drawing attention to

[1] cf. a similar discussion in Wilson, 1951, p. 97.

the relationship involved which gives one man the power to curse the other. A firestick elder would begin 'May the fire I kindled for you hate you' (*mikimbai nkima naaipiraka*); a ritual leader cursing his phratry age mates would begin 'May the name I gave you (i.e. at the *ilmugit* of the name) hate you' (*mikimbai ntai nkarna ai natangamaka ntai*). A bond brother, instead of the usual *aramenye*, would address the man he is cursing as 'Fellow of our home' (*ltungana lenkaji ang*) and then pronounce his curse. And a mother's brother would begin 'Son of my sister' (*layin lenkanashe ai*): it is said that he would not want to curse his sister's son to death and would first of all bless him with life, and then curse him with bad luck in marriage or with insanity; or he might bless the knife which slaughters cattle, implying that the other will have to kill off all his stock one by one. Certain immigrant families from Rendille (*lais*, pl. *laisi*) have a potent curse which varies from family to family; they begin by invoking God, 'God help me, God listen to me' (*Nkai teretoki, Nkai tiningoki*) and then pronounce their particular curse.

A man who has been justifiably cursed is said to have *ngoki*: he is in an unpropitious ritual state which can only be removed by offering the curser a placatory gift in order to secure his blessing. *Ngoki* also hangs over those who have committed certain heinous offences such as manslaughter or allowing a parent to die in poverty through neglect; but unlike the man who has been cursed, the impending misfortune which hangs over them can never be removed and ultimately leads to their deaths – even if they live to a ripe old age in the meantime.

One Samburu tried to convey to me the isolation and inevitable fate of a man with *ngoki* in the following picturesque terms: 'His herds may multiply, and his children may grow to be strong and healthy, green grass may grow around his home and rain may fall wherever he goes. But every man knows that he has *ngoki* and that either he or his children will suffer. No man will follow him and he will live alone.' And others sometimes say, 'When a man has *ngoki*, God throws him away'; this implies abandonment and a withdrawal of protection rather than divine retribution.

When a curse has been pronounced, the death of the curser

187

does not remove the *ngoki* from the other; it only makes matters worse since true reparations can never be made, except with some close kinsman acting on the dead man's behalf which is felt to be a makeshift arrangement. Once a curse has been pronounced the matter is in the hands of God until there is a blessing. This may account for an apparent lack of accusations of cursing in the society. To accuse another man of being responsible for misfortune because he has resorted to the curse is tantamount to admitting oneself morally in the wrong. If this man is held to have a potent curse then such an accusation showing gross disrespect could easily lead to worse misfortune, and if he has no potent curse then a very serious wrong must have been committed. Sorcery, on the other hand, can be practised by any man who is unscrupulous enough without any initial wrong. The following example should make the differences between sorcery, cursing and unpropitious behaviour quite clear.

39.* As was noted on pages 31 and 64 Seletu was generally considered a mean man. In 1957 he shared a settlement with an age mate of the same clan, Dapar. Nothing is known of the friendship between the two up to this time, but the fact that they did live together suggests that they were on reasonably cordial terms. Then 30 of Dapar's cattle died and he accused Seletu of having killed them by sorcery and cursed him. The local clan elders met and Dapar pointed out to the others that Seletu's father had immigrated from the Tiamus of Lake Baringo where sorcery was practised and that Seletu himself had visited this area a number of times recently. The elders considered that Dapar's accusations were serious and as Seletu equally vehemently denied the accusations they did not feel justified in taking any direct action. They therefore decided that they would 'curse the space' (*a-dek mpash*) between the two elders which would bring misfortune to either of them if he had meant to harm the other, whether this was Seletu through sorcery or Dapar through deliberately malicious slander.

Shortly after this incident, Seletu was visiting the settlement of another elder, and on leaving the hut he forced his way through a gap in the side of it instead of using the main entrance. His only explanation was that he had mistaken this hole for the entrance. But the other elders argued that this could have been unpropitious, and misfortune could fall on the owner of the hut, his wife and children. Seletu was not accused of practising sorcery on this occasion, but the elders insisted that he should perform a ceremony to purify the hut. Seletu killed one of his own sheep, splattered the hut with the chyme, and smeared its fat over the sleeping hides. The elders then came and blessed the owner of the hut and his wife and children. It was felt that this was sufficient to protect them from the consequences of Seletu's unpropitious action.

In 1958 Seletu became seriously ill and he died the next year. His death is understood to have been the result of the curse of the elders and is a clear indication that he was a sorcerer. That being the case, it is now generally accepted that his forcing his way out of the side of the hut of another elder must be a sorcerer's way of transferring *ngoki* (his unpropitious ritual state) to another man: he must have known that unless he did this the curse of the elders would eventually kill him.

In this example we are perhaps justified in assuming that Seletu had no intention of practising sorcery on Dapar's cattle or of leaving the hut through a hole in the side: in the second incident he was a fairly old man and on the verge of what proved to be his final illness. But he was generally recognized as a mean man and his non-conformity in small everyday matters accompanied by a series of chance events ending in his own death appears to have roused public opinion to such a degree that they are now prepared to believe that he was a sorcerer.

In his original curse Dapar may have been genuinely enraged by what he thought to be Seletu's sorcery. However, in the discussion which followed he is described as having tried to justify his curse, and an awareness that he must muster public opinion to his side is likely to have affected his aguments. Both sorcery and cursing are ways of resorting to supernatural forces to achieve destructive ends, but whereas public opinion does not condone sorcery at any time, it can condone a curse in exceptional circumstances. Dapar would have had to persuade the elders that these were exceptional circumstances if he was to retain their respect. Public opinion at the time appears to have been uncommitted on Seletu's unconventional exit through a hole in the side of a hut. It was neither laudable nor immoral. But it was almost certainly unpropitious and he was made to perform the cleansing ceremony in order to avert misfortune. Since it has been established that he is a sorcerer, however, his action is clearly seen as a sorcerer's trick and is regarded as wicked.

All forms of unexpected misfortune, from disease among cattle to early deaths among humans, may be interpreted as significant. Disasters, which we would ascribe to chance, the Samburu ascribe to cursing, sorcery and unpropitious actions or objects. It is rare, and certainly improbable that an individual who suffers misfortune has not in the past violated some prescribed rule of behaviour which could explain it. The extent to which the Samburu are prepared to accept metaphysical explanations for chance events is indicated by the following figures. A reliable informant maintained that of 80 early deaths of elders in his clan, 49 were not necessarily due to any discernible supernatural cause. But he accounted for the other 31 deaths (nearly 40% of the total) in the following ways: 11 were due to an unresolved curse (three by bond brothers, three by the elders, one by a mother's brother, one by a firestick elder, one by an age mate, one by a mother, and one by a brother's widow) of which nine had been pronounced on the dead men themselves and two on their living parents; two followed automatically from a homicide committed in one case by the dead man himself and in the other by his living father; six (and possibly two others, making eight altogether) followed automatically from some unpropitious action, one from the possession of an unpropitious ox, and four from a close relationship with an unpropitious person (only one unpropitious person was involved in the deaths of all these four); four died from sorcery, and one from Turkana witchcraft. He accepted the possibility that the unexplained 49 deaths could be due to supernatural causes if only all the facts were known.

In recounting stories of sudden and untimely deaths or losses in a herd, the Samburu frequently point to some previous happening for which the sufferer had been cursed. But in most cases of cursing, the pronouncement of the curse is a signal for a meeting of the local clan group (or groups if two clans are involved) in order to resolve the issue immediately before misfortune occurs. It seems unlikely, then, that there are as many unresolved curses as one is led to believe from an examination of *past* misfortunes. My own impression was that the disturbances which were assumed to have led eventually to misfortune, had in many cases been resolved at the time, but in retelling the story this fact was conveniently forgotten. If there is misfortune and the sufferer has recently offended someone with a potent curse over him then it is concluded that the violator has *ngoki* even though no curse was pronounced or intended, as in example 6. In fact, just one minor violation against any person with a potent curse may be sufficient to explain misfortune which the violator suffers for the remainder of his life. Perhaps it was used to explain why the steering on my Land-Rover failed completely only half-an-hour after I had refused to give a bond brother a lift or why my tent caught fire after I had found I had no money to give a mother's brother. The problem here is not how it is that the Samburu so often manage to find a supernatural reason for a man's misfortunes, but why they should choose to find it in one case and not in another.

It can only be a matter of speculation whether these Samburu metaphysical beliefs are less widely held today than in the past or if they are changing in any way. They do seem to be well suited to a society in which unexpected and sometimes severe misfortune is frequent; and the fact that for the past 40 years the Samburu have been better protected from misfortune than at any other time in their recent history does suggest that some of their metaphysical arguments may be losing their cogency. Certainly, the content of some of these beliefs appears to be changing and appears to have changed to some extent even in pre-European times. There is a case, for instance, of one man who refused to kill his first-born twins and against all predictions he has since prospered greatly. Other Samburu, however, point out that he is of Dorobo descent and they affirm that they will not at this stage abandon the practice of killing first-born twins, although they concede that they may be prepared to do so if a number of other persons follow this example without apparent misfortune. Conversely, as old beliefs are discarded, new ones arise, as occurred in the instance of Seletu's sorcery – leaving a hut by a hole in the side may be a way of evading the effects of the curse.

Similar reasoning may not be confined to cultural beliefs: it may also affect structural relationships, as is shown in the following examples where there is an extension of a ritual brotherhood.

40.* Several generations ago Bukunoi's ancestor left Loisilale clan and associated with Lorogushu phratry. Close social ties have persisted between this lineage and Loisilale and on at least one occasion, Bukunoi has personally supported the marriage suit of a Lorogushu age mate with a girl of his former lineage group inside Loisilale and helped to ensure its success.

Ltoiyo clan are bond brothers of all Lorogushu, but Bukunoi regarded himself as sufficiently distant not to have to recognize the tie and one of his sisters was married to an Ltoiyo elder. On one occasion he asked this elder for a heifer and on being refused, he tried to take his sister away by force, but was prevented by the other Ltoiyo elders. He then developed a skin disease from which he eventually died in 1959. It is now popularly maintained that this was because his relationship with Lorogushu had been so close that the bond brotherhood with Ltoiyo clan implicated him to some extent, and his dispute with the Ltoiyo elders had the same unpropitious consequences as it would have had with any Lorogushu. Other members of his lineage living with Lorogushu do not as yet address the Ltoiyo as their own bond brothers, but it is generally acknowledged that no more marriages between the two will take place and it seems likely that this is a first step towards acknowledging the relationship.

41.* Kalasi, an elder whose ancestors had only recently immigrated to Lorogushu from the Rendille, was approached by a daughter of Ltoiyo clan for a goat to give her children to eat. He refused her, arguing that he was not a full member of Lorogushu and so had no bond brotherhood with Ltoiyo clan. The other Lorogushu elders then reminded him that Bukunoi had thought the same way and he had since died. With this argument they persuaded him to give the woman a goat.

Once again one has an example of a critical event which serves to consolidate membership of an adopted clan. In example 11 it was a dispute which precipitated this; here it was a misfortune.

The Samburu themselves see the content of their beliefs

changing as old beliefs are shown empirically to have no validity and new ones are formulated from their latest experiences. This, they maintain, is the inevitable path to a completer knowledge of what things are to be avoided. But they do not question the underlying assumption that human behaviour and supernatural forces interact with one another, and I have no evidence which suggests that they are beginning to question it.

Public Opinion and the Curse

The use of the curse is primarily in the hands of the elders. It is a sanction which is thought to bring severe misfortune for even a very minor offence. Only a mean man quite insensitive to public opinion would be prepared to resort to it without extreme provocation. It might be considered justified in one or two exceptional cases. One man, for instance, was quite unscrupulous in demanding stock from men who had married his bond sisters, and the deaths of three children of these families were ascribed to his curse. When he became ill and eventually died while still a young man, it was assumed that he had in turn been cursed by his bond brothers for his behaviour.

A curse, then, does not necessarily rally public opinion to the side of the curser; it may merely draw attention to the fact that something is in dispute and that this has led to a final appeal to destructive supernatural forces. Nor can the elders always persuade the curser to withdraw his curse in the interests of avoiding misfortune and restoring social harmony.

42.* It became known that Keseker's senior wife was pregnant by Leritem, a member of the opposite alternation and therefore her classificatory son, and it seemed that this explained the deaths of two of her children: the pregnancy was unpropitious. In his fury Keseker cursed both Leritem and his own wife; the woman ran away to her parents' home and died shortly afterwards. Keseker now refuses to accept any placatory gift in return for his blessing. There is little the other elders can do: they recognize that Keseker is embittered by his recent misfortunes and he always has been known as a hard and implacable man, thought by many to be mean. They have done their best to help Leritem by giving him

193

their collective blessing, but they cannot bring him out of his unpropitious ritual state: only Keseker can do that.

A man who wishes to gain the sympathy of the other elders can more effectively do it by stopping short of actually pronouncing the curse, thereby demonstrating that he is restraining himself in not resorting to it. The following example concerns Letuno, a mean man, and his more worthy half brother Piliyon, who were the protagonists of example 4.

43. When Letuno was a moran, he showed considerable disrespect towards his half brother Piliyon on a number of occasions. Piliyon, the head of the family, then let it be known that he would curse Letuno on his marriage. Letuno tried to marry three different girls and each time he was told by the kinsmen of these girls that they would never agree to his request until he had put matters right with his half brother: the curse could affect the fortunes of the wife and children as well as the husband. After the third failure, Letuno returned to Piliyon and asked him for his blessing and this was given publicly. In his very next quest for a wife, Letuno was successful.

This particular case is not complicated by any chance misfortunes which might have been ascribed to supernatural forces. It simply shows how one man succeeded in drawing general attention to the way in which his younger half-brother was disregarding his obligations towards him as the head of the family. If Piliyon had actually pronounced a curse instead of merely threatening it, then he might himself have been generally criticized as unduly harsh and it might have been harder to arrive at a final reconciliation with Letuno. By only threatening to curse his marriage, Piliyon effectively ensured that Letuno would not be able to marry within the society until he had changed his attitude, for the elders of any lineage he tried to marry into would hear of the threat long before they had agreed to his suit. But Letuno was in no immediate personal danger; he did not have *ngoki*. Furthermore, Letuno was quite helpless in the matter: even if he had personally disbelieved in or doubted the efficacy of the curse, he could not alter the situation so long as the majority of elders still believed.

Cursing the marriage of a junior kinsman is a quite common way of drawing attention to some unjustified slight. Kuracha followed the same course when one of his sons refused to obey him and stay herding the cattle; a blind man, Leteneto, (blind, it is said, because he had refused six elders permission to use his water hole and had been cursed) followed this course when his younger brother took back a cow he had previously given him as it had turned out to be a particularly fertile beast; Letuluai is still following this course because a classificatory sister's son recently refused him hospitality. It is also a method that can be adopted by a man who wants to avoid cursing a bond brother: Lelema was cursed in marriage by a bond brother who was also an age mate of his father for stealing a goat, and after being unsuccessful in his quests for a wife, he admitted his guilt and gave the other a heifer in return for his blessing.

A man would not normally wish to draw attention to a rift between himself and some junior kinsman for this would reflect on the good name of the family where loyalty and mutual trust should prevail. Other elders normally hesitate to interfere in the domestic relations between brothers or a father and his sons as differences between them can usually be settled without bringing them to the general attention of the elders. But when a curse is involved then the matter is too serious and the possible consequences too dangerous for the others to ignore. A curse on a kinsman's marriage may be ignored up to the time that he wishes to marry, but at that point the reconciliatory blessing must be made in public so that there is no longer any doubt that the curse has been removed; and, incidentally, the matter has been brought to the attention of the elders by the senior kinsman who effectively airs his grievance.

In such cases of bitterness between close agnates it is only the senior who can act in this way. If it is the senior who is at fault by abusing his privileges, then the only approved sanction that the junior can take is to assert his own independence as quickly as possible, and everyone will appreciate his motives and not criticize his action. If he tries to take active measures too soon or too drastically then they will only criticize him for showing disrespect and any curse which the other pronounces on him will be justified. In the above examples both Letuno and Kuracha appear to have acted in ways which might have been condoned from older and more independent men.

195

The curse on the marriage of a man is generally pronounced in the following way. 'I will bless you in life and in health. I will bless you in cattle and good fortune. But you will never marry.' It can only be made by men who are related to the offender in such a way that they have a potent curse, and it is made so as to appear coupled with a blessing: a clear indication that no direct curse is contemplated.

But the majority of men with a grudge against another are not closely related and they have to resort to an even more indirect means of threatening the curse. Once again this concerns the marriage of the offender. It is known to the Samburu as 'waiting on a col' (*a-any ndikir*), because it is thought to be similar to a strategy in defensive warfare when the moran would wait for the advancing enemy to cross a range of hills by one of the suitable paths: by guarding strategic cols – gaps in the ridges – a few moran could effectively bar the progress of a much stronger enemy. Correspondingly, a man who harbours a grievance against another may wait until his adversary proposes to marry a girl whom he has the power to curse, and then he may refuse to allow the marriage by threatening to use this curse. With this threat it is possible for him to veto the marriage of any daughter of his clansmen, phratrymen, brothers by descent, bond brothers or age mates, and of any daughter of these daughters. Such girls are his classificatory sisters, daughters, and their daughters: they are, in fact, precisely the girls that he is prevented from marrying himself by rules of exogamy and incest, and for any typical elder they could amount to one-quarter or even one-third of all marriageable girls. The elder 'waits on a col' until his adversary tries to marry one of these girls and then he announces that the marriage must not take place, for if he curses the girl at her marriage then this combined with her husband's offence will have a disastrous effect on her and on her children. This sanction is very popular among the Samburu and is probably more common than the direct use of the curse. It is therefore discussed in considerable detail in the following pages.

44.** A moran, Kaisan, hit a boy of his clan with his knobkerrie without real justification. The boy's father, Lomere, informed the other elders that although he was a firestick elder and could curse

Kaisan, he would not resort to this, he would merely 'wait on a col'. Some time later Kaisan went to Mount Ngiro (some 90 miles from the scene of the original incident) to ask to marry a girl living there. But her father was a member of Lomere's age-set and Lomere had sent word that he would veto the marriage. The elders at Mount Ngiro informed Kaisan that until he had settled his dispute with Lomere they could not give him the girl.

In a similar way another firestick elder, Kingeyo, refused to allow a moran to marry the daughter of an age-mate, because at one time he had refused him permission to use his water hole. In this second example, the marriage later took place when Kingeyo agreed to accept a heifer from the moran. This is the conventional payment in such instances.

Often an elder harbours a grievance secretly and only brings it to the attention of the other elders when all the preparations for marriage have been made. This is a particularly effective way of bringing his grievance to the general notice of the public, and usually of obtaining satisfaction.

45. Three moran of Pardopa clan stole a goat from Aruata, a firestick elder of Makalilit clan. Aruata could not prove their guilt conclusively and he did not threaten to curse them; however, he secretly waited on a col.

Two of the moran married girls that he had no power to refuse; but then the third was promised a daughter of one of his age mates. He waited until the ceremony had actually been arranged and the bridegroom had asked the bride's father to make the final preparations for her circumcision. Then, and only then, Aruata came forward to forbid the marriage. The bridegroom maintained that the theft had never taken place, but offered Aruata a heifer to placate him. Aruata refused the heifer saying that he would only be satisfied with a full confession. The bridegroom would not change his attitude and the marriage was held up for some time.

One of the other two moran involved in the theft heard of the incident and he went straight to Aruata to confess the guilt of all three of them. He knew that out of loyalty to his Club mates, the bridegroom would not want to confess even at the risk of spoiling his marriage, but this did not hamper the other two, who had less to gain from confessing. Aruata accepted the confession and said that he only wanted a male calf as a token gift from each of the three thieves.

This is a particularly dignified incident: the bridegroom had risked his marriage out of loyalty to his age mates, and one of them had confessed to the theft out of loyalty to him. Aruata had shown shrewdness and generosity in the way in which he had handled the matter. The incident had a final outcome which left no rancour or disgrace with any party.

An interesting feature in this example is that Aruata would not accept the conventional heifer without a confession from the thieves, and that once he had obtained the confession he accepted a far smaller payment than he might have done: he could have demanded a heifer from each of the three culprits. The issue at stake in this instance appears not to have been simply a desire to obtain a placatory gift, but rather a desire to obtain a full confession. The importance of a confession is that once it is obtained then the matter is clearly at an end and the accuser has justified his action in the eyes of his fellow elders. Having obtained this satisfaction he may be prepared to accept merely a nominal payment.

Sometimes when a cordial social relationship has developed between a man and his maternal kin, his power of veto may be extended by courtesy to the daughters of these men. He has no power to curse these girls, but at his request his mother's brothers may agree to oppose the marriage of one of his adversaries. It is only likely that he will ask them to do so if he knows he can rely on their support.

> 46. Letiten had grown up inside his mother's brother's clan, Pardopa. At his request, the elders of this clan agreed to reject the suit of one of his adversaries for one of their girls. This adversary, an age mate of his, had been prominent in foiling Letiten's earlier attempt to take back his own wife after having divorced her.

Letiten has not, as yet been so completely accepted as a full member of Pardopa clan that he can ask that a girl of some other sub-clan than his mother's should be refused in marriage.

Even a wronged elder who prefers the calculated way of waiting on a col to the more impetuous way of the curse must be able to justify his actions if he is to retain the respect of the other elders. It is quite common that men fail to do this.

47.* When Titian was a moran, he accompanied a friend who seduced the wife of a clansman, Leraren. Ever since he found out, Leraren had borne a grudge, and when he heard that Titian wanted to marry the daughter of one of his age mates, he vetoed the marriage altogether and refused any placatory gift, even although Titian had not been the seducer. Leraren vowed at the same time that neither Titian nor his friend would ever marry a daughter of his age-set. This caused considerable criticism among the other elders of his clan who considered his action quite un-justified and mean, but they could not force him to withdraw his veto and later Titian married some other girl.

Several years later in 1958, Leraren's second wife was raped and murdered, and in some quarters it was rumoured that this was perhaps due to an unvoiced curse by his clansmen who dis-approved of his general meanness and in particular of his spite-fulness against Titian. When Titian married another wife, again the daughter of a member of Leraren's age-set, Leraren did not attempt to veto the match after all. It is understood that he would not dare to air the same grievance again.

If all elders were to use their powers of vetoing marriage in this unscrupulous fashion then marriage among the Samburu would become virtually impossible or the sanction would lose its effectiveness. Incidentally the misfortunes which Leraren and his brother Seletu (page 189) have recently suffered are thought to derive partly from the bad feeling they have aroused among Pardopa elders generally. Their father was an immi-grant from the Kunguan clan of the Tiamus tribe who are bond brothers to Pardopa clan – a fact which Seletu and Leraren have tended to ignore. A further moral to be drawn from this inci-dent was that at the time of his wife's murder, Leraren was not sharing his settlement with any other man. Only mean men choose to live alone in order to avoid interference in their affairs from their neighbours, but this also means they forfeit their protection and are liable to meet with misfortunes of this kind.

Situations can arise where a man may be justified in waiting on a col so far as the immediate circumstances of the case are concerned, but it would be unwise for him to adopt this course. If, for instance, he is having a difficult time with his wife's kinsmen then he would be ill-advised to veto the marriage of one of their girls to an adversary of his, even if there is an obvious way of doing it (e.g. if she is the daughter of an age mate or of a kinswoman): this would only increase the strain between himself and his affiness whom he should respect.

If he were to try to interfere in the marriage of a maternal kinsman this would not only be considered ill-advised, but also reckless:

48.** Loyan suspected five moran of Masula phratry of stealing a goat and he decided to wait on a col. However his mother *and* both of his wives belonged to this phratry and by antagonizing the Masula elders both he and his children would be in danger. Eventually one of the moran wished to marry a girl of Ltoiyo clan, bond brothers to Loyan's, and he vetoed the marriage. The father of this moran told him to accept a heifer with his blessing (as a classificatory mother's brother), but Loyan demanded a confession of the theft before giving way. His own clansmen, although they supported him in the debate with the Masula elders, in private persuaded Loyan to accept the offer of the heifer or he would be cursed by his maternal kin. Loyan still intends to oppose the marriages of the other four moran on each available opportunity and this demonstrates to everyone what a fool he is. Commenting on the incident one of his clansmen said: 'A goat is not worth a human heart.'

Loyan was acting unwisely and his clansmen pointed out to him that his maternal kin might threaten to use their curse. But they never did this, possibly because it would have prejudiced their chances of success in the marriage suit: men who wish to marry should always be on their best behaviour, especially towards people who will be their distant affinal kinsmen if the marriage takes place. The offer of a heifer with a mother's brother's blessing in return for Loyan's compliance was totally different from the threat of a curse.

In another case where a man tried to veto the marriage of an elder two age-sets senior to his own and hence a firestick elder, he was sternly criticized by the other elders and persuaded to withdraw his objection and accept a gift. Respect for seniority in the age-set system is perhaps the most transcending of all Samburu values. But even so there is no harm in waiting on a col for a man who is only one age-set senior provided there is full justification in taking this course, and cases of this sort have been recorded.

It is quite common for a man to wait on a col for an age mate (e.g. example 46) but no cases have been recorded of any one who has harboured a grievance in this manner against an age mate dating from the days of their moranhood. If he tried to do so, then the other elders would wonder why he had not settled it at the time in the approved manner of the moran. It would be tantamount to admitting either that his grievance was never really justified or that he had not the courage to attack or challenge the other. Even an elder would not want to admit to having been a coward in the days of his moranhood: an affair in which he was degraded is best forgotten.

This sanction is only effective because the total society is of such a size that any man who keeps his ears open can expect to hear of the proposed marriages of his adversaries. But from time to time other men know that he is harbouring a grievance out of sheer spite and wilfully leave him in ignorance or even try to mislead him.

49.** When a moran of Lngwesi clan approached the Lorogushu elders for marriage with one of their girls, they gave their consent and advised him to be cautious in preparing for the marriage as one of their bond brothers of Ltoiyo clan, a notoriously mean man, had already vetoed unconditionally the marriage of one of the moran's brothers after being refused marriage to one of his sisters. They felt that it would be harder for this man to veto the present marriage unconditionally if negotiations had been completed before he heard about it.

A man who does happen to miss hearing of the marriage of an adversary before it has taken place can still try to insist on an immediate divorce under the threat of his curse. It is unlikely that he will obtain a divorce but he will almost certainly be offered a placatory gift.

50.* In a disagreement over the repayment of a dead brother's debt, the local clan elders had persuaded Letuluai to give way to Modo as the issue was slightly unpropitious. But Letuluai still bore a grudge, and he only heard that Modo had married a girl of his phratry after the event. He demanded the immediate return of the bride to her parents threatening to use his curse over her. He was later persuaded to accept a heifer from Modo in return for his blessing.

It is not certain, of course, than an offender will ever propose to marry a girl whom his accuser can veto, and the latter may feel he is justified in making sure of obtaining satisfaction by vetoing the marriage of a brother or a son of the other to any of these girls. He may even try to refuse the marriage of more than one girl to more than one man; but this is always liable to lead to general criticism.

51 (follows from example 15, page 45). After Kingeyo's attempt at marriage by *fait accompli* with a daughter of Kotet had failed, he tried to interfere with three successive marriage proposals by three of Kotet's sons: two of the girls were of Kingeyo's phratry and the third was the daughter of a girl of his clan. In the first case he accepted a heifer from the suitor and withdrew his veto; in the second case he demanded a heifer, but was persuaded by his clansmen to accept a blanket; in the third case he asked for some gift, but was persuaded by his clansmen not to raise the issue again and the marriage took place without opposition. According to one informant, the husband of this third girl later offered Kingeyo a heifer so as to mollify any hidden rancour which might have the effect of a curse on his wife. Kingeyo is known to be an immoderate man and it is quite in keeping with his character that he should try to interfere with three marriages instead of one; but it has also led to criticism among the elders of all clans.

52.** When one of Kotana's sons, a moran, was accused before a government court of having stolen stock in a raid on a European ranch, it was commonly assumed that it was Lerima, an elder with a government appointment, who falsely reported him. He was acquitted on insufficient evidence. Later when Lerima wanted to marry a girl of Kotana's phratry Kotana vetoed the suit altogether, and when Lerima's brother also tried to marry a girl from this phratry, Kotana again wanted to apply an uncompromising veto. In the second case, however, the elders of his own clan eventually persuaded Kotana that he had already aired his grievance against the real culprit and should allow the second marriage to go through.

It is worth noting that in this example, as in example 48, it was the father who acted on behalf of his moran son, in one case to apply the veto and in the other to try to settle it. Moran simply do not have the seniority or even the ability to dispute the intentions of the elders in matters of marriage. In example 52, both Lerima and his brother were firestick elders and it would have been very unwise for Kotana's son to have taken the initiative in opposing their marriages.

In the hands of some men, the power to interfere with one another's marriages leads to the building up of private feuds reminiscent to some extent of the conflicts of the moran. Elders outside these disputes disapprove of this and try to discourage the protagonists from prolonging the issue. Example 46 appeared to be of this nature and so is the following example:

> 53.* A dispute at a water hole had brought Sutilai (a junior elder) and his brother Asuman (a moran) into conflict with another junior elder, Peyon. The fault had been mainly with Peyon and the matter had been resolved by the elders then and there.
>
> Peyon then married a girl of Sutilai and Asuman's phratry, and Asuman married a girl of Peyon's phratry. When he discovered this, Peyon went to Asuman threatening to curse his wife and was given 30 shillings in return for his blessing. This infuriated Sutilai and he has announced that he intends to take away Peyon's wife and force a divorce. At present the outcome is undecided: Sutilai has the support of some of his own age mates of his phratry and Peyon has said that if he loses his wife he will curse Asuman's wife. Asuman himself is in a vulnerable position and does not attempt to support his brother Sutilai.

A man may succeed in convincing the other elders that he has a legitimate grievance and is entitled to veto a marriage altogether, or to accept a payment for his acquiescence, or to hold up negotiations for a while. But in the eyes of other men, far more worthy is the man who entirely forgives his adversary and does not demand a payment.

> 54.* Kajole told the other elders that he intended to veto the marriage of a girl of his phratry to a moran who as a government employee had reported him for trespassing his cattle into an area officially closed to grazing. The moran was sent by the girl's kinsmen to settle the matter with Kajole before approaching them

again. He apologized to Kajole and offered him a heifer, but Kajole told him he would withdraw his veto without any payment and he blessed the moran. His action was praised as a generous and worthy one.

55.* Damayon is a well liked worthy man of his clan and one of the few firestick elders who has really endeared himself to the moran. One moran of his clan, Pinte, struck Damayon's son and stole a goat, and later this moran proposed to marry a daughter of Damayon's mother's brother. Damayon is on extremely cordial terms with his mother's clan (see example 7) and no one had any doubt that if he were to ask them to refuse a daughter in marriage then they would comply with his request, even although he has no direct power of vetoing this girl.

At a meeting at which the proposed marriage of Pinte was being discussed by his clansmen, Damayon announced that he realized that he could effectively oppose the marriage if he wanted to. But he pointed out that this would not benefit the clan in any way and he intended to overlook the incident. He would not curse Pinte (as a firestick elder) and he would not interfere in his marriage, but he could have resorted to either measure if he had felt so inclined. Damayon's reputation remained as high as ever and Pinte told the other elders that he intended to make him a gift to show his gratitude.

Damayon's worthy attitude towards his clan does not extend to the whole society: he harbours a grievance against a moran of another clan who has stolen a sheep of his, and says that he has no intention of letting pass any opportunity of vetoing a marriage so far as this other moran is concerned.

It is with gestures similar to this that Damayon has built up and maintained his popularity within the clan. Unlike Leraren in example 47, he showed a willingness to help the marriage of a clansman instead of hindering it, although he, at least, had a genuine grievance.

The quest for a wife is a long and expensive manoeuvre, owing largely to the high degree of polygamy which leads to competition. And the inescapable convention that no man should seek to marry more than one girl at a time only prolongs the period if he is unsuccessful a number of times. It is not inevitable, although quite common, that his suit will be blocked by a man waiting on a col. But even when no uncompromising opposition is expressed in discussion, all those clansmen of the girl who know him or know of him may raise points in his favour and points against him, judging him from his past behaviour.

No doubt the forced marriages which occasionally take place in this society are correlated with the sheer inability of some men to marry the women they want, or even to marry at all. With the ever possible threat of an adversary waiting on a col, a man is forced to adhere to convention if he wishes to marry several times and build up a large family. Moreover, whether or not he believes in the general efficacy of the curse, he is powerless to challenge it when those who have the power to prevent his marriage retain the belief.

A man with a curse hanging over him is not likely to find it easy to marry: no Samburu would want their daughters to suffer the misfortune of his *ngoki*. This is probably one reason why Leritem, the elder who had been cursed by Keseker (page 193), was having considerable difficulty in obtaining a second wife. But as we have seen, there may be other objections to a man's marriage. Discussions on marriage are probably more commonplace than on all other topics. The merits and demerits of each suitor for a particular girl are discussed by her clansmen in the various local clan groups where she has close agnatic kinsmen. If they have been informed that some man is waiting on a col for him, then he is told to settle the matter before his suit can be considered further. In settling the issue, he may ask for a discussion of the local clan group of his adversary and make his placatory offer. When the matter is raised in the presence of other elders, it is harder for the adversary to refuse this request altogether or to demand too heavy a payment, and once it has been settled it will also be harder for him to raise it again in future. For these reasons the suitor is not likely to try to settle the matter with him in private.

The importance of obtaining the general approval of public opinion in one's actions draws attention to the high value placed on conformity which pervades the whole society. A moran who wishes to marry and settle down to elderhood cannot do so until he has clearly shown that he is prepared to

205

conform with the conventions of elderhood. His rash escapades during moranhood may be accepted by the elders as characteristic of young men, but if he has provoked offence in any quarter then he may find his way to marriage barred by those he has offended. It is their indiscretions as moran in particular which men tend to be faced with when they find difficulty in marrying. The quest of one moran, for instance, for a particular girl was not only forbidden at first by his blind brother Leteneto (see page 195), but also subsequently by two other men he had offended who were waiting on a col (one a bond brother of the girl and the other a brother by descent). As they mature, moran realize, that they must conform with their social obligations if they ever wish to marry, and this is almost certainly a significant factor which moderates their behaviour as they prepare for elderhood.

The Clan and the Curse

This is a convenient place to reiterate some of the conclusions of Chapter Two where the relevance of clanship to marriage was discussed, and to add a number of points emerging from the present chapter.

The boundaries between clans are more definite than at any other level of segmentation. A dispute within a clan can generally be resolved equably by the elders of the local clan group: They are anxious to preserve harmony and they apply pressure on any dissident clansmen to conform with their decisions. There is, moreover, a general spirit of compromise within the clan which makes it less likely that elders will come into conflict in the first place. Co-operation and a display of generosity are norms most Samburu adhere to when dealing with clansmen.

But Samburu clans are not in any way isolated from one another: in most areas their local clan groups are interspersed as shown on page 21, and this brings members of various clans into daily contact in the ordinary course of their lives. Between clans there is not this same spirit of compromise or readiness to co-operate, and a discussion on some issue bringing two clans into dispute is quite likely to be inconclusive; a temporary decision may be reached, but the issue may still be raised again on a future occasion by one dissatisfied party (as in examples 4G, 50 and 53). The general distrust for outsiders, fanned as it is by new disputes and by recent developments of old disputes maintains a social distance between clans which tend to live apart, migrate apart and be somewhat self-contained.

At the same time unless a clan can maintain high moral standards in dealing with other clans, its members may find that they obtain wives less easily and fewer people compete to marry their girls as they are no longer regarded as worthy. This is as true of its attempts at interfering with marriage arrangements as it is of any other aggressive form of behaviour. Abuse leads to abuse and a lowering of standards and respect.

Tension between different clans was correlated in Chapter Two with marital ties which inevitably cut across clan boundaries and are subject to constant strain. In this chapter it has been shown that when a man has a grudge against a member of another clan, he can bring this to public attention by opposing the latter's marriage to a girl of his own clan. His objections call for a discussion within the clan itself and may bias the other elders against the suit. He may even make this the opportunity of airing his grievance without actually vetoing the marriage. It is important at this stage when a new tie with another clan is being negotiated that any grudges against the suitor should be brought into the open and settled before the marriage is allowed to take place. In this way, differences of opinion between members of different clans tend to be raised and settled in a piece-meal fashion whenever a marriage is contemplated. As a result, one issue between clans does not necessarily add to the indignation caused by another issue and build up the tension between them. On the whole, it would be true to say that these tensions are seldom less than a hidden resentment and seldom serious enough to lead to open hostility. Moreover, the constant need for migration and dispersal inevitably dampens local strains

Tensions between clans that do not intermarry cannot be related to marriage in this way. Moreover, where grievances do exist between them, it is not so easy to wait on a col since the only girls a man can refuse a member of a linked clan are daughters of his age-set (examples 45 and 47). Several factors serve to prevent tensions between these clans from mounting seriously. Those which belong to the same phratry do have an uneasy alliance. They regard one another as outsiders, but it is still common for one clan which is poorly represented in an area to become closely associated with a collateral clan which is well represented. Thus a number of Makalilit moran in the Lbarta area belonged to the Pardopa Club and performed in the Pardopa *ilmugit* of the bull ceremony there (pages 92–4). It was inconceivable that the affray between the Pardopa and Makalilit clans in the Sonia area (pages 113–14) should spread to Lbarta for this very reason. Outside the phratry, clans and segments which do not intermarry are predominantly bond brothers and should avoid any action liable to antagonize one another. In other words, they are less likely to come into conflict even than the collateral clans of the phratry. It is worth noting that bond brotherhood is also a fairly common cross-cutting tie between collateral clans, as shown on pages 72–3, and this also inhibits any open hostility between them.

Now one of the most common ways in which such linked clans impinge on one another is at the proposed marriages of each other's girls when they are waiting on a col. The attitude of the close kinsmen of these girls to such interference from outsiders is indicated in examples 44, 48 and 54: they were wholly indifferent to the breach itself, and in each case told the suitor that he must settle his differences with his adversary before they could promise him their daughter. Sometimes, as in examples 11 (page 40) and 49, they even tried to help the suitor overcome the objections of the outsider. There is considerable resentment at this outside interference, especially when the suitor is a popular one; it is not an issue which they feel implicates their own relationship with him.

An interesting feature of bond brotherhoods is that while bond brothers prefer to avoid one another and not to interfere in one another's affairs or make use of their powers of moral coercion unduly, there is less reticence shown by a man who is waiting on a col when he sees a chance to veto his adversary's marriage to a bond sister, and in practice this appears to be a comparatively frequent – possibly the most frequent – way in which bond brothers exercise coercion over one another.

Waiting on a col is one of the most important mechanisms of social control among the Samburu, and it now becomes possible to relate it to the size of Samburu clans and the number of cross-cutting ties in the segmentary structure. The various inter-clan ties have the effect of reducing the proportion of the total number of girls in the society which a man can marry, but at the same time he has a wider power to interfere in the marriage of a larger number of girls if these are sought by his adversaries. If there were fewer clans or more inter-clan ties than there are then finding a suitable spouse might become increasingly difficult; or if, on the other hand, there were more clans or fewer inter-clan ties then it might be harder for men to obtain satisfaction by waiting on a col. This is not to say that the practice of waiting on a col could not occur under these conditions, but it does at least imply that the marriage regulations of the society, the power of the individual to obtain satisfaction by waiting on a col, and the popular attitudes towards conformity and avoiding the direct use of the curse might well be rather different from what they are. Evidence supporting this is given in Chapter Ten (page 298).

Summary

Real power in the society is vested in the elders and their control over the moran in particular rests entirely on the general belief in their curse. The ability to curse gives each elder a power of a sort, but real prestige among the elders is obtained by not resorting to it in the interests of better relations between men, especially within the clan. This is the way of the worthy man, and worthiness first and foremost is necessary to have influence over one's fellows. Thus one is presented with the apparent paradox that the power of the elders which is based on their ability to curse is their weakest tool in any attempt to gain influence over each other, since in threatening to use it, they cut themselves off from their fellows.

The indirect ways in which they make use of their curse to gain satisfaction over an adversary or assert control over a junior kinsman once again draws attention to marriage and the problems it involves and opportunities it gives. The various aspects of marriage have been a constant theme throughout this study, and before the ceremony itself is considered in detail, more must be said about the women of the society, who are the pawns of this game played by the elders.

Chapter Eight

THE STATUS OF WOMEN

THE previous chapters have largely concentrated on the masculine aspects of the society with constant reference to the various implications of marriage and polygamy. The present one is intended as a supplement to these, drawing attention to the status of women in the society, and introducing a topic which is discussed more fully in Chapter Nine where the marriage ceremony itself is described.

Girlhood, Marriage, and the Father's Clan

Among their children, the Samburu place a greater value on sons than daughters. Sons remain associated with their father's homestead, and as he grows old they take over the duties of looking after him and managing his herds; whereas daugthers are married away from the homestead while still quite young and from this moment they may be regarded to some extent as outsiders. In addition to this, a man's lineage is perpetuated through his sons but not through his daughters.

The greater importance of a son is implied in the ceremonial observances which follow his birth: these are richer in detail than those for a daughter. From the very first week of his life a boy is allotted a male calf and at least one heifer as the foundation of his herd, whereas a girl is allotted nothing for she has no inheritance rights in her father's herd. The Samburu say that a man with daughters but no sons is a poor man, and find some mystical explanation to account for the fact that he has no male heirs.

Conversely there are certain disadvantages in having a family of all boys and no girls. From the point of view of the father, it means that his closest ties are restricted to his own clan and he is more closely bound up with the fortunes and misfortunes of that clan; whereas if he has a number of daughters married elsewhere, then in times of hardship he can legitimately come to his daughters' husbands for help, as their closest wife-giving affine. From the point of view of the clan in general, it is an asset to have many girls married elsewhere, for, apart from the economic advantages of having plenty of wife-receiving affines and 'sisters' sons' to exploit, their own negotiations for wives are strengthened when they can point to previous ties which have been made with the same lineage and can ask for a return favour. Inevitably, the father of a number of girls who have been married into good families elsewhere has an enhanced status among his own clansmen. It is worth noting that in blessing a man and his wife so that they may have children the other elders sometimes say: 'May they be like *kerin.*' *Kerin* are beads worn by moran and elders which are alternately light and dark in colour. The elders are blessing them with an indefinite number of boys alternating with girls: this is the most propitious assortment of children any woman can have.

A girl is brought up to avoid all elders including even her own father. She is made to accept this situation almost as soon as she can speak, and, according to the Samburu themselves, rather sooner than she can have any clear idea of what is happening. At first, this avoidance entails a certain modesty in the presence of elders: she should sit in a decent posture and not play too freely. From the time she is perhaps six, she should sleep only in huts where there are no elders, not even her own father. Later, by the time she is about ten, she should have sufficient respect for elders to avoid them on all occasions: she should leave the hut when one enters and keep away from them when outside. She would only speak to them when they address her first. This is only slightly modified in the presence of her own father and close kinsmen: she might not actually leave the hut when they enter, but she certainly would not sit on the sleeping hides when they are sitting there and would step down from these hides before they step up on to them.

This avoidance is more outstanding than any other among the Samburu: that between bond brothers or between moran and married women only entails certain aspects of their behaviour; that between girls and elders is almost complete. It is at its height where it involves the father's age-set: under no circumstances would a man marry the daughter of an age mate or enter into a familiar relationship with her after her marriage. But he might assert himself as a 'father' in protecting her marriage, as occurred in example 4.

One possible explanation of this avoidance is that older men are well aware of the sexual attractions of young women: besides referring to them in their gossip, they also marry girls who are often younger than some of their own daughters: and hence the avoidance of daughters. This does not, however, explain the avoidance between elders and girls in general, nor does it explain why this particular avoidance does not appear to have been recorded elsewhere in other societies where polygamy is high (e.g. among the Turkana or the Nyakyusa). It is, I suggest, largely to be seen as one more aspect of the competition for wives that exists and all that this implies in social control and realizing social ambitions.

In the first place, the system can only work if women are resigned to their position. They must accept the fate that their fathers and elders of their clan decide for them unconditionally. This can only be done by subordinating them from a very early age and maintaining this up to the time of their marriages.

Secondly, though there is seldom any difficulty in marrying a girl off, it is not so certain that in every case an ideal suitor will present himself. In order to attract a worthy man, or even better, a number of worthy men to choose from, she must have certain qualities promising in a wife: she should have a marked sense of respect, so that she will automatically accept any difficulties her marriage entails. Furthermore, in order that there shall be a popular demand for the girls of a lineage and clan in general, it is essential that each one shall reach a standard which will maintain the reputation of the lineage. In other words, just as there is a pressure on men to conform with certain ways of behaving within a lineage and clan so that they may all make good marriages and marital bonds, so there is a pressure to bring up their daughters in the best traditions of the society.

The reputation of both lineage and clan hinges on the extent to which they can maintain their standards.

A girl's relationship with her father is a weak point in this avoidance; for it is commonly acknowledged that they have very strong feelings of mutual affection, an admission which is evident from time to time when they hear bad news of each other. It is said that if a father sees anyone – even his own wife – beating his daughter he will want to beat this person in his fury. Occasionally, it is rumoured of an elder who does not avoid his daughter sufficiently that he has incestuous relations with her. In order to avoid such aspersions, he and his daughter must observe the necessary avoidances strictly. They do it because it is expected of them by the remainder of the society and not because of their own spontaneous sentiments towards each other. Not to do so would excite local gossip. Thus, this avoidance relationship, in so far as it entails father and daughter, cannot be explained adequately in terms of sentiment, but only in terms of social expectation. And where it entails the elders in general, it should be regarded as an aspect of tension between them and the girls[1] rather than as a consequence of such tension.[2]

The expected behaviour and attitude of a man towards his daughter makes it quite impracticable for him to be directly responsible for her education: he cannot both avoid her and teach her, and if he really loves her as much as is commonly supposed then he may be unwilling to castigate her as necessary. Her education is in the hands of her mother. As a part of the avoidance with her father, she must be taught not to run to him when her mother has beaten her or even to cry out in his hearing. She must not look on him as an ally in her distress, as it would indicate that whenever she suffered any frustration – as would frequently happen after her marriage – it would be to him that she would turn for help, exploiting his fondness for her and endangering her own marriage. Once again this insistence is not to be explained in terms of spontaneous sentiments, but only in terms of social expectation. If at any time the father is dissatisfied with the progress of a girl in acquiring

[1] cf. Fortes, 1953, p. 19.
[2] cf. Radcliffe-Brown, 1952, p. 92 ff.

the necessary sense of respect, he may tell her mother to do something about it and even stay away from her hut for some time to allow her greater freedom in beating the girl, which could never be done in his presence; but he would not intervene in the girl's education more directly. By the time she is fit to be married at, say, the age of 17, it is hoped that she will have acquired a full sense of respect for all elders and that her moral education will be complete.

The strict upbringing of a girl contrasts considerably with that of a boy. At precisely the age at which a girl is circumcised and married, a boy is circumcised and becomes a *moran*, but *his* social education has barely begun. The respect he shows towards the elders is perfunctory. Before he is fully grown, he may giggle, sulk, lie and even run away when addressed by an elder. It is only later on, as a moran, that he really begins to acquire a sense of respect. In certain ways his moral education is almost 10 years behind that of a girl. He is kept from being the parent of a family that much longer and his social maturation is delayed rather than accelerated.

In contrast to their depressed status *vis-à-vis* the elders, girls enjoy an unusually high status among moran. The moran are inevitably attracted towards them and the fact that there are more than twice as many moran as adolescent girls may well increase competition among them for the favours and praises of these girls.[1] It is the taunts of girls and their praises which are largely responsible for inciting many moran to steal stock; and it is competition over them which frequently leads to fighting and affrays. Once a moran has a mistress of his own, then both his prestige and his honour are implicated in the relationship and the fidelity of the girl.

It is worth noting that in common with the moran with whom she associates, a girl is placed in a position of considerable frustration and has good reason to resent her lot. She has no choice in determining her future marriage which will entail breaking any relationship with her moran lover and separation from her parents' home and clan; she will go to live in a strange land

---

[1] In 1958, corresponding to each unmarried girl between the ages of 13 and 17½ years, there appeared to be 2·5 moran between the ages of 17½ and 33 years. (These figures were extrapolated from the demographic data in the appendix.)

among strangers. Any resentment and feelings of insecurity which this entails could conceivably help to account for her behaviour prior to marriage where she taunts the moran, encouraging them to behave in ways which are against the best interests of the society. The vying between the sexes is only one aspect of their game. There also seems to be an implicit antagonism towards social order and society in general expressed in their songs. It was the girls who were most reluctant that the Kiliako age-set should abandon blooding their spears long after there had been political security in the area, and who refused to accept a man's serving in the King's African Rifles and buying cattle with his wages as an acceptable substitute for stealing cattle. The girls do not simply want the moran to show bravery – killing a lion single-handed requires far more courage than stealing a cow and yet has never been extolled in the Club songs – they seem to want something that is disruptive to the social order under which they are placed.

The enhancement of a girl's status within the Club ends with her marriage. The relationship she has enjoyed with her lover is totally different from the one she will develop with her husband: it was formed and maintained largely out of sexual attraction with a variable element of mutual affection and implicating the honour and prestige of the lover within his Club, whereas marriage is a serious domestic relationship having more far-reaching issues. The Samburu realize that the two can never be the same. Lovers tend to treat each other to some extent as equals and either can terminate the relationship at will, whereas within the family, the husband should be the undisputed master; marriages between a man and his mistress lead, they say, to battles (*arabal*). For this reason many moran who profess to be very fond of their mistresses and are not restricted from marrying them by the rules of clan exogamy admit that they have no desire to do so. A few, with the consent of their senior kinsmen, are prepared to take this risk. But the clear majority have no choice in the matter as they are of the same clan as their mistresses and therefore cannot marry them. This fact helps to condition both them and their mistresses from the moment they become lovers to accept that their affair has no future and is bound to end in separation.

A girl is not brought up to marry her lover or the man of her choice. She is brought up to create one more marriage tie for her kinsmen, and it is in their best interests that she should have all the qualities expected of a good wife: a sense of respect, competence in fulfilling her household duties and the makings of a good mother. It is not forgotten that if she has been brought up in the best traditions of the society then she can in her turn hand on her merits to her own daughters. A well brought up girl is an investment for her husband in the years to come as much as she is an investment for her kinsmen. A man whose daughters are well prepared for a good marriage may take a justifiable pride in them, and they are one more attribute of his worthiness among his fellows.

Marriage negotiations are conducted without reference to the girl's personal feelings. She may learn from her mother of the various suitors who are asking to marry her, but her father does not inform her of her forthcoming marriage until he and the other elders have unanimously agreed to accept a particular man and the preliminary negotiations have been completed.

After her marriage, she remains on very much the same terms with her clansmen as before, although the relationship is inevitably more distant and she must be treated as a wife and not just as a girl. Her clansmen will try to help both her and her husband to adjust themselves to marriage by not demanding too much of them and by interfering only when they feel this is really justified. The husband will not generally live with them, but when he does it may be to help her settle down to her new life or it may be with less concern on her behalf and more concern for the marriage itself: any intractable or wilful traits in her will be suppressed in the presence of her kinsmen. He may consider that she will come to accept her new status more easily and that domestic harmony will be attained more effectively by impelling her to show respect in her parents' settlement than by treating her more harshly in his own. Sooner or later they will generally return to live with his clan.

Every married woman has her own hut, which is avoided to some extent by all her classificatory fathers and brothers. The former include all members of her father's or her husband's father's age-set and generation, and the latter include other members of her natal clan and linked clans. Her classificatory fathers would avoid sitting on the sleeping hides of her hut, and if they are almost strangers or have a very pronounced sense of respect they would avoid her hut altogether. Her classificatory brothers do not avoid any part of her hut and may specifically come to it to ask for food, but they would never sleep there unless she is beyond child-bearing, by which time she normally has a sleeping hide of her own. Her new interests are largely confined to the family she is rearing, but she still retains a diffuse and occasionally strong tie with her natal family and clan. Just as her brothers look to her husband for hospitality and occasional gifts, so she may look to them for help when she is destitute. The Samburu do not stress the power of the curse that she has over her 'brothers' to the same extent that they stress the power of the curse that they have over her and her children, but if any of them were to ignore her when her need is great then this would be to betray the ties of clanship formed early in life and misfortune could result – possibly as a result of her curse.

As a married woman, she is an ally among outsiders to her 'brothers', just as they may be allies to her at critical moments in her husband's home. Even at times when tension between the two clans is considerable, 'sisters' and their husbands are expected to fulfil their obligations of hospitality. On one occasion, during the heated arguments and threats between two clans that followed a marriage by *fait accompli* earlier in the day, the transgressors retired to the huts of kinswomen previously married to the bride's clan to refresh themselves with milk. They found this the most natural thing to do. At other times when a man wishes to marry a girl of a family closely associated with one which a kinswoman of his has been married to, he may confidentially ask her for an honest opinion of this girl's worth as a potential wife. At other times he may ask her how other 'sisters' married in the same clan are behaving and how they are being treated. She is a link between her husband's and her father's clans.

A Woman and Her Husband's Clan

The difference in age between a bride and her husband is

commonly anywhere between 10 and 40 years, the average difference being of the order of 20 years;[1] in other words, a woman's husband is typically more than twice her age at marriage, but it is not unusual for him to be more than three times her age.

If he is relatively young, belonging in fact to the age-set of her former lover (and more than one-third of all women are married to such men[2]) then she will find least difficulty in adjusting herself to married life: he and his closest friends are all of an age and disposition which is well known to her, and the wives of these friends are in a similar position to herself. If, however, the husband belongs to a more senior age-set then she finds herself having to live with the type of man she has been taught as a girl to avoid and even fear. The prospect of being married to an elderly man is one which women admit terrified them before marriage.

On her marriage, her relationship with elders who are not her classifactory fathers inevitably changes. She must still show respect for them, but not necessarily complete avoidance. With members of the same alternation as her husband (apart from his full and half brothers) she may develop a relationship of privileged familiarity. If her husband is of a senior age-set then this adjustment is hard to make. In addition to associating with elders whom she previously had to avoid, she must now avoid moran of the age-set with whom she previously associated: this is not a matter of respect for the moran themselves, but for her husband who may otherwise suspect that she is having clandestine affairs with them. Once these moran become elders, then she may find them, especially those of her husband's alternation, congenial companions. A large number of children borne by widows (jurally the sons of the dead husband) have been begotten by members of the age-set with which she previously associated.

A woman may consider herself lucky to be married to a young man, but she has little chance of evading marriage into a completely strange social group who live in an unfamiliar part of the country: this is almost inevitable, because clan exogamy

---

[1] Figures based on the clan census, see the appendix.
[2] Loc. cit.

and corporateness encourages virilocal marriage. After her marriage, she should not expect to be free to return to her parents' home, except for very occasional visits, ever again. The strictness of her upbringing does not merely instil into her those attitudes expected of a good wife, it also prepares her for the worst ordeals her marriage may entail – marriage to a much older man, and removal to a distant and seemingly unfriendly part of the country.

The normal way in which an elder keeps his wife under his control is by beating her as he thinks necessary. He is unlikely to curse her as this would implicate their children and cattle. The Samburu are very critical of those elders who have cursed their wives for this very reason. It is also debatable whether the threat of a curse would be as effective in controlling a woman who is driven in desperation to run away as it is in controlling the moran. Fear of the curse is not an attitude which is as thoroughly instilled into women as it is into the moran: with the lesser physical strength of women, this is not absolutely necessary, whereas with the greater physical strength of the moran, it is.

A wise man does not beat his wife on any pretext, nor does he do it in a moment of annoyance unless immediate action seems necessary. An elder once pointed out to me signs of disrespectfulness in the speech and behaviour of his junior wife. She was sulky rather than openly defiant. The present place was not, he argued, a suitable one to beat her: there were no good trees to cut a whip from and she might feel tempted to run away to some of her clansmen living nearby. But when they migrated to a new area he had in mind then the opportunity would present itself and he would take it. This long-sighted planning by a man who was gentle by nature was consciously aimed at changing the attitude of his wife towards him. He recognized her peevishness as dating from the death of a previous child, and had not wanted to treat her too harshly at first; but now that two years had elapsed and she had borne him a further child, he felt he was justified in his action without any implied malice.

The presence in a settlement of people a man should respect

gives his wife some degree of protection, whether these are his affines, his clanswomen or members of the other alternation. The respect shown between alternations is not confined to sexual avoidance (page 94), there is also an element of privileged coercion in special circumstances. Thus, if a man starts to beat his wife and she runs to the hut of an elder of the other alternation and asks for his protection, then this elder is more or less obliged to intercede on her behalf and the husband is obliged to respect his request. When men of the same age but opposite alternations are by themselves, their behaviour may be relaxed; but if their wives are present or are indirectly implicated then a certain restraint is shown by everyone. The principle of alternations affected the outcome of example 3 (page 33) where the other elders of Kimiri's settlement persuaded his wife not to run away after he had beaten her. Prominent among these was Kisaiton who was of the other alternation to Kimiri, and he promised to intercede with Kimiri on her behalf. Kisaiton was only a classificatory son of Kimiri and also of a junior age-set, but he could demand a certain respect from both of them in these critical circumstances.

An elder should also respect his married kinswomen and these may intercede on his wife's behalf to protect her.

56.** In the settlement described on pages 17–19, Lekiso started to beat his junior wife for negligence. This took place outside her hut. Partuala, his classificatory sister, came and stood between the two, facing Lekiso with her arms raised sideways. Lekiso could not have beaten his wife without hurting Partuala and he stopped beating altogether. He said later that he had done this out of respect for his 'sister'.

In this example, intervention by either of Letuluai's wives would have had a similar effect, as Lekiso and Letuluai were of opposite alternations. However, these were both much younger women than Lekiso and might have been too overawed by his seniority to dare to intervene. My impression of the incident was that Partuala had acted in this way out of friendship for Lekiso's wife, knowing that she had it in her power to stop the beating. As a girl she had been associated with Lekiso's Club and consequently did not regard him with awe.

It is evident that the presence in one settlement of classificatory sisters (of the same clan) and of classificatory parents and children (of the opposite alternation) has a stabilizing influence on the various marital relationships that offsets the constant wranglings between husbands and their wives. The elder in particular is obliged to show a greater respect for his wife than he might otherwise do. A number of Samburu sub-clans, perhaps about one-third of the total, do not have alternations: they are jokingly said to have 'a bull's alternation' (*ltalepa lolaingoni*), as bulls also do not differentiate between females of their own and other generations when serving them. Such sub-clans are criticized by those that do acknowledge alternations for not having a sense of respect. This criticism can be interpreted in two ways. It may imply that persons of adjacent generations have indiscriminate sexual intercourse with one another's wives (i.e. their 'mothers' and their 'daughters-in-law') and beget incestuous children. But it may also imply that members of clans without alternations are less liable to respect their own wives, when there are fewer people with powers to restrain them.

In time a woman becomes familiar with life inside her husband's clan, and comes to regard it as her own. She makes friends among the other wives, she grows accustomed to the company of elders who visit her hut, and above all her energies are devoted to rearing a family of her own. As a new-comer to the clan she was in a completely novel situation and was obliged to show a marked respect to many men. In the course of time, the older men whom she should respect die and younger men, whom she knew as children, become elders. She acquires a certain seniority with age and can expect some respect from everyone.

When her sons are circumcised, she acquires a special status which is displayed by certain ornaments she wears on her head. By now she is well established in her husband's clan and as an oldish woman and a 'mother of moran' she is not obliged to avoid members of her son's age-set. It is to her hut that these moran come to drink milk, to sing and to discuss news from other parts of the country and news of particular members of their Club. Sexual topics are, of course, avoided in her presence and there is no relaxation of the food prohibitions observed by the moran. These middle-aged and old women listen with some interest to the conversations of the young people and even join in. It is a new association which appears to give them considerable satisfaction: the moran are, after all, the social group on which so much attention converges from all quarters, and they carry much of the latest news from other localities. Sometimes mothers of moran use slang words introduced by the moran which even the elders do not know.

One aspect of the relationship between moran and their mothers should be borne in mind: it is to their mothers that they first make the vow that they will avoid food seen by married women. Thus the avoidance between moran and married women initially takes place in their own homes, and it is said that even when this restriction is lifted by the blessing of the elders after marriage, many men still find it embarrassing to eat in their mother's presence and try to avoid it. Once again this draws attention to the fact that the association of the moran with the bush also implies their extrusion to some extent from the family. At an *ilmugit* ceremony, the ambivalence of this relationship is expressed where on the one hand each moran is specifically attached to his mother's hut, and on the other hand he is associated with the *ilmugit* enclosure in the bush.

The circumcision of her oldest son to make her a mother of moran is often a significant step in the progressive estrangement between a woman and her husband. The husband, now a senior elder, generally prefers to dissociate himself from the moran – apart from his own sons – and is likely to avoid her hut. It is just at this time that he may decide to take on another wife so as to have a wife and hut of his own free from the comings and goings of the moran. Not all elders follow this course, however: a large number of them continue to take an interest in the activities of their sons after they have become moran. This is particularly true of the older men who have a less pronounced interest in the affairs of the elders and have stopped marrying young girls who may attract lecherous young men.

The rights of a woman and her sons in the herd which the husband allotted her when they were first married, and the extent to which the husband is free to manipulate these rights to his own advantage (Chapter Three) are fair indications of her status in her own hut and in her husband's homestead. Her allotted herd is the source from which her sons, with her acquiescence, build up herds of their own, and this common interest unites them against the efforts of the father to use the cattle of this herd for his own ends, and against any of her kinsmen and others who come to beg beasts from it. The husband may have the final word in alienating stock, but as the sons mature they have an increasing right to build up herds of their own which he should respect. Ultimately, the interests of these sons is their mother's interest, for their prosperity is hers and their marriages are her assets. In so much as they, as brothers, tend to remain associated after their marriages to an extent which half brothers do not (see page 15), it is the link through their mother which unites them.

A woman with married sons has an honoured position in any of their homesteads, and is respected for her seniority and looked after by their wives, while she for her part can help them in a number of small ways. It should be noted, however, that owing to the late age at which moran marry, a woman is commonly over 70 years old before the youngest of her sons marries – if she is still alive. Her position with regard to her sons is sufficient to give her a powerful curse over them. It is said of one man that he was killed in a raid because he had whipped his mother and she had cursed him, and of another that the reason his wife did not bear him any children for many years was that he had taken cattle from the herd of his brother's widow (ultimately derived from the mother's allotted herd) and his mother had cursed him. These are exceptional cases, however, and most Samburu show a great affection for their mothers and are on cordial terms with them.

A woman depends on having sons of her own to assert her

rights in the allotted herd. Examples have been cited where these rights have not been respected by the husband (page 55), by his close kinsmen after his death (page 65) and by his senior son by another wife (page 25). In the first two instances, it was the adult sons who later found ways of returning their stock, but in the third where there were no sons the matter could not be disputed.

When she has no sons, a woman's allotted herd is eventually taken over by her husband's heirs and she is left dependent on them. She may return to her natal clan if she wants or if she has a daughter she may accompany her on her marriage: inevitably, she has a close bond with each of her daughters, but her position in her son-in-law's settlement is that of an outsider and rests entirely on this one relationship. This freedom of a woman without sons of her own corresponds to a certain lack of definite status. She is no longer obliged to remain with one group and tends to be regarded as a necessary liability rather than as an honoured dependent.

Reciprocity Among Women

The friendship which one wife showed for another in example 56 by protecting her from her husband is one illustration of the support women give one another at critical moments. The tension between the sexes, and in particular between elders and their wives, is not only correlated with a virtual conspiracy among stock friends to exploit the herds of one another's wives; it is also correlated with a general sympathy and mutual support among the wives. The depressed status of women puts them at a great disadvantage, but by loyalty to one another at difficult moments they can at least improve their position somewhat.

Even co-wives who by the very nature of their relationship are placed in a position to compete for the favours of their husband generally become friends rather than rivals. This is partly encouraged by the custom of allotting each woman a herd of her own, and so long as her rights are respected there can be no rivalry between co-wives for property. It is also encouraged by the custom which constrains a man to be reasonable with all his wives, distributing his favours in an equitable manner.

A triangular relationship between a husband and two of his wives in which each women competes with the other for his favours, while he tries (or does not try) to remain impartial is not common among the Samburu, even though two-fifths of the married women have just one co-wife. The more usual relationship is of a strong bond between the two (or more) wives who support each other against the husband. A wise man does not try to break this bond, but uses it as a basis on which to maintain harmony within his homestead. He must resign himself to being an outsider to the bond that tends to unite all women and accept it as an inevitable consequence of the enormous social barrier that separates him as an elder from them:

57.** After the marriage of Nirorol (described in the next chapter), her husband, Darapul, tried unsuccessfully to come between her and his first wife, Kioban, with whom he persistently quarrelled. He made it fairly apparent to everyone that he intended to favour Nirorol unnecessarily. However, Kioban also made friendly gestures towards Nirorol, offering her a considerable number of cattle from her allotted herd (she had no sons of her own and was not likely to have any). Nirorol quickly responded to this offer of friendship and made it quite clear that she did not want unfair attention from Darapul, even at the risk of offending him.

Within a matter of days of meeting each other for the first time, Nirorol and Kioban were clearly firm friends, and Darapul had to accept the situation as it stood.

In this example, Darapul was not at first behaving in his own best interests; and the other elders of the settlement, all members of the same clan, kept a wary eye on his homestead during those first few days and discussed the matter among themselves, although they did not find it necessary to interfere.

A woman should accept the seniority of her senior co-wives and above all of her husband's mother. They should all cooperate in the duties of the homestead. If there is any antagonism between them then the polygamous husband can always divide his family into two homesteads and, if necessary, keep these in different settlements. Some informants have suggested that when a man splits his homestead, wives should be assigned alternately to different homesteads or that the senior wives should belong to one homestead and the junior wives to another. In practice, however, the co-wives are divided from one another so as to keep friends together and to separate rivals, and also to divide their joint skills and abilities evenly. A peevish junior wife may be assigned to the same homestead as a senior wife whom she respects, and women married from the same clan may be left together. Similarly, the custom that the husband's mother should be cared for by the most recent wife of her youngest son is often modified when she dislikes this particular wife or has formed a close friendship with another of her daughters-in-law.

Women born into the same clan are expected to help one another in the difficulties that face them when they have been married elsewhere, especially if they are closely related. Their sons call one another by the special term (*arnashe*) and if they have known one another since childhood they continue to treat each other with special familiarity and even joking playfulness: they are at the same time often members of totally unrelated lineages and yet united by a common tie through their mothers and stand in a common relationship to the same group of maternal kin.

All married women are united to some extent in their opposition to the elders. Adultery, for instance, is a constant source of strain between elders and their wives as it is between elders and moran. According to the elders, young wives tell one another of their private love affairs and keep one another's secrets; even a senior wife beyond child bearing is understood to keep secret the affairs of her younger co-wives so as to retain their friendship; or at the most she will warn them to moderate their lusts and show a greater discretion; and at no time does she concern herself with the affairs of the wives of other men. A really old woman with a married son might, however, tell him about the infidelities of his wives if she finds out, as she is said to be jealous on his behalf. The following incident related by elders shows clearly some of the general concern about adultery.

58.* Kitosion, a senior elder, found a moran talking with his youngest wife in the yard of his homestead one night. They sprang apart when they saw him, and the moran ran away into the bush as Kitosion lashed out with his staff at him. Kitosion called the other elders of the settlement and under relentless questioning on the matter the woman broke down and admitted that the moran had been trying to seduce her, but she denied that any seduction had taken place. The elders refused to believe her, and questioned her further. One of them, Keseker, a particularly bullying elder, demanded that she should tell him what moran had been seducing his own wife: she had little resistance left to offer and she answered this question.

Later, there was considerable hostility among the women of the settlement against this one woman, who, they felt, had acted indiscreetly in the first place, arousing the inquisitiveness of the elders, and then had given away some of their secrets for no good reason.

A final aspect of the bond which unites women is to be seen in their songs and dances, some of which suggest a joint hostility towards the elders, and these seem to be a valuable and perhaps necessary form of tension release. Two of these deserve special mention. The first is a series of songs sung by women during male or female circumcision ceremonies. They stand outside the hut in which the boy or girl is resting after the operation and with considerable amusement and laughter they sing ribald songs which refer to the impotence of old men and to the licentious intentions of visiting elders to their huts. The second (*ntorosi*) is a song which is said to give them fertility and cure barrenness in women. They collect together in a large band of perhaps 20 and dance their way from settlement to settlement. Their song is a form of coercion, similar in a number of ways to the boys' circumcision song. In performing it they not only confer fertility on themselves, but also a general prosperity on the families of those men who grant them their requests for a sheep to eat or smaller presents such as tobacco, red ochre or money; and they curse a man who refuses them any gift when they come and sing at his homestead, or who does not allow his own wives to join them. In deciding to sing at the homestead of a particular elder, the women may be influenced by his richness, by the infertility of his wives or even by the fact that he is notoriously harsh with his wives. If it is found out that an elder maltreats his wife for her part in the song, then he may be singled out as a victim on a future occasion. And if he is cursed by the wives for refusing to comply with their requests then the other elders persuade him to give these wives an ox to eat in return for their collective blessing. The words of the song are a prayer to God for children, and in places are openly obscene. If in their journey around the countryside the women come upon an adult male by himself they may grab and manhandle him. This song is not frequently sung, but when it is, the elders prefer to keep well away from the women and to comply with any requests they make. They argue that the song will quickly wear itself out and the women will return to their domestic duties without trouble.

Similar reversals in the behaviour of women where they went round the countryside singing lewd songs and maltreating any men they met have been recorded among the Zulu and neighbouring tribes, although in these instances the avowed intention was the earth's and not their own fertility as with the Samburu. Gluckman has related such reversals to the depressed status of women in these societies, pointing out that they can have a positive value in maintaining social order when there is an underlying conflict; but he also suggests that such conflict could not be stated openly or condoned in a weak system where it is liable to disrupt the system.[1]

These comments seem particularly pertinent to the Samburu. Both their wives and their moran sing songs which imply a certain rebellion against the established social order. And it may be significant that whereas the Samburu are willing to condone these songs from their women who remain essentially under control, arguing that they bring fertility, they do not always condone those of the moran (page 147), even though some of these songs are regarded as a part of the heritage of the moran and form an integral part of certain ceremonies. The moran are not so completely under control as the elders might wish (e.g. example 38).

[1] Gluckman, 1955*b*, Chap. 5.

The meanness of women is a constant topic of conversation among Samburu elders. The respect they show towards their 'fathers' and 'brothers' is not extended to elders in general, and they are deceitful and selfish. A man is expected to treat his guests and visitors with a generous display of hospitality, denying himself and his family in order to offer them food. A wife should also behave with the same magnanimity, but it is rather unusual for her to do so. She is more concerned that she and her children should feed well and is likely to violate the norms of hospitality and to lie unashamedly to any elders. Elders sometimes refer to a particular mean or quarrelsome man and point out that he had no father to bring him up as a boy: his meanness is seen as the product of a woman's rearing.

Conversely, the women say of the elders that they are mean: they alienate stock allotted to their wives for their own private ends, they bully them and they take little notice of their requests. 'Meanness' ultimately depends on how the speaker himself chooses to use the term. It is evident from these mutual accusations that elders and wives have different sets of values based on competing interests, and that this is a source of tension in the society.

Throughout much of the day, women sit together in the shade of a tree inside or close to the settlement, gossiping and often doing some handiwork. The elders sit or lie in the shade of another tree rather farther from the settlement and gossip and hold their discussions. The two groups remain separate and usually out of sight of one another, and each is engrossed in its own affairs and its own view of the world. The elders gossip group has a certain atmosphere of dignity and authority, for it is there that all important decisions are made during discussion and only elders may join it. The women's gossip group has no atmosphere of dignity or authority: small children play around it and it is joined by girls of all ages and a myriad of flies. Elders do not care to associate with it and the moran avoid it altogether. It was not possible to collect any first hand material on the gossiping of women during my field work, but my impression and that of the elders was that it was confined to domestic affairs and long and detailed accounts of recent conversations and happenings. It would not proceed to discussing serious matters of importance as the gossiping of elders frequently did.

On the whole I found women were quite ignorant of many aspects of the total society and usually unhelpful as informants. Outside the affairs of their own family circle they often showed a certain indifference. They were less inquisitive than the males and less quick to grasp situations. They found it harder to comprehend my remarks and questions. I had the impression that they had never been encouraged to show much initiative of their own, and this was a quality which they simply had not developed; any inborn tendencies to this had been baulked by the strictness of their upbringing. Their demeanour was sometimes listless and frequently sour. They often lacked the general conviviality and warmth that typified the adult males, and it was only with the ameliorating circumstances of middle-age that they tended to acquire it – and many never did. Samburu is essentially a man's society and from the male point of view women are inferior and politically uninfluential. Patriarchy is the norm.

Summary

Women throughout their lives have a generally depressed status and this is instilled into them from a very early age so that even the most assertive among them ultimately accept it as a basic fact of existence. It prepares them for marriage which may be regarded as the critical turning point of their lives when they cease to be girls, sisters and daughters in their natal home and clan and become wives and mothers in their husbands' homes and clans possibly many miles away. As they raise families of their own, they acquire a certain status within it and can look forward to living with and depending on their sons for the remainder of their lives, sharing with them the concern over the allotted herd against the predations of the husband and others.

In other words, the notion that women are chattels does not refer to the older, well-established wives so much as to girls and newly wed women. It is only before their marriage has acquired a certain stability and before they themselves have gained a certain status within their husbands' clans, that they are commodities to be bargained for. With increasing age, they have stronger rights of their own.

We now turn to the ceremony which marks the critical turning point of their lives and examine how it prepares them for the unknown times that lie ahead.

Chapter Nine

SOCIAL ATTITUDES AND CEREMONY

THIS chapter is primarily concerned with the effects of ceremony in its broadest sense on the social attitudes of the participants. In the first two sections a detailed account and analysis is given of one particular marriage: apart from the presence of a European (myself), this marriage seemed a typical one, and the points to which I draw attention generally valid. The discussion later turns to other ceremonies observed by the Samburu, and includes in its scope allied forms of behaviour such as dancing and debating. In order to analyse these more fully, I rely to a large extent on a book recently published by a psychiatrist. I do this without apology, as it seems to me that it may not be possible to understand the social function of ceremonial behaviour more fully than we do at present without turning to the findings of psychologists; and other social anthropologists have followed a similar course. I would like to emphasize at the outset that as a non-psychologist, I am only suggesting how an approach might be made to appreciating Samburu ceremony, even if in the text I seem to be too specific and decisive on various points in order to avoid continual circumlocution. The general theme of this study is supported by the various points made in this chapter, but it in no way relies on them. At the worst, this chapter may be regarded as a convenient way of presenting more material on the ceremonial aspects of Samburu society.

Darapul's Second Marriage

59.** In 1959, Darapul, a member of Pardopa clan, married for the second time. This was the culmination of negotiations between him and the elders of Parakeno clan into which he married. It was a critical change in the life of the bride, Nirorol, a girl of about 16: she was married into a new clan and to a man who was perhaps 35 years older than herself, and she was removed to an area of the district where conditions were hotter, drier and harsher than she had ever known.

A kinship diagram of the various persons implicated in the marriage is drawn below in order to facilitate discussion: Darapul was a member of Pardopa clan and Nirorol, the girl he proposed to marry, of Parakeno clan. There had previously been two other marriages which had some relevance to this one. The first was by Legilen, the father of Nirorol, whose junior wife, Sienti, was the daughter of Opori, an old and respected member of Pardopa clan. The second was by Saguya who lived in the same local clan group as Legilen and had married a girl of Darapul's phratry (Lorogushu). It was quite evident to everybody that Darapul's chances of success were

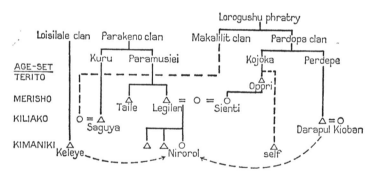

Kinship Diagram: Darapul's second marriage.

enhanced by Legilen's marriage to Sienti, which placed him under a diffuse obligation to comply with the requests of members of Pardopa clan as they were his wife-giving affines. I had been adopted into the same lineage group as Sienti's father, Opori: my own relationship to Legilen was, in fact, that of a fairly close wife-giving affine. In asking me to accompany him during his marriage negotiations and later at the marriage itself, Darapul was drawing attention to this other marriage, and hence to Legilen's obligations towards him.

234

Saguya's marriage was of less immediate importance. He was not closely related to Legilen, and his wife was not a close kinswoman of Darapul. But Saguya and Darapul were age mates; they had known each other as moran (about 1922–36) and had remained on cordial terms since then. The fact that Saguya had married into Darapul's phratry strengthened the bond between them. Saguya showed a ready interest in Darapul's suit, and though he could not effectively influence other members of his local clan group to accept him as the most promising candidate for Nirorol, he could at least give Darapul frank advice, telling him how the other elders of the local clan group were disposed towards him, what they thought of the other suitors, and how he should act. The relationship between Darapul and Legilen was a delicate one at this time, and it was essential that Darapul should have some friend in the vicinity to whom he could turn for advice and hospitality. Saguya was ideally placed to offer these.

Darapul had a second friendship which he could use to his own advantage. This friend was Legilen's elder brother, Taile. Taile lived in the same part of the country as Darapul and knew only too well how rich he was. Darapul obtained his ready support for the suit very early in his negotiations, and he and members of his local clan group treated Taile with great courtesy from that moment, knowing how important it was to retain his support. Legilen was an elder of perhaps 60 years, but Taile was still his older brother and his views had to be respected.

Darapul's initial negotiations with Taile started in March or April 1958; and he first went to Legilen's settlement to ask the elders of his local clan group to consider his suit the following June. By September it transpired that these elders had rejected him in favour of a moran of Loisilale clan, Keleye. Legilen had been especially impressed with this moran and had opposed all other suitors: other elders of his local clan group had decided to support him. For several months it was taken for granted that so far as Darapul was concerned the matter was at an end. But Keleye made the grave mistake of not coming to Taile to ask his permission. He simply took the promises of Legilen and the elders of his local clan group as decisive. This mistake seems to have been due to his inexperience as a moran in handling important affairs. In December Taile announced that he would unconditionally oppose Keleye's suit; it was also rumoured that he had a personal grudge against Keleye's clan and would have opposed the match in any case. By January 1959 it was generally accepted that as Keleye could not marry Nirorol, Darapul was the next most eligible man.

The exact process by which the Parakeno elders resolved their differences of opinion to reach this final decision is not known among Pardopa elders. It is generally accepted as having rested on the divergent views of Legilen and Taile. Both had the power to veto any choice made by the other; but it is unlikely that either would have been prepared to be so determined on having his own way as to offend the other permanently (as has occurred in one or two other recorded cases). It seems more likely that Legilen was prepared to accept Taile's veto on Keleye, and in giving way to him on this occasion he was strengthening his own right to be firm on some other matter of disagreement.

Darapul was anxious by now that he should marry Nirorol as soon as possible before anything else occurred. He went to Legilen's settlement in February to tell him to prepare to perform the marriage that month, but he was overcome by illness (probably pneumonia precipitated by the colder climate where Legilen lived) and the marriage was postponed. Darapul recovered quickly, but as a member of the White Cattle moiety, he could not propitiously marry during the March full moon (*Soom*). Consequently, it was April before he could marry, and this time he was successful.

It had been a full year since he first started negotiating for the girl, and only now was he practically certain of marrying her. The following diary of events refers to the marriage itself. The times of day are only approximate.

17th April. 3.00 p.m. Darapul arrived at Legilen's settlement and formally asked him to extend his hut in order to circumcise Nirorol in six days' time. This would be the fifteenth evening after the new moon had first been seen – the most propitious time for girls to be circumcised and married. He was accompanied by four other members of his clan, one of whom was the principal best man (*chaplkera*), and the others, including myself, took over the duties of best man at certain points, but not in the important parts of the wedding ceremony itself. That night Darapul's party avoided sleeping in Legilen's settlement and went to another Parakeno settlement about a mile away.

18th April. Darapul and Legilen made final arrangements for the ceremony. Then Darapul's party split up to visit various local clan groups of their own clan and agreed to meet again at Legilen's settlement on 23rd April. In point of fact, however, they remained in casual contact with one another during the intervening period.

23rd April. Surprisingly enough, the ceremony had not been deferred even for one day and the circumcision of Nirorol was to take place that evening. This would be preceded by a short ceremony in which she and her lover broke their relationship, from which time they should respect one another as 'brother and sister'. And it would be succeeded by her marriage to Darapul on the next day.

The hut of Nirorol's mother had been extended to make room for a circumcision couch, raised 18 inches off the ground and placed between the sleeping hides and the donkey pack frames (see diagram on page 19). This hut is referred to here as the *circumcision hut* (*nkaji elatim*).

4.00 p.m. Moran of Legilen's clan gathered to take their formal leave of Nirorol, and they went to the hut of a mother of moran inside Legilen's settlement and only 10 yards from the circumcision hut. Foremost among these was Nirorol's lover who was required to break the relationship between them. He had previously killed a sheep and with its fat and some red ochre powder he made a thick paste. He then daubed this paste on to Nirorol's head and shoulders, and on to a girl's (unworn) apron and skirt. He was helped by other members of his Club. Other girls of the area (of all clans but mostly Parakeno) then came to this hut and several of the moran daubed the remainder of the paste onto their heads and shoulders. While they were doing this, the moran sang the song, *ntira*, which amounted to an ineffectual curse on the bridegroom, saying that an unpropitious ox would bring disaster to his herds, that his bride would shortly run away from him, and that he

237

would lose his reason and wander from place to place without purpose. Legilen's own moran sons stayed away from this as the curse indirectly implicated their own father and close kin. Eventually three moran were dragged away from the hut shaking violently and were held firmly by their Club mates. One of these was Nirorol's lover, and when he had recovered sufficiently, he rose to his feet and strode away from the settlement. He was not seen again during the marriage.

5.00 p.m. A woman from the circumcision hut went over to this hut and called Nirorol, who left it and followed her back to the circumcision hut. Milk mixed with water was poured over her outside the hut and she entered and sat on the circumcision couch. Legilen's cattle were then driven through his gateway into the settlement and the operation (clitorodectomy) was performed by a skilled Dorobo woman.

This ended the ceremonial duties for this day. Darapul and his party watched the whole performance from Saguya's yard which was on the opposite side of the settlement to Legilen's. They commented on each phase and were particularly intrigued (and appeared slightly anxious) to see what Nirorol's lover would do when he recovered from his fit of shaking, and they watched him slowly disappear into the distance. Nirorol was now a circumcised but unmarried girl (*siromolei*), and if any determined man wished to marry her he might try to do so by *fait accompli*. For this reason, she was to be married the very next day; and in case there were any attempts at marriage by *fait accompli* (for instance by Keleye, the rejected suitor), the groom's party agreed to keep a careful watch for suspicious signs during the night.

24th April. Most of the ceremonial activities of the marriage were performed on this day. Only the most important details are enumerated here.

6.30 a.m. Darapul and the principal best man left Saguya's gateway. They were dressed in ceremonial clothes, which consisted of blue or green beads across their foreheads, women's brass ear-rings, a woman's apron, strips of lion-skin at their knees, red ochre on their heads, and they each carried a staff and a club. The best man led the sheep of the bridewealth, and other members of Darapul's party followed behind and drove the marriage ox (*erukoret*) and a heifer of the bridewealth. They arrived at Legilen's gate and waited until it was opened by Nirorol's mother. Two women came to take the shoes, staves and clubs of Darapul and the best man, and they led away the sheep; these were all put inside the circumcision hut where Nirorol was still resting on the circumcision couch. Darapul and the best man were given two other staves. The remainder of the party drove in the ox, threw it on its right side, and killed it in front of the circumcision hut. In this act of killing the ox, the marriage was accomplished, although ceremonially it had only just begun. Darapul and his party spent the remainder of the morning cutting up the carcase and sorting out various parts for various categories of people: the elders, the wives, the bride's mother, the woman circumciser, the women who held Nirorol's back and her leg during the operation, the woman who would shortly sew her marriage skirt, the women who collected the shoes, staves and clubs of Darapul and his best man, uncircumcised boys and a blacksmith: each have certain parts of the carcase allotted them, and there was a prescribed way in which certain of these parts had to be cut and presented. Moran, uncircumcised girls, the bride, members of the groom's age-set (apart from those who are kinsmen of the bride) and other members of the groom's marriage party abstained altogether from this meat. One or two elders who were particularly familiar with the ceremonial details stood by, ready to offer their advice.

11.00 a.m. The work of the groom's party was almost complete, and Legilen, dressed in ceremonial clothes identical with those of the groom and best man, was blessed by other elders of his clan as father and guardian of the bride, just outside the doorway of the circumcision hut; while doing this they put butter on his head. Then Legilen and his clansmen went inside this hut, and he gave them all some tobacco and they blessed the hut. These elders then went away to the bush to a spot well concealed from the settlement and ate their portions of the marriage ox communally. Elders of other clans who cared to come along shared in this meal.

12.00 a.m. By now women from neighbouring settlements had gathered to claim meat from their allotted portions of the marriage ox to take back home with them. They collected together just outside the doorway of the circumcision hut, shouting, laughing and chanting their lewd circumcision songs gleefully, led by Nirorol's mother.

The afternoon is normally devoted to dancing by the various social groups, but these dances are not specifically confined to ceremonial occasions as were those of the morning.

2.00 p.m. The women came together to dance, and elsewhere the girls, still wearing the red ochre from the previous day, performed the same dances. The younger elders might have come to dance with their wives, but on this occasion (as on many others) they did not.

3.00 p.m. The dance of the moran, normally the most spectacular of all activities at a marriage, began, but it was slightly disappointing. The Parakeno moran of Legilen's local clan group had mostly gone to support a member of the Club who was marrying on the same day elsewhere, and the Pardopa moran, who might conceivably have come to support Darapul, had also neglected it in favour of other marriage dances. There were only seventeen moran in the dance, belonging to three different Clubs, and no one of these Clubs predominated over the others. The dance quickly progressed from the first tense stage of dances of display to Club dances without any dramatic incident. But there was a vitality missing from the dance and it never developed sufficiently for it to reach the third stage of 'boys' dances'.

One important feature of the day's celebrations was the presence of Opori, Legilen's father-in-law. Legilen had sent one of his moran sons to Opori's home (some eight miles away) to try to persuade the old man to come to the celebrations, and Opori, although he was possibly 75 years old, had come along. Among other things, this gesture by Legilen seemed to draw attention to the fact that he, under a diffuse obligation to Pardopa clan for giving him a wife (Sienti), was acknowledging this obligation by giving one of his own daughters to them in marriage. Throughout the celebrations Opori was given a place of honour by everyone, even in the elders' meat feast which had been provided by his own clan and from which many other Pardopa elders abstained.

8.30 p.m. (when the moon had risen). Darapul formally

presented the heifer driven that morning into Legilen's yard to Legilen. Each touched the beast and said *pa-kiteng* (*nkiteng*=a cow) alternately four times, and this now became a reciprocal term of address between them. Then they went into the circumcision hut with the other elders. The sheep handed over that morning lay by the circumcision couch, and Darapul formally presented it to Nirorol's mother. Each repeated *pa-ker* (*nker*= a sheep) alternately four times, and this too became a reciprocal term of address between them.

The final discussion and handing over of the bride now took place. On the sleeping hides in the corner farthest from the door sat Nirorol's mother, and next to her Nirorol herself was lying, apparently asleep. Darapul sat next to Nirorol, and the best man and other members of the marriage party next to Darapul on the extreme right of the sleeping hides behind the circumcision couch. Legilen and members of his local clan group sat on the floor of the hut around the fire. The discussion lasted more than two hours and was aimed primarily at convincing Nirorol that she must accept the marriage. Elders of her father's clan, including her father, addressed her in stern and persuasive tones, and relentlessly drove home the same point again and again and forced from her the correct replies. The following is a reconstructed version of one of these addresses.[1]

> *Elder:* Nirorol (pause) NIROROL.
> *Nirorol (replying all the time in a listless manner)*: Sir.
> *E.* Do you know who this man is? – *N.* Yes.
> *E.* Is he your husband or isn't he? – *N.* Yes, he is.
> *E.* Do you want him or don't you? (*pause*) Say you want him – *N.* I want him.
> *E.* Do you know why we are giving you to him? Do you know it's because we love you, and we want you to have a good husband? Do you know he is a rich and worthy man and will look after you? (*pause*) Say yes. – *N.* Yes.
> *E.* And your lover. Where is he? Where are his cattle? Could he make a good husband? Wouldn't he beat you all

[1] I was unable to get a tape-recording of any of these addresses, and it must be emphasized that this is a reconstruction. The various points raised by the speaker and the way in which the girl was at times confused in her replies was typical of a number of occasions of this sort which I attended, including Nirorol's marriage.

the time, and starve you, and make you work hard?
(*pause*) Well? – *N*. Yes.

E. Nirorol. – *N*. Sir.

E. Do we love you or don't we? – *N*. Yes.

E. Haven't we brought you up all these years, fed you,
protected you, made you one of us? – *N*. Yes.

E. Doesn't that prove that we love you? – *N*. Yes.

E. And now we are giving you to this man in marriage.
Doesn't this prove we love you? – *N*. Yes.

E. Would he want to marry you if you were not of a worthy
family, if he did not know that you would make a good
wife? – *N*. Yes –

E. WHAT? (*other elders ejaculate and call out: Say No.*) –
N. No.

E. Why do you think we gave you to him and not to one
of the other suitors? Wasn't it because we love you and
respect him? (*pause*) Well wasn't it? – *N*. Yes.

E. And now we have brought you up to make a good wife,
are you going to make a good wife to him? – *N*. Yes.

E. Are you going to bring your family credit as a good wife,
as your 'sisters' have done? Are you going to show your
thanks for all that we have done for you? – *N*. Yes.

E. Do you realize that by doing all these things, you will
show that you are still one of us and we shall always bless
you, but if you disobey us then you will show your in-
gratitude, and we will curse you? – *N*. Yes.

E. Do you know that when we blessed your father this
morning and put butter on his head, we gave him the most
powerful blessing and curse that anyone has over you? –
N. Yes.

E. Do you want him to use that curse? – *N*. (*inaudibly*) No.

E. What did you say? – *N*. (*more loudly*) No.

E. And when you go away, will you do everything your
husband tells you to do? – *N*. Yes.

E. Fetch the water for him? – *N*. Yes.

E. Look after his stock? – *N*. Yes.

E. Bring up his children? – *N*. Yes.

E. Will you keep away from all Kimaniki (moran) and
forget your lover? – *N*. Yes. Etc.

Legilen was the first speaker to address Nirorol and subsequent speakers kept referring to her obligations to him. Saguya also addressed her. These addresses were interspersed with discussion between the elders of Parakeno clan and those of Darapul's party, agreeing on the general principles of a successful marriage, and how Nirorol should be treated. It was on this theme that the discussion was concluded and there was a general blessing.

11.00 p.m. Most of the elders then left the hut, leaving only the bride, her mother, the bridegroom and three of his party (at other marriages simply the one best man) in the hut. The sleeping arrangements were similar to the positions occupied during the discussion, the order being from left to right (facing the back of the hut): Nirorol's mother – Nirorol – Darapul – the best man and other members of Darapul's party.

25th April. 2.00 a.m. While the others slept, the best man rekindled the fire in the hut and started to stew certain portions of meat taken from around the chest of the marriage ox. He was helped at intervals by other members of Darapul's party and by Nirorol's mother. This took them nearly four hours.

6.30 a.m. (dawn). One or two elders came to the hut to give Nirorol personal advice similar to that of the night before and to bless her. Darapul and his party left the hut to drink milk at Saguya's hut.

10.00 a.m. Darapul and the best man returned to the circumcision hut, and a woman shaved some hair from each of their temples and from Nirorol's temple, and mixed these together on a stool. By this act Nirorol was transferred from her father's family to her husband's. Previously she would have shaved her head if her father had died; now instead she would shave her head only if her husband, Darapul, died.

11.00 a.m. Darapul and the best man ceremonially led Nirorol away from her mother's hut. They went to Legilen's gateway where they were given their shoes, staves and clubs back. Then they left the settlement, and passed between two lines of elders (of all clans) who blessed them. Walking slowly in a wide arc to Saguya's gateway, they halted four times. At each halt, the best man found some greenery and placed it on the ground for Nirorol to sit on. After perhaps two minutes they would continue the procession: first the best man, clearing away all stones and pieces of wood from their path, and then Darapul, the groom, and finally Nirorol, the bride with red-ochred head and shoulders and carrying one of the aprons her former lover had covered with red ochre. She was obliged not to look back towards her mother's hut, not to stumble or cross rough ground (hence the best man's precautions) and not to touch the ground with any part of her body or clothing except her feet. She only had a staff to help her sit down and rise without using her hands. This procession ended at Saguya's hut, which they entered. Meanwhile the elders concluded their blessing and went into the circumcision hut to eat the meat which the best man had stewed during the night.

Throughout the day other elders came into Saguya's hut to give the same advice and warnings to Nirorol. Among these, Opori showed great consideration for the girl's feelings. It also became evident on this day that Nirorol's stepmother, Sienti, who was probably not more than five years older than she was, was a close friend of hers, and as a kinswoman of Darapul, she could enter the hut and comfort her.

Darapul's party and Nirorol were now established in Saguya's hut. It was the first occasion that Nirorol had been left informally alone with her husband or members of his party. Darapul himself seemed to be rather embarrassed with the situation and tended to leave the others to make the first attempts at conversation with her. Nirorol (as she later admitted) was rather scared of them, but her emotions were obscured by the same listlessness that she had shown the previous evening, and she continued to say nothing except when replying to any questions more or less automatically. She spent most of the time lying down apparently asleep.

That night Darapul and his party and bride slept in this hut and Saguya and his wife slept elsewhere. (Saguya could not sleep in his own hut for two reasons: first, as host to his age mates and secondly, as a 'brother' to Nirorol, he was obliged to sleep elsewhere. And his wife, as 'sister' to Darapul and his clansmen, had to sleep in another hut also.)

26th April. 8.00 a.m. A short ceremony was performed among Saguya's cattle (the groom, best man, bride and a girl each touched four female cattle, four calves and a bull with their staves) and the two men were then able to take off their ceremonial garb. This also released Nirorol from the ritual prohibitions she had been required to observe on the previous day.

27th April. 10.00 a.m. A special blackened skirt had now been made for Nirorol to wear and she was free to leave with her husband. The elders saw no harm in the journey being made by my car. Other members of Darapul's party found reasons for staying to visit their clansmen in the area, and I was handed the responsibilities of best man from this point.

28th April. 4.00 p.m. We eventually tracked down Darapul's settlement which had moved a number of times since we had left it. Darapul and I entered the settlement while Nirorol remained outside. I was then sent to ask her in. She refused. Then Darapul's senior wife, Kioban, and his brother's widow went to offer her a heifer each from their allotted herds, and eventually she complied. Sitting in Kioban's hut she was given a child to nurse on her knee. For the time being the ceremonial aspects of the marriage were concluded.

Example 57 (page 226) follows directly from this account. Nirorol spent one month in Kioban's hut, and then was allotted her herd of cattle and the other women of the settlement helped her to build her own hut on the same day.

Analysis of Darapul's Marriage

In the above account of Darapul's marriage I have confined myself to observed events without particular reference to the sentiments of those involved. The details of the ceremony conform broadly with Van Gennep's three stages of a 'rite of passage' – separation, transition, integration[1] – although it would be an over-simplification to divide the total ceremony into three distinct stages. For the groom and the best man, the period over which they wore their ceremonial clothes was one of transition where they had to behave and be treated in certain ways, and where they performed all the necessary parts of the ceremony to form the new marital relationship. For

[1] Van Gennep, 'Les Rites de passage', 1909. These are the terms used in the English translation by Vizedom and Caffee, 1960.

Nirorol, at least three rites of passage can be distinguished: the first was when she broke her relationship with her lover (separation), crossed to the circumcision hut (transition) and was circumcised to become a woman (integration); the second was when she left her mother's hut (on 25th April – separation), walked in procession to Saguya's hut under certain ritual restrictions (transition) and then finally performed the small ceremony among Saguya's cattle which removed these (on 26th April – partial integration into Pardopa clan as a wife); and the third was the territorial passage from her parents' home to her husband's when the whole party were under certain ritual restrictions (e.g. not to sleep in the bush and to wear only certain clothes). The total ceremony formed a transition from her status as a girl, mistress and daughter to her new status as a wife and potential mother in a completely different social group.

The point which Van Gennep emphasizes is that the transition of an individual from one social group to another is generally enveloped in ceremony which follows the lines of a rite of passage, and that in primitive societies differences between social groups tend to be more accentuated than in advanced ones, and hence the greater importance of rites in such societies.

In the present section I propose to discuss certain possible psychological implications of these transitions, and their relationship to ceremony. In order to do this, it is first useful to summarize relevant points in a recent book by William Sargant. This is *Battle for the Mind: A physiology of conversion and brainwashing* (1957).

Sargant is primarily concerned with the physiological mechanisms which make it possible for the beliefs and attitudes of individuals to be modified or radically altered, and this leads him to consider the physiological basis of techniques of political and religious conversion. He first of all draws attention to Pavlov's experiments on dogs, especially his later ones. Pavlov's earlier experiments had shown that certain behaviour patterns (conditioned responses) could be built up in dogs under controlled laboratory conditions. In his later experiments he examined ways in which these behaviour patterns could be removed and supplanted by new ones. He found that by submitting the dogs to abnormal mental stress, or by debilitating them in some way (such as by inducing excessive fatigue, fever, intestinal disorders or by castrating them) a breakdown could occur which would interfere with their normal conditioned responses. Sargant refers to this breakdown as 'transmarginal'. Pavlov also found that while these dogs were in a transmarginal state, new patterns of behaviour might be induced in them which would remain after recovery. These new patterns tended to be more permanent in dogs of an inherently stable temperament than in others, and *not* vice versa.

Pavlov evidently felt justified in applying his conclusions on animal behaviour to processes of human thought,[1] and Sargant has no hesitation in doing so,[2] equating positive and negative conditioned responses with positive and negative emotional attitudes. Pavlov found that during some floods in Leningrad when a number of his laboratory dogs were nearly drowned, some of them no longer responded to stimuli to which they had previously been conditioned, but were highly sensitive to the sound or sight of trickling water. Sargant makes it clear that similarly the emotional attitudes of men towards one another or towards ideologies may alter when they are subjected to abnormal mental stress, and that these changes may remain when the cause of anxiety is removed: the two situations are, he says, analogous. He also notes that this change is liable to be more permanent if the subject has a stable personality, and if he tries at first to oppose the change. Mental stress may be produced by fasting, ordeal, threats, prolonged social isolation, debilitation or torture; and under these conditions brainwashing in both religion and politics and eliciting confessions are quite practicable. It is only necessary to force the subject to accept the fact that there is no other way of achieving peace than to accept what is being indoctrinated.

I have drawn attention to this book by Sargant because it seems to have particular relevance to the ordeal which Nirorol went through in the course of her marriage. At first there were the months of uncertainty when apparently one suitor and then

[1] Sargant, 1957, pp. 6, 12, 18–19, 37.
[2] Ibid., pp. 7–8 and Chap. 2.

another was chosen as her husband, and then there was post-ponement when Darapul became ill and might die, and finally in the space of less than 48 hours, her relationship with her lover was completely broken, she was circumcised (debilitation), subjected to a long and exhausting harangue by the elders, made to leave her mother's hut to which she had been attached all her life in a slow procession which after her circumcision looked both painful and exhausting, and from that moment onwards she had to associate closely with unknown men who, as elders, she had been taught all her life to avoid. It was, I suggest, an ordeal which could easily drive her to a transmarginal state and implement the sudden change of status from a girl in her parents' home to a wife in the care of much older men who were also strangers.

At the time of the ceremony, I had not read Sargant's book. My impression was that she was suffering from shock which accounted for her inert behaviour. On the 25th April shortly after she had been transferred to Saguya's hut and we were alone together in the hut, Nirorol told me that she was ill and afraid. During the marriage, the two notions which I believed may have impressed her most were first that every stage of the performance down to the finest detail was in the hands of the elders, and secondly that her only way of retaining a place in society and even of surviving at all was to accept her change in status and transfer to a new social group as inevitable. Whatever freedom she had been allowed with the moran, ultimately she was nothing more than a pawn in the hands of the elders.

The address by the elders on the evening of the 24th April reiterated all the duties and attitudes required of her as a wife, and she responded in a listless and automatic way, sometimes giving the wrong answers and sometimes not answering at first. Sargant draws attention to the listless and confused attitudes of soldiers suffering from battle fatigue.[1] As previously noted (page 142), the verb used by the Samburu for this kind of address, *a-ikok*, also means to 'hit a person in a sore place', and Sargant points out the necessity of finding a 'sore spot' to work upon in

---

[1] Sargant, 1957, pp. 23 and 29.

brain-washing for religious and political ends.[1] In this instance, the sore spot was her relationship with her lover and her obligations towards those who had nurtured her. The address was conducted as if the elders really wanted to help her, and all she had to do was to accept her new role.

If Nirorol was suffering from shock at the time of the address by the elders (24th April), then it is also interesting to note that on the 29th April, less than a week after her circumcision she was sitting among the women of Darapul's settlement and showing evident enjoyment at having made friends with them so easily. For the first time since the ceremony, her own shrewd and blithe personality (unusually so for a Samburu woman) asserted itself. The speed of her apparent recovery was noted by everyone with approval.

During the ceremony, Darapul was not subjected to the same severe mental stress. The marriage affected his relationship with Nirorol, her clansmen and to some extent with his own clansmen, but it did not portend a complete disruption of all his existing social ties. Nor was it an entirely novel situation, for he had married once before. But he did have some cause for anxiety: his first wife had not borne him any sons and was not likely to do so now; he was emaciated and had recently been severely ill (at the time it had been rumoured that he had died); he had been negotiating for this marriage for a year and Legilen had at first rejected his suit. The requirements of the ceremony and the chidings of both his own party *and* Legilen's clansmen only served to increase his discomfort.

Before the ceremony members of his own party continually asked him why, when he had spent so much money on buying presents for his future affines, he had not bothered to buy himself a new cloth to wear for the ceremony, indicating that he was either a pauper or mean: his present cloth was dirty and torn. They also criticized the condition of the marriage ox he was providing and pointed out that it was so thin that Legilen and his clansmen would take offence, and his mother-in-law would scorn him for his meanness. They then found difficulty in obtaining suitable strips of lion-skin for him to wear at his knees. Legilen's clansmen increased his discomfort by reminding him

[1] Ibid., p. 145 (religious) and p. 158 (political).

that they had somewhat unwillingly agreed to his marriage and by asking him for further gifts: they could stop the marriage even at this stage. He soon had to part with a new blanket he had bought himself and he also promised certain gifts of stock and money. In recounting these incidents afterwards, Darapul maintained that these men had had every intention of interfering with the marriage if he did not comply with their eleventh hour requests.

All this occurred on the 17th–18th April, and Darapul had five days in hand before the circumcision in which to put things right. He went to his various friends in the closest Pardopa local clan groups and borrowed strips of lion-skin to wear at the ceremony, and begged two oxen. One of the oxen was to replace his own scraggy marriage ox, and the other was to sell at a cattle sale which was rather conveniently being held at Maralal at the time. With this money he bought himself a new cloth and various gifts for his affines to fulfil at least some of his promises immediately.

His initial anxiety was maintained throughout the ceremony. He was constantly reminded what he should do. He afterwards admitted that he, like everyone else, had wondered if something would go wrong: Nirorol's lover might refuse to break the relationship, even threatening anyone who tried to come and fetch her for circumcision with his spear; during the night of the 23rd–24th April someone might try to accomplish a marriage by *fait accompli*; the marriage ox might be thrown on the wrong side when it was to be killed or it might be found to have some disease when it was opened up; Nirorol might refuse to comply with all that was expected of her during the ceremony or she might slip during the procession from her mother's hut to Saguya's, and so on. Any of these might have some unpropitious effect on the marriage. The whole ceremony had a profusion of detail and the main participants were constantly reminding one another what should be done next and showing some concern from time to time when matters appeared almost out of hand. One or two elders watching the proceedings offered their advice, but this was not always consistent and occasionally added to the confusion. Darapul's role in the ceremony was an active one, unlike Nirorol's which was passive. It was an occasion which attracted a large number of people and Darapul could not avoid being a central figure of attention.

The ceremony permitted certain forms of ritualized protest as when the moran cursed Darapul in their song before and while the circumcision took place, and on the following morning when the women gathered to sing lewd songs at the expense of the elders. As suggested in Chapter Eight, these may well have been useful ways of releasing tension for the singers. But for Darapul they could only serve to heighten his embarrassment: the curse of the moran, though harmless, was directed at him, a firestick elder, and it implied that these moran did not respect him as much as they might other firestick elders at whose marriages they might be silent; and the songs of the women though not specifically directed at him were led by his mother-in-law and sung at the expense of all elders and he was as prominent as any elder on this occasion. His mother-in-law, incidentally, was popularly nicknamed *Nkuba* by the women (a Samburu feminine form of the Swahili term for a chief), because of her skill in leading women's dances; thus Darapul had a double reason for regarding her with some awe.

In addition there was the possibility that some blunder by Darapul would be interpreted as a sign of discourtesy towards Legilen and other members of his clan: it was important that Darapul should wear a new and clean cloth, provide a fat marriage ox, keep away from Legilen's yard except when required to be there, make the right sort of comments during the discussion when Nirorol was being harangued, and maintain a modest bearing throughout the ceremony. He was a centre of attraction and had to be constantly on his guard against such mistakes.

While we were still at Legilen's settlement, Darapul was generally subdued and evidently embarrassed in Nirorol's presence. Once we were clear of the settlement, however, with the bride in our possession he became suddenly elated and started to behave more naturally towards her.

The marriage did not imply a fundamental change in social status and a completely new set of social ties for Darapul as it did for Nirorol, and the minor anxiety he exhibited, caused as much by his embarrassment as by real fears, was not of the same order as her shocked state. But the marriage did implicate his relationships with a number of persons, and the anxiety created by the occasion may well have helped him to orient his attitude towards these persons. Sargant's constant reminder is that at a time of mental stress when men's higher nervous systems are strained beyond the limits of their normal (conditioned) responses, they may be unusually susceptible to suggestion, which may lead to a change in their attitudes. In other words, the anxiety exhibited by Darapul may be expected to have increased his willingness to accept the suggestion – implicit in every action of the ceremony – that his marriage entailed a new set of relationships.

This general approach to ceremony may be compared with the views of Malinowski and Radcliffe-Brown as to the relationship between ceremony and anxiety. Malinowski, referring to 'magical' rites with some specific end, maintains that these are performed in situations in which there is considerable uncertainty from chance factors, and that they serve to allay anxiety and give confidence.[1] Radcliffe-Brown points out that the opposite may also be true: that the rites and associated beliefs may induce anxiety in situations where it might otherwise be absent.[2] Radcliffe-Brown then fits this into his general theory of the social function of ceremony, which is that ceremony (rites) serves to 'regulate, maintain and transmit from one generation to another sentiments on which the constitution of society depends.'[3] For instance, taboos observed by the parents during pregnancy and childbirth among the Andamanese may, he says, engender anxiety in the father; but anxiety over childbirth is a sentiment he should have and hence the taboos help to maintain appropriate social sentiments. If one is to fit this theory to the Samburu marriage ceremony, then the occasion should have filled Darapul with a respect for his affines. This is not altogether consistent with the only joke I heard during the whole ceremony which was that when Darapul had formally handed over the sheep to Nirorol's mother in the presence of all the other elders inside her hut, he

---

[1] Malinowski, 1948, pp. 59 ff.
[2] Radcliffe-Brown, 1952, pp. 148–9.
[3] Ibid., p. 157.

had inadvertently broken wind – an expression of true sentiments. In fact, as I have tried to show, the one sentiment which
the ceremony seemed to succeed in instilling into Darapul was
not so much one of respect for his affines as of a certain degree of
anxiety.

In his analysis of ceremony, Radcliffe-Brown is concerned
with the maintenance and transmission of sentiments rather than
with a marked change in sentiments and he regards anxiety as a
sentiment appropriate to specific occasions rather than as a
means of modifying social sentiments to a new set of relationships. Here, I am suggesting that at a time when social relationships are undergoing change, the uncertainties of the occasion
which Malinowski saw as a cause for anxiety, and the beliefs
and ritual prescriptions which Radcliffe-Brown saw as an
additional cause for anxiety may serve to induce a mental state
in the participants which implements these changes; changes
which Van Gennep realized to be disruptive to social existence.[1]
They increase the suggestibility of the participants so that they
come to accept the changes.

In an extreme instance when a ceremony marks a fundamental
change in social status, as when a girl is married, it has been
shown to be more than a temporary embarrassment, it is a
relentless ordeal. Darapul's anxiety merely served to extend
sentiments which he already had (towards his first wife and her
kinsmen) in new directions; Nirorol's ordeal may have served
to instil into her altogether new sentiments.

This general approach to Samburu ceremony has certain
affinities with Turner's treatment of his Ndembu material.[2]
Turner has suggested that where conflict leads to a mounting
crisis and ultimately to a realignment of social ties, the process
commonly follows a set pattern which he has called 'social
drama'. The ceremonies we have examined here are of a
different order, since they concern the conflicts that *arise from*
prescribed changes in relationships and shifts in status, rather
than conflicts that *lead to* such changes. But, both Ndembu social

[1] Van Gennep, p. 3. It is not altogether clear whether Van Gennep regarded
such changes as a possible source of 'discomfort or injury' because of the action of
supernatural forces, or because of purely social ones. I have taken him to mean the
latter.

[2] Turner, 1957, chapter 4.

drama and Samburu ceremony are only intelligible with reference to the structural forms of the two societies, they are critical points at which relationships (and hence attitudes) are changing, and anxiety over these changes becomes evident. Samburu ceremony, then, is not a social drama in Turner's sense of the term; but it could be regarded as a controlled social drama in which the element of individual spontaneity and freedom is heavily suppressed.

Boys' Circumcision and Ilmugit Ceremonies

It was shown in an earlier chapter that male initiates experience both a change in status and a mental ordeal during circumcision. This provides further material on which to consider the present hypothesis that Sargant's work is applicable to an analysis of ceremony. Sargant does consider the ordeal that initiates undergo during initiation rites in West Africa and New Guinea, and the inculcation of new social attitudes.[1] The present section is largely a confirmation of the points he makes by extending his arguments to the Samburu.

The period preceding circumcision was shown to be one of considerable strain for the initiates: the prospects of pain involved in the operation and the possibility that they might flinch seemed to be a greater ordeal than the operation itself; and the way in which elders and moran were losing confidence in them as the time drew near must have increased their apprehensiveness. During the 24 hours before the first circumcisions they were generally subdued, a number of them shivered, at least one of them developed a facial twitch and another a fixed frown.

The thought present in everyone's mind at this moment was whether any initiate would flinch, and this entailed honour. In so much as the anxiety created by the ceremony could induce any new attitude in the initiates it might well be the association of this notion of honour with their new relationship to family, clan and age-set. Honour would not be an entirely foreign notion to them, but the gravity and intensity of the ceremony could introduce a new significance. Might it, I wonder, explain

[1] Sargant, p. 94.

to some extent why honour is of such importance during moran-hood? Almost as if by accident, it becomes the crucial issue during circumcision, but the very fact that it is a crucial issue could, it is suggested, have a pronounced effect on the values accepted by the initiates after their circumcision.

The material available does not seem to justify any analysis along the lines of circumcision as a symbolic form of castration to prepare the initiates for the years of bachelorhood that lie ahead. But, nevertheless, it is still worth noting that circum-cision is a form of debilitation sanctioned and organized by the elders which precedes a time when the initiates are to be subordinated to the will of the elders. And one other aspect of the ceremony which may well have impressed them was that in every detail and at every stage, it was under the control of the elders, especially the firestick elders. The initiates had to do at each stage what they were told. From beginning to end they seemed thoroughly bewildered. They had no idea what signifi-cance their actions had, whether these were to avoid mystical misfortune or show respect to the elders; they only knew that to flinch meant dishonour. Thus a second notion which may have been instilled or reinforced at this stage was that they belonged to a society which was controlled by the elders.

The period of change-over is one full of intense interest for the Samburu. It has far-reaching implications for most people in the society and concerns not only their membership of various age grades, but also, in certain cases, of clans. It is a time when boys living with their maternal kin may be recalled by fellow initiates of their father's clans, and when elders whose wives have been married previously to other men may want their sons to be circumcised young so that the first husbands can no longer exercise any claim over them. The circumcision cere-monies are the climax of this change-over which altogether takes a number of years. On page 105, the concern which elders and moran showed during the circumcision of their close kins-men, especially at the prospect of their own sons and brothers flinching, suggests that the situation was sufficient to revive their own ingrained notions of honour associated as it was with circumcision, the lineage and the herd. It seems possible that this anxiety may have helped to induce them to accept the change in relationships which this change-over involved. *Once everyone could be made to accept it*, it would be fully accomplished and the problems it raised would be solved.

A characteristic feature of moranhood which follows initiation is that it constantly points back to it: for the age-set system, circumcision can be regarded as an 'initial situation': words commonly used with reference to this system, *lmurani* (a moran, warrior) and *murata* (an age mate, the correct reciprocal term of address to any age mate who is not known by a more familiar term) are basically similar to *lmura* (a penis) and *emuratare* (circumcision). In *ilmugit* ceremonies, too, there is an identical layout of the settlements (see page 92) to that of circumcision with an emphasis on the order of birth of full brothers and performance by each Club separately. And, of course, the *ilmugit* ceremonies are in the hands of the elders.

In order to consider the social function of *ilmugit* ceremonies, it is convenient to follow Chapple and Coon's elaboration of Van Gennep's 'rites of passage'. Chapple and Coon point out that certain ceremonies are performed periodically and do not mark any change in social relationships.[1] They refer to these ceremonies as 'rites of intensification'. The authors state that in rites of passage, individuals are conditioned to adapt themselves to a new pattern of interaction that follows from a change in social relationships, whereas in rites of intensification, the existing pattern of interaction is periodically reinforced.[2] Sargant also draws attention to the need for new doctrines to be consolidated through periodic reinculcation and communal meetings (and hence the relative permanence of Wesley's sect and the impermanence of Billy Graham's). In certain respects Chapple and Coon's rites of passage correspond to Radcliffe-Brown's 'transmission of sentiments' and their rites of intensification correspond to his 'maintenance of sentiments'.

It is with reference to rites of intensification that the *ilmugit* ceremonies can most clearly be understood. The hypothesis here is that at circumcision certain values were instilled into the initiates, and that these are reinstilled at the periodic *ilmugit*

[1] Chapple and Coon, Chaps. 20 and 21.
[2] Ibid., pp. 484 and 527.

ceremonies. The elders regard *ilmugit* ceremonies essentially as times when they can gather the moran together and harangue them. They are a means by which the moran can gain a sense of respect. This, they often say, is the prime purpose of *ilmugit* ceremonies. It was only when I asked them specifically what would happen if the ceremonies were not held that they said it would be unpropitious.

It cannot be denied that certain *ilmugit* ceremonies are also rites of passage, but their principal function does appear to be the reinforcement of the notion of a sense of respect rather than a fundamental adjustment of social relationships. Of the three types of *ilmugit* ceremony previously distinguished (pages 164–6), the first type, performed at each point of promotion of the age-set, was a rite of passage as well as of intensification; whereas the second and third types, performed respectively when mis-behaviour was expected from the moran and when their cor-porate unity and morale were low, were rites of intensification pure and simple. This is quite consistent with the suggestion in Chapter Six that the *ilmugit* ceremonies brought the moran into a specific relationship with the remainder of the society, thus counteracting the tendency for anomie to develop among them.

Chapple and Coon's distinction between rites of passage and rites of intensification is perhaps a little too rigid, and they overlook those aspects of a rite of passage which serve to maintain social sentiments and make it in a sense also a rite of intensification. Thus the ceremonial behaviour of the moran at a marriage, in putting red ochre on the heads and shoulders of girls, singing *ntira*, abstaining next day from the meat of the marriage ox and dancing in the afternoon does not accompany any change in social relationships for most of them. Their behaviour must be regarded as a rite of intensification in which the notion that they must all, sooner or later, relinquish their mistresses and allow the elders to dispose of them as they wish is reinforced. Any anxiety which a marriage ceremony evokes for these moran should be regarded, in fact, as a temporary climax of the mental stress to which they are subjected throughout their moranhood rather than as a direct result of the specific change in social relationships of this particular occasion. The part played by girls in a marriage has a corresponding function of instilling into them the same notions with regard to their own future marriages.

It is worth noting that Chapple and Coon treat rites of passage and intensification as being intelligible in terms of Pavlovian psychology, and throughout their work they emphasize the relevance of Pavlov's 'conditioned responses'. They outline his findings in an early chapter, but make no mention of his later experiments which form the basis of Sargant's book, and in neglecting this they seem to have missed a very important aspect of these ceremonies: the relationship between anxiety or transmarginal states and the reorientation of social attitudes.

In trying to account for the nature of symbolism in ceremony, Chapple and Coon point out that through the mechanism of conditioned responses men come to associate certain objects with certain patterns of interaction (social relationships); they then follow Radcliffe-Brown in suggesting that through this association such objects acquire a symbolic significance in ceremony and the ceremony reinforces the relationships involved. These objects are largely derived from the technology of the society in question.[1] Thus immediately before an evening circumcision of either a boy (page 105) or a girl (page 238), the cattle of the homestead have to be driven into the yard; and it may be argued that the cattle, an essential part of Samburu economy, are closely associated with the family, and the status of the initiate with respect to his or her family is undergoing a change; furthermore on her circumcision and marriage a girl is replaced by new acquisitions to the herd (her bridewealth) which incidentally she should avoid, and after his circumcision a boy with no father or elder brother can alienate stock from the herd without reference to his guardian: in other words the status of an initiate with respect to the herd also changes. Similarly, the sharing of meat by moran at an *ilmugit* ceremony might be related to the importance of food in the society, confirming their solidarity and fellowship through commensality rather as Robertson Smith argued.[2]

[1] Chapple and Coon, p. 508.
[2] Robertson Smith, p. 265.

Sargant, on the other hand, suggests another approach to the study of symbolism which supplements this one. He points out that just as Pavlov's dogs caught by the floods became highly sensitive to the sight or sound of trickling water, so in primitive societies men may have become sensitive to objects or actions originally associated with their initiation.[1] It follows that such symbols would acquire a far greater emotional significance. This may account for all those characteristics of moranhood which, it was noted, are associated in the first place with initiation ceremonies. The cattle driven through the gateway before circumcision are more than just the means of subsistence for the family over which there is a change in rights and duties: they become associated with family honour. Similarly, it is not just shared meat at an *ilmugit* ceremony which brings the moran into closer fellowship: there are also those countless occasions when they must go hungry together, even when food is available, and share many other anxious and dispiriting moments. These also serve to bring them together (page 131).

Van Gennep notes that in any rite of passage, there tend to be many stages which can broadly be classified as a process of separation–transition–incorporation.[2] Initiation rites can, he notes, last as long as six years in exceptional cases.[3] But unaccountably, when discussing early material available for the Masai tribe,[4] he fails to note that the whole period of moranhood, with its many ritual prohibitions and ceremonies, can be regarded as an extended period of transition between circumcision when a youth is separated from his mother's home and his eventual incorporation into his own home many years later, after his marriage.

Among the Samburu – and I assume that the situation is essentially similar among the Masai – circumcision is a rite of separation, moranhood with its prohibitions, association with the bush and *ilmugit* ceremonies is a prolonged rite of transition, and the final blessing by the elders when a man is allowed to

---

[1] Sargant, p. 97.
[2] Van Gennep, p. 11.
[3] Ibid., p. 81.
[4] Ibid., pp. 84–7.

relax the food restrictions of moranhood is a rite of incorporation into elderhood (along with other rites of this stage).

'Rites of transition' is the term used by Chapple and Coon and by the recent translators of Van Gennep's work for the second stage of a rite of passage. But Van Gennep himself refers to *'rites de marge'*. The term *marge* is particularly apt when referring to the separateness of those implicated from the remainder of the society: they have a marginal position. The ritual and social separateness of the moran from the remainder of the society has been stressed previously. Throughout their moranhood they are marginal. And the duress under which they are continually placed may perhaps be regarded as a counterpart of the anxiety noticed among participants in other rites of passage.

Dancing

In Chapter Five some mention was made of the dances performed by the moran, but apart from outlining the context in which they occurred and certain tensions which they revealed, no closer analysis was made of them. In order to do this here, other aspects of Sargant's work are considered.

Sargant does not give a succinct account of the psychological implications of dancing, but in different parts of his book he does refer to two types of dances which are clearly distinct. The first type he associates with religious cults, where the excitement of intense rhythmic drumming and dancing may lead to the physical and emotional collapse of a performer, who believes himself – or is believed – to be possessed by some supernatural force; if the dancing is skilfully led by a priest, a transmarginal state may be induced in the dancers increasing their suggestibility and this may have the effect of maintaining their religious beliefs; in exceptional cases these beliefs may even be implanted in the minds of outsiders.[1] Stripping this type of dance of certain cultural elements such as the presence of a priest, the belief in supernatural possession and beliefs which are specifically religious, one may perhaps regard it as one in which the performer is excited to the point of a transmarginal breakdown. The second type of dance is a means

[1] Sargant, pp. 89 ff.

by which nervous energies built up through previous mental stress may be released: this type, one gathers, is more spontaneous than the first type and has no associated beliefs.[1] Sargant calls a process through which nervous energies can be released by the term *abreaction*.

Now both of these types of dancing seem to be present among the moran as previously described on pages 120 to 127, and they correspond broadly to the various phases through which a single dance was seen to evolve.

The initial phase of a daytime dance when members of different Clubs come together is one of the dances of display. In the presence of rivals, the moran are said to be angry and they boast of their own prowesses as potential warriors and of their achievements as stock thieves. This frequently leads to shaking among a number of moran and occasionally to fighting. Honour is at stake during this phase; and in so far as these dances increase anxiety among the moran sufficient to cause them to break down it is their notion of honour which they associate with them. This phase seems to correspond closely with the first type of dance described by Sargant where attitudes (this time the notion of honour and not any religious beliefs) are reinforced through inducing a transmarginal state.

During the second phase of the dance when Club dances are performed, the girls play a definite role. These dances again take the form of vying, but this time between the sexes and not between different moran or Clubs, and they are more relaxed and playful. In so far as the honour of the moran is not implicated during this dance and they perform it with an obvious elation, it corresponds to the second type of dance described by Sargant where nervous energies are released. At the same time, this dance may be sufficient to instil Club notions and the value of stock theft into the minds of certain moran, as suggested in the statement by one moran quoted on page 127, and to this extent it belongs to Sargant's first type.

The third and fourth phases, those of 'boys' dances' and what I have called 'play', are entirely ones in which nervous energy is released rather than built up, and no ideas or values are expressed.

[1] Ibid., p. 52.

Now this process bears a striking resemblance to the abreaction induced in patients suffering from combat exhaustion and shell shock during the second world war in order to cure them.[1] Under drugs they were encouraged to re-live the combat experiences or analagous and even imaginary situations until they entered a transmarginal state when repressed emotions associated with the incident could be released and they would be cured. In order to achieve a satisfactory abreaction it was necessary first of all to bring their repressed emotions to a head.

Among the Samburu moran, as I see it, they are driven into a transmarginal state by the display dances of the first phase and the notion of honour which divides them from each other is brought to a head and released. These dances are explicitly associated with aspects of their life which concern their honour, and it is honour which, since the time of their circumcision has been their most treasured and their most brittle value. Only once this has been achieved can they relax sufficiently to enjoy the dances of the later phases without showing animosity. But they are still divided as a group from the girls, and in the second phase of the dance, by a similar though less dramatic process, this barrier too is broken down leading to a completely relaxed relationship between the dancers.

It is fairly inevitable that the moran should have to work off the tension that separates them from one another before they work off the tension that separates them from girls: any lessening of the tension between sexes *before* a lessening of tension between moran would only produce an increased rivalry and tension among the moran. Viewed in the context of the general strain under which they are living during their moranhood, these dances can be seen as a temporary though valuable outlet for these nervous energies. In a sense their behaviour becomes progressively juvenile in the course of the dance: the strains under which they live are the product of their society and upbringing, and by lifting these strains they become little more than children again.

Not all dances of the moran conveniently follow this general pattern. A number of moran may leave the dance during its first phase after a bout of shaking or the dance may end in a

[1] Sargant, pp. 42 ff.

minor affray: in such instances the build-up of tension during this phase has led to a different type of tension release which does not allow further more relaxed phases. On the other hand, in the moran dance performed at Darapul's marriage to Nirorol, there was no increase in tension during the initial phase, and significantly, the dance did not progress to a more relaxed phase: it just petered out without having achieved anything. This is also common.[1]

Shaking

It has been noted that shaking may be exhibited by the moran on various occasions: several moran shook during an initiation ceremony when they were about to be replaced by a new age-set (page 105); several moran of one Club shook during a dance when they were being outvied in front of their own girls by the Club which had come to take away one of their girls in marriage (page 123); and several moran shook at the final moment when a girl (a mistress of one of them) was being taken away for circumcision and marriage (page 238). When they shake, the moran say that they are angry and want to assert themselves in some way and it is worth noting that all these situations were ones of frustration for those who shook.

At first they shiver (*a-ikirikir*=to shiver), and then they either recover from this or the shivering gives way to uncontrolled shaking (*a-ipush*=to shake) at which point they have to be forcibly held from possible violence or hurt to themselves: the subjects themselves claim to have lost all consciousness once they have started to shake. The term for 'to be angry' is *a-goro*, which is the inflexive form of the verb 'to strangle' (*a-gor*). During the dances of display in particular, where the moran say they are angry, their chorus is a rhythmic growl –

---

[1] Radcliffe-Brown has suggested that the dance is a means of producing harmony among the performers by joint action (1922, p. 235).

Professor Evans-Pritchard has contested this view, pointing out that harmony is not always achieved, and he regards the dances as a means of canalizing the forces of sex into socially harmless channels (1928, pp. 456 ff.).

Each of these points may to some extent be applied to Samburu dancing: disharmony prevails at first; and the initial phase serves to break this down, allowing harmony and a sexual outlet to be achieved in the later phases.

almost a suppressed bellow not unlike a bull's – and at each sound they press their heads forward and up so that their throats are considerably constricted; this corresponds fairly closely to their behaviour when shaking. Thus there seems to be a definite verbal association between the emotion they associate with this (anger) and the behaviour they display when shaking.

The three situations quoted above are not only ones of frustration, they are also ones in which the moran are constrained to act in certain ways rather than give way to their most natural impulses which might have been to attack the initiates (as one of them tried to do), to attack the moran of the other Club (as occurs from time to time), or to prevent the elders from taking away the girl for circumcision (which is occasionally done by a moran, guarding his mistress with his spear until he can be coerced by other moran and elders to allow events to take their inevitable course).

Initiates awaiting circumcision may shiver, so may a moran when woken up or suddenly surprised, or when being blessed by elders. Moran on a criminal charge before a government officer are said sometimes to shake and so are Samburu soldiers serving in the King's African Rifles when on parade or under ambush. The army officers who have reported that the Samburu shiver under ambush have also praised them as exceptionally fine soldiers. Shivering is not a sign of cowardice on the battlefield any more than it was among the initiates immediately before their circumcision. Mpaayei writing of shaking among the Masai states that 'a warrior goes into a sort of shaking trance, which makes him irresistible in battle, but quite irresponsible'.[1]

The Samburu regard shivering and shaking as signs of manliness, an indication of the assertive qualities expected of the moran. As they settle down to elderhood by degrees, they cease to shake altogether and shivering is very unusual.

Shaking is now examined as a form of transmarginal breakdown brought about by a combination of mental stress *and* the susceptibility of moran to it. The period of moranhood is one of

[1] Mpaayei, 1954, p. 53.

duress, and shivering and shaking seem to occur mainly in situations when duress is rather greater than usual.

It is first necessary to realize that the moran are predisposed to shaking. It is expected of them especially in certain circumstances. As they grow up they may start to shiver and even shake before they have been circumcised, and as they settle down to elderhood they cease to do so. That shaking may perhaps be regarded as a conditioned response is confirmed by the ex-K.A.R. soldier who said that being on parade was like being on display in a dance and this was what made them shiver. In other words, although the situations in which moran break down and shake may often be ones where their higher nervous systems are strained beyond the limits of their normal conditioned responses, the way in which they respond to these situations is conditioned and they are prone to the same sort of breakdown in other less critical moments.

Secondly, shaking occurs in situations where they are under duress, and at such times their suggestibility is increased. This accounts for the fact that when one moran breaks down in a shaking fit, others may quickly follow suit. This was particularly evident in the first two of the three examples quoted above.

Now, following Sargant's general analysis, a transmarginal breakdown may have one of two consequences: it may accompany a release of nervous energy (abreaction) or it may accompany a change or an intensification of sentiments.

When a moran shakes at a dance and is led away from it, but later rejoins the dance in its subsequent phases, then his shaking may perhaps be regarded as a form of abreaction; it has relieved him of his nervous energies in a more dramatic, but essentially similar manner to the other dancers.

At other times there may be both release of tension *and* an acceptance of a new state of affairs, and this seemed to occur in the other two examples quoted above. At the initiation of the Kishili age-set, the minor affray and shaking among the moran seemed to accompany a release of the general anxiety even though only two of the 17 circumcisions had been completed. The senior moran told me afterwards that they had hated that day more than any other in the course of the change-over, but they now accepted the fact that a new age-set had indeed been brought into being. At the marriage, the shaking of the bride's lover may have accompanied a similar release of anxiety *and* a changed attitude towards his relationship with his mistress: their affair was now utterly at an end.

In other contexts shaking may accompany a reinforcement of existing sentiments. The most intense shaking which the moran are said to experience occurs when they eat large quantities of meat and soups mixed with certain roots in the bush. They maintain that it is these foods which cause a state of general apprehensiveness and the slightest shock can make them shake violently. This may be followed by a week or 10 days of apathy, during which period the very smell of women or anything associated with the settlement will, they say, make them vomit. They are associated with the bush and they have eaten foods which no married woman has been allowed to see. It would seem that their experience has made them unduly sensitive to the avoidance they must observe with married women and its association with the food they eat, and has intensified their association with the bush. It is said that when a moran eats some meat and later finds out that a married woman has actually seen it, he will vomit with disgust.

The blessing which follows a harangue by the elders is liable to produce shaking, and this also occurs at a time when the expected sentiments of the moran are being reinforced by the elders. The following blessing of the moran was given at the *ilmugit* of the bull ceremony performed by the Pardopa moran at Nkaroni in 1958 (see the map on page 92):

60.** For about 10 days before the performance of the *ilmugit* ceremony, the elders and moran periodically held separate discussions; and the moran were given four or five harangues, each lasting several hours. The main theme of these harangues was that the moran did not have a sufficiently developed sense of respect and that this retarded them in their progress to elderhood. This was, they said, most apparent from the open way in which they stayed close to certain settlements where there were attractive young wives and from the large number of accusations of adultery recently levelled against them. They argued that it was dangerous for the moran to provoke the anger of the elders by their bad behaviour since this might tempt them to use their curse. They urged the moran to discuss the matter among themselves so that they could reaffirm their sense of respect. In their own discussions the moran did in fact acknowledge the essential truth of the accusations levelled against them and did not express any open or hidden hostility for the elders.

At about 9.00 p.m. on the evening before killing the first ox in the ceremony, the moran were called over to the elders' enclosure for a blessing. There were about 25 elders of all age-sets and 40 moran of the Kimaniki age-set. This was preceded first by separate discussions by the elders and by the moran, and then by a harangue. At each new stage of the evening's activities a spiral kudu horn was blown by a moran at the instigation of the elders. Finally, it was time for the blessing. To the sound of the horn an intense fire was built up between the elders and the moran: the former protected their bodies from the heat by drawing up their blankets, but the moran only had short loin-cloths and were exposed to it.

Two firestick elders, one of them the redoubtable Keseker, led the blessing invoking the protection of God on the *moran*. 'May *Nkai* look after you. . . . May *Nkai* give you life. . . . May *Nkai* look after you. . . . May *Nkai* give you peace. . . . May *Nkai* give you good fortune. . . .' etc. The invocations were very similar to those quoted at greater length on page 178. At each pause the other elders waved their up-raised staffs and chanted, '*Nkai* . . . *Nkai* . . . *Nkai* . . .' rhythmically, and continued to do so even when the invocations were drowned by the general tumult. A moran was also blowing the horn in time with the rhythmical chanting.

As they began their invocations, the two leading firestick elders splattered the bodies of the moran with a mixture of milk and water. The touch of the cool liquid on their bodies exposed to the heat of the fire caused many of them to squeal and jump. And immediately three started to shake and perhaps a dozen started to shiver. Relentlessly the blessing continued, and the gasps of the shaking moran and the chant of elders and the sound of the horn practically drowned the words of the invocation. Some shaking moran partially recovered, and others started to shake and had to be held. Eventually the moran blowing the horn fell shaking and had to be held by about five other moran. Another moran picked up the horn and started to blow, but he began to shake immediately, and the horn was taken over by a third moran who had some difficulty in keeping the time and just blew it continuously. After about six minutes, there were five shaking moran who were being forcibly held by both moran and elders, and a dozen other moran who were either shivering or shaking. There was no moran who was not either shivering or shaking or holding a shaking moran. At this point the blessing stopped.

In this incident, the blessing started abruptly and there was a sudden and relentless build-up to the climax which was maintained throughout. At one moment, the moran were standing half-naked before the blazing fire and waiting, and then it started; their heated bodies were suddenly stung by the cool mixture of milk and water, the leading firestick elders were shouting the invocations of the blessing more or less at them, the other elders were chanting 'Nkai . . . Nkai . . . Nkai . . .', and the horn was blowing almost deafeningly in time with the chant. The association of so many of these features with circumcision and the power which the elders hold over them may well have been sufficient to increase the apprehensiveness of the moran and induce shaking. It has much in common with the circumcision operation where each initiate has first to wash himself quickly with a similar mixture of milk and water, and then he is suddenly surrounded by a crowd of shouting elders excitedly telling both the initiate and the circumciser what they should do. The constant use of the horn, only used at ceremonies, important discussions, or when some enemy raiders are discovered in the vicinity, added to the impressiveness of the occasion, and it, too, has powerful associations for the moran: they say that the sound of it, especially in the presence of the elders, makes them feel angry and want to shake. In other words, such features as the mixture of milk and water, the horn, the concentrated attention of the elders may retain their potent associations from previous occasions. It also seems feasible that any extent to which the elders managed to impress the moran with the weight of their power over them on this occasion when there was a blessing would also engender a greater dread of their curse. Paradoxically, both the curse *and* the blessing over the moran are oppressive, and not as complementary as they may seem at first sight.

Another important factor which may have helped to induce the shaking was the rhythmic chanting of the blessing, for 'certain rates of rhythm can build up recordable abnormalities of brain function and explosive states of tension sufficient even to produce convulsive fits in predisposed subjects.'[1]

Sargant pays particular attention to John Wesley's techniques of gaining converts among his hearers. And certain aspects of Wesley's meetings resemble to some extent the harangue quoted above. Wesley would first agitate his audience with threats of eternal hellfire (just as the elders warned the moran of the unpropitious consequences of their behaviour) and then he would suggest to them that salvation could be gained through conversion (just as the elders would persuade the moran of their general security from ill-fortune once they acquired a sense of respect). Wesley's preaching would have a powerful effect on his hearers: 'Some sunk down, and there remained no strength in them; others exceedingly trembled and quaked; some were torn with a kind of convulsive motion in every part of their bodies, and that so violently that often four or five persons could not hold one of them.'[2]

Sargant points out that religious conversion, political conversion, or for that matter conversion to any absolute philosophy, have similar basic physiological explanations although the contents of belief may belong to quite different spheres. It is quite natural, then, that the inculcation of certain values in the moran, such as honour, respect, avoidance of married women and acceptance of their own childishness compared with the maturity of the elders, should have a similar basis. And as was stated earlier, the gaining of respect is one of the prime purposes of *ilmugit* ceremonies, harangues and blessings; and the moran acknowledge this purpose.

A further possible cause for shaking is suggested by the Samburu themselves. This is that the roots which the moran mix with their soups do in fact have certain properties which cause shaking. In other words, it may be that these roots are similar to the drugs which Sargant and others have administered to their patients to induce an abreaction. In order to examine this possibility, samples of the four most potent roots, according to Samburu reckoning, were collected and sent for laboratory

[1] Sargant, p. 88.
[2] Sargant, p. 82. Quoted from Wesley's 'The Journal of John Wesley'.

testing, and in every case the findings were wholly negative.[1]
Thus, accepting these tests as conclusive, the roots appear to
have no chemical properties which might induce shivering or
shaking, and one is forced to conclude that this behaviour has
a purely psychological and social explanation. The drug
explanation offered by the Samburu may be excluded.

The Discussion

It is even possible that at these occasions when the elders
establish and maintain their ascendancy over the moran they
also condition them to accept as a matter of course all decisions
made by elders in discussion, and that the moran retain this
acceptance *after* they have settled down to elderhood.

My impression was that the great majority of Samburu elders
were prepared to follow the decisions made by other elders in
discussion without questioning the wisdom of this or even
bothering always to listen too attentively to what was being
said. It was sometimes bewildering to notice a complete change
in attitude among informants after an important discussion.
Beforehand they would state certain firmly held views on such
topics as grazing schemes or the moran or stock theft, and would
go apparently determined to present these views. At the discussion itself many of them would remain silent throughout.
And when afterwards some quite different course of action had
been agreed to by the elders they would recount the new views
with apparently as much conviction as before and without any
show of insincerity or embarrassment. It was as if they identified
themselves completely with this new view without any question
of having previously thought differently. It would seem that in
their discussions as elsewhere, the Samburu are most susceptible

---

[1] The first three roots tested which are said to make the Samburu shake were
lkitalaswa (Myrica kilimand scharica Engl. var. macrophylla Engl.), *lkinyil*
(Rhamnus prinoides l'Herit), and *seketeti* (Myrsine africana L.) ; and the fourth which
is said to make the moran unusually quarrelsome was *loiraur* (Cussonia sp.). I am
very grateful to Dr. John A. Lock of the Pharmacology Department, Makerere
College for making these tests, identifying the plants and for permission to quote his
results. Dr. Lock writes, 'None of them shewed any central nervous system stimu-
lant effect when extracts were injected intra-peritoneally in relatively large doses to
mice. All, however, shewed a purgative action.' I can vouch for the purgative
action.

to suggestion and this is very consistent with the emphasis on conformity in the society.

The formal etiquette of discussion among the elders has already been presented (pages 175 ff.). It was noted that they may discuss general topics of interest during their gossiping, but when some issue is raised about which a collective decision is required then the gossiping turns to debate. During the debate, the other elders may start shouting at any man who does not follow the correct etiquette or who indicates that he does not agree with the view of the majority. Apart from the practical use in deciding issues, debates also provide a means for men to air and work out their grievances.

It is now suggested that the very atmosphere created in a debate has many features in common with ceremony – both its collective and ritual aspects – and these may be sufficient to predispose the participants to adopt a unanimous attitude. Any man who obstinately does not agree is liable to become the focus of interest and coercion. A debate at which a really serious issue is at stake is also liable to be one in which argument is fierce and prolonged, and anxiety is raised to fever pitch.

If discussion is to be viewed alongside the other topics of this chapter, it would seem to be a combination of abreaction in which certain anxieties are allayed or worked out, of adjustment to a new state of affairs as dissident participants come to accept the views of the majority, and of a rite of intensification in which certain ethical and social principles are asserted and confirmed in public.

Misfortune and Beliefs in the Supernatural

It should be evident from Chapter Seven that Samburu beliefs in the supernatural influence their behaviour considerably. If they did not believe in the efficacy of the curse then the society and existing mechanisms of social control would be altogether different. These beliefs are instilled into all Samburu from a very early age and are constantly reaffirmed in their conversations with one another. It has already been shown that in a ceremonial context these beliefs add to the general anxiety of the occasion.

271

The maintenance of these beliefs is worth some consideration as they do appear to have a considerable degree of permanence in spite of evidence suggesting that specific beliefs occasionally change. In this chapter the primary concern has been with the assimilation of new social attitudes. Following Sargant it has been suggested that this is possible because at times of mental stress an individual is more prepared to accept new ideas and attach an emotional significance to them than at other times. As a corollary to this it follows perhaps that unexpected misfortunes could produce the necessary mental stress for a new belief to be suggested and accepted. 'The anxiety engendered by the Fall of France, the Battle of Britain and the Blitz created a state in which large groups of persons were temporarily able to accept new and sometimes strange beliefs without criticism.'[1] The following incident illustrates the suggestibility of the Samburu following an unexpected tragedy.

61.** After the Masula moran at Ngelai had attacked the elders (page 158), discussions were held by the Masula elders, to decide what disciplinary measures they should take against the moran in addition to the fine imposed by the administration.

One night in this area, a moran was lying inside a hut and he heard a commotion in the yard. He left the hut to investigate it, and he was killed instantly by a rhinoceros which had broken into the settlement. No one would touch his body, even to lay it in the correct mortuary posture. They packed their huts and left the settlement site in the small hours of the morning.

Rumours of the incident travelled around the countryside quickly during the next day, and the elders gossiped about it in earnest tones. To them any violent death was unpropitious, but that of a moran inside a settlement was doubly unpropitious, for moran should only die in the bush. A few days later, I was told that this particular moran had played a most unpropitious part in the affray. The immediate cause of the affray had been the jealousy of one man over his wife. During the affray, this moran had led an attack against the hut of this wife, howling like a hyena as he wrecked it. The combination of his wrecking the hut (an unpropitious action, especially if intentional), howling like a hyena (an unpropitious animal), joining in an affray against the elders (highly unpropitious) and being cursed by the elders had, they said, led to his death in a most unpropitious manner.

[1] Sargant, 1957, p. 36.

Up to the time of this tragedy, however, I had not been told of the hut wrecking incident. Altogether, I am not convinced that the hut ever was wrecked, and if it was then it seems a remarkable coincidence that a moran who led this attack should have been killed so unexpectedly so shortly after the affray (a matter of two months). It is even just possible that this moran never actually took part in the affray – he appears to have evaded the administration's work party set up for the worst offenders. It seems far more plausible to assume that the people in the locality, shocked by the death of the moran, were prepared at the time to accept any wild theory as to the supernatural cause of his death. And once such a theory had been accepted it remained an unquestionable demonstration of the powers of the supernatural – and of the curse of the elders.

This is, I suggest, a regular pattern of events following any sudden misfortune among the Samburu, and it is worth noting that those who are likely to be most shocked by the event and hence most prone to suggestion, in other words the relatives and companions of a man who has been unexpectedly killed, are also the people who are best placed to spread rumours of his actions prior to his death. It is, perhaps, in a society in which sudden, violent and unexpected deaths and misfortunes occur that such beliefs in the supernatural are most likely to be maintained. In other words, where an element of unpredictability is built into the economic or social life of a community, one might expect certain anxieties to be generated which serve to perpetuate ritual beliefs and activities, and counteract any rational forces that might otherwise destroy these irrational beliefs.

One type of ceremony which is notably absent from this society is an elaborate mortuary ceremony after any death, even that of an influential elder. The disposal of the corpse is essentially a simple affair compared with some of the other ceremonies referred to in this work, and it is accomplished discreetly. There are, it is true, certain stringent restrictions placed on the principal mourners; but these are totally negative in character and are not accompanied by any public ritual. A plausible explanation to this is that the death of either a man or

273

a woman does not precipitate a critical change in social organization or intense competition for property. It was noted in Chapter One that homestead composition is fluid in character and that the Samburu are essentially dependent on one another so that the death of one person, even of the stock owner of a homestead, need only lead to a local readjustment, and this can follow a familiar pattern. And it was noted in Chapter Three that the laws of inheritance are essentially rigid, and they are enforced by the local clan elders who strongly oppose any attempt at evading them. Thus, while a death may affect certain people profoundly, it is unlikely to present them with insurmountable problems or affect their relationships with other people. They are encouraged to react to it in certain stereotyped ways and it does not create a social problem. It does not, I suggest, call for any collective ceremony.

Summary

Van Gennep described primitive societies as tending to be ones in which there was a considerable differentiation in statuses; and inevitable changes in status were accompanied by ceremony. The Samburu, with their age grade system through which age-sets are promoted in a series of jerks, and the tense social boundaries surrounding their clans which have to be crossed at every marriage, are no exception to this. Changes in status are inevitably disruptive to the society and engender anxiety amongst those most closely affected.

Sargant, following Pavlov, has pointed out that anxiety accompanies an increased suggestibility and this may induce a change of attitude or reinforce existing attitudes of those concerned. And hence one infers that the anxiety brought about by changes in status help those concerned to adjust themselves to the new relationships involved. But the Samburu have a number of additional devices which serve to increase this anxiety largely by overawing those most directly concerned; and these, it has been suggested, implement the change in attitude necessary for a change in status to be accomplished.

The devices through which the participants are overawed include physical debilitation (circumcision), haranguing, blessing and insisting on the meticulous performance of ceremonies which perplex by their profusion of detail and dismay through the mystical beliefs which surround them. The participants find public scrutiny turned in their direction and this makes them intensely aware of certain important social values such as honour and a sense of respect, for the possibility of shame and ridicule hangs over them. Any permitted form of ritual protest by other people less directly concerned may serve to heighten their embarrassment.

But such ceremonies need not only be regarded as a means of transmitting and maintaining social sentiments (Radcliffe-Brown) or facilitating change in status in a society where status differences are very pronounced (Van Gennep); they may also be regarded as a means by which elders, by accident or by design, assert and maintain their control over the remainder of the society. Respect for the elders and for the will of the elders is perhaps one of the most significant sentiments induced in the participants, who are made fully aware that society sanctions the occasion and all that it implies. Ceremony, in the hands of the elders, is another means by which they retain their power.

Chapter Ten

THE SAMBURU AND SOME NEIGHBOURING TRIBES: A COMPARISON[1]

THE Turkana, Dorobo and Rendille are neighbours of the Samburu, and a very brief comparison between certain features of their social systems and corresponding features of the Samburu social system provides a useful confirmation of a number of points raised in this study. Because they are their neighbours, the Samburu themselves are quite aware of these differences and of certain correlations between them; this is particularly true of their understanding of the Dorobo and Rendille with whom they have had close social relations over a long period, but it is less true of their understanding of the Turkana.

I. The Turkana

The Turkana are the north-western neighbours of the Samburu. Over a narrow strip to the west of Baragoi the two tribes are to some extent interspersed and they remain on terms of uneasy coexistence. Both are pastoral tribes, but with very different languages, customs and social systems. In looks also they are quite distinct: the Turkana have dark skins, coarse features and masculine physiques, whereas the Samburu have lighter skins, finer features and a slighter, more graceful build.

---

[1] A fuller account of the relations between these tribes is given in *The Survey*. Here I am only concerned with comparing social systems. I rely on material from my own field-work in discussing the Dorobo and Rendille, and on Dr. P. H. Gulliver's two monographs (Gulliver, 1951 and 1955) in discussing the Turkana.

I. The Turkana

It has already been suggested that the tensions which are visible in the Samburu age-set system may be regarded as a counterpart to those which are reported between close agnates among the Turkana (page 134). Both societies place a high value on polygamy and this necessitates a comparatively late first marriage for men. Among the Turkana, men want to draw on the family's herd in order to provide bridewealth for each marriage, and this brings them into competition with their brothers and even with their father. The Samburu must also build up a herd before they can marry, but the age-set system prevents young men from marrying for some time and this inhibits competition for stock within the family: by the time a moran is permitted to marry he has normally had ample opportunity to found a herd of his own. Thus, the tensions inside the family which tend to occur among the Turkana tend to be absent among the Samburu. And conversely, the tensions between age grades among the Samburu tend to be absent among the Turkana where the age organization is neither strong nor restrictive. The Samburu regard the lack of discipline within the Turkana age-set system and the tension that exists within their families with disgust. This is essentially the attitude of a society in which the emphasis is on conformity for a society in which competition is more evident.

There is a second striking contrast between the two societies which is also related to family solidarity, and this concerns the transfer of stock. Among the Turkana bridewealth is a heavy burden, and a single marriage may impoverish a man who has to pay approximately one-half of it from his own herd and beg the rest from his closest kinsmen.[1] A typical bridewealth payment among the Turkana would amount to 50 head of large stock, or in other words about one and a half times the size of a typical family herd, or about 14 times the number of large stock per person in the society,[2] as compared with about six head of large stock (excluding calves) among the Samburu, which is less than one-tenth the size of an average herd and about one-half the number of large stock per person in the

[1] Gulliver, 1955, pp. 231 and 239.
[2] These figures are inferred from Gulliver, 1951, p. 15, and 1955, pp. 38 and 229.

277

society. Gulliver presents a picture of families being impoverished through the marriage of one of their males and gradually rebuilding their herds through natural increase and the marriages of daughters and close kinswomen until they have sufficient cattle to marry again.

The effect of the bridewealth on the economy of the Samburu household can be ignored. A large number of stock – perhaps 35 head of large stock and a similar number of small stock – is allotted to the new wife from the husband's residual herd, but the stock remain inside his total herd. It is with the number of cattle he has available to allot his wife that he impresses his potential affines and not with the bridewealth he pays them. It is quite possible that over the decades which follow a marriage, the close kinsmen of a wife will beg more than 30 head of large stock from this allotted herd, and ultimately the figure obtained from her husband and his heirs could be of the order of 50 large stock and 100 small stock. Spread out over a large number of years this does not constitute a heavy burden. It is just a constant source of irritation to each Samburu and his sons.

Social relations between affines are also quite different in the two societies. Among the Samburu, a wife's kinsman must be respected and his predatory visits are unwelcome. He is an outsider who is popularly held to be only interested in exploiting her allotted herd. Whereas Gulliver says of the Turkana: 'All in-laws, of whatever degree, are known as "ekameran", s: "ngikamerok", pl. This comprehensive term indicates a general relationship of mutual help in all walks of life, plus close emotional ties of a very strong order. Turkana like to talk about their in-laws with an avidity and pleasure that is quite remarkable in comparison with their normal taciturn nature. I have never come across a case of really bad feelings between in-laws, nor of refusal of one to help another in whatever way.'[1] This could never have been written about the typical relations

[1] Gulliver, 1951, p. 103. Elsewhere, Gulliver notes a certain asymmetry in which the father-in-law is the 'superior affine' with greater claims for assistance (1955, pp. 205–7). This asymmetry is equivalent to what I have called the wife-giving/wife-receiving relationship among the Samburu. But whereas for the Samburu this is overriding, Gulliver stresses that for the Turkana in their day to day relations the asymmetry tends to be overlooked and mutual help and reciprocity is the norm.

between Samburu affines. *But,* ignoring the remark about 'their normal taciturn nature', it might very well be said of the relationship between close agnatic kinsmen. This contrast is even more striking when conversely one compares the Turkana relationship between brothers with the Samburu relationship between affines. Among the Turkana: 'Brothers are looked upon as people who are trying to better themselves at one's expense. "When your brother comes to see you, you know that he wants something. He may want a goat or a cow. And having got it he goes off again," said one man to me.'[1] This statement which Gulliver quotes from one of his informants is very close to the statements which I collected from the Samburu when they were describing their relationships with their wife-giving affines. In other words, there is a general similarity in the relationship between Samburu *agnates* and Turkana *affines,* and conversely between Samburu *affines* and Turkana *brothers.*

This inversion of relationships between the two tribes is perhaps correlated with the differences in marriage payments. Among the Turkana, a large number of stock is transferred from the herds of the bridegroom and his closest kinsmen to those of his closest affines. While on the one hand he competes with his brothers and close agnates for stock with which to marry and their relationship becomes strained, on the other hand he forms strong personal bonds of reciprocity with his wife-giving affines based on the heavy transfer of stock to them which has impoverished him, and they become his 'stock associates' (similar to stock friends among the Samburu).[2] The Samburu do not transfer large numbers of stock to their affines at marriage and the bulk of the bridegroom's herd remains inside his homestead. He does allot his bride stock to which her kinsmen have limited claims, but between agnates there remains a cordial relationship of reciprocity, and rather than compete, they support one another both in their marriages and in many other ways.

Clanship to the Samburu is a logical extension of the ties between close agnates. They regard all their clansmen as

[1] Gulliver, 1951, p. 102.
[2] Gulliver, 1955, p. 204.

brothers. The Turkana also have exogamous clans and there is a diffuse belief in ultimate descent from one founding ancestor. But clanship does not appear to have a greater significance for them than this; a man will only seek hospitality from a clansman if there are no affines, close kinsmen or 'best friends' living in the area, and to the traveller 'the clansman is only one degree removed from a stranger.'[1] In other words, a Turkana regards a clansman almost as an outsider, whereas a Samburu regards any person other than a clansman as an outsider: once when I was being taken to a strange area by another Samburu and we were seeking hospitality for the night, he entirely ignored the fact that he had close maternal kinsmen, close affines, and even age mates in the area, but led me to the settlement of a distant clansman who happened to be living there. The sort of bonds which the Turkana form with their affines, Samburu cultivate with their clansmen. For the Samburu, strain and partial avoidance with his affines reinforces and is reinforced by his cordial ties with his clan; whereas for the Turkana, affines tend to be on cordial terms and clanship has less meaning. Stock owners in both societies are free to live with whom they please, and it is hardly surprising that whereas a Samburu commonly lives with his clansmen, a Turkana appears to do so with his affines.[2]

It is possible that the differences between the two societies in their affinal bonds account for differences in the status of women. Among the Turkana: 'In many cases a wife is the moral equal of her husband in their informal relationships.'[3] Although her status is admittedly rather inferior to that of men in non-domestic affairs. Among the Samburu, the status of women is inferior in every way to that of men. This is not to be explained in terms of the rate of polygamy as the Turkana have a rate which is high even in comparison with that of the Samburu,[4] and this also implies that there is a considerable age difference between men and their wives. It can most logically be explained by reference to the cordial relationship which exists

[1] Gulliver, 1951, p. 70.
[2] Ibid., 1951, p. 122; and 1955, p. 204.
[3] Ibid., 1951, p. 215.
[4] Ibid., 1955, p. 243.

between affines among the Turkana: the wife is the pivotal point of this relationship and if her husband lives with her close kinsmen then this consolidates her position. Among the Samburu, the corresponding social tie for each man is with his clan, and his wives are peripheral to this. Indeed, it is from his clansmen that he gets help in exploiting the herds he has allotted to his wives. The differences in the position of women in the two societies may account for the fact that whereas the Turkana regard adultery as an offence comparable with homicide, the Samburu approve of it under certain circumstances, especially within the clan (page 94).

In this section it has been possible to relate some striking differences between the Samburu and the Turkana to differences in the rights in property transferred at marriage. Among the Turkana there is a heavy bridewealth payment which brings close agnates into competition in order to marry and creates a close economic and social tie with the kinsmen of the wife, apparently enhancing her status. Among the Samburu, the initial bridewealth is low, the bulk of the herd is retained within the clan, and close social and economic ties are maintained between clansmen; conversely a man's relations with his affines tend to be strained as they constantly strive to exploit their rights in his herd. The transfer of rights over the women (i.e. at marriage) is the crucial issue of both the strong bond existing between affines among the Turkana and the strain existing between them among the Samburu.

II. The Dorobo

Before the advent of British administration in the area there were a number of small groups of people who subsisted mainly by hunting and gathering although they did at times have a few sheep and goats. These groups were known to Masai speaking tribes such as the Samburu as *Ldorobo*, a term which seems to correspond more or less with the Nandi *Okiek* and the Boran *Warta*, and which the Europeans have coined as *Dorobo*. In recent years, these groups have been confined to certain reserves and have been encouraged to take up cattle husbandry. In northern Kenya there are five such groups in the

Doldol reserve, seven in the Leroghi reserve, one, the Suiei Dorobo, on the Mathews Range, and one, the Elmolo, on the south-eastern shore of Lake Rudolf.

Apart from the Elmolo who are fishermen and atypical in a number of ways, there is considerable uniformity among these groups, and intermarriage and intermigration between them is common and has been for many generations. They speak Masai and like the Samburu share many Masai customs and beliefs.

For comparison with the Samburu social system, the Suiei Dorobo who live in the Mathews Range and are fairly representative of the other groups are briefly described. In spite of recent economic changes in their way of life, their social system appears to have altered little from its traditional form.

The Suiei Dorobo

Previously the Suiei Dorobo were closely associated with the Laikipiak Masai, and when in the 1880s this tribe was dispersed by the Purko Masai, a number of survivors settled among the Suiei and became Dorobo themselves. The Samburu, living to the north, moved into the area formerly held by the Laikipiak over the next two decades, but apart from a few stragglers who had lost their herds through epidemic and became Suiei, they did not establish friendly relations with them for some time.

In 1936, when the Suiei were suffering in a severe drought, the administration tried to settle them at Wamba and encourage them to cultivate *shambas*. This was not a success and they were later allowed to take up cattle husbandry, a livelihood which they still retain although they are on the whole less successful at this than their more experienced Samburu neighbours. This change has not interfered with their bee-keeping activities, and they still obtain small stock from the Samburu in exchange for honey-beer, and hand-made artifacts, such as wooden stools and buckets for watering cattle. Some Suiei informants have maintained that in the past they could live through the wet seasons without hunting, simply on honey, roots and the small stock that they obtained from the Samburu, and in earlier times from the Laikipiak.

All over the Mathews Range where the Suiei live, hills, hill-sides, valleys, strips of land and even certain trees are individually owned; and the owner has the sole right to cultivate bees on his own territory, or to pass these rights on to anyone else. He may allot trees or portions of his land to his sons, his affines, his friends, and to any stranger who comes to settle down in his neighbourhood. On his death, his property is inherited by his sons. In theory, the whole of the Mathews Range is divided into areas, each of which is owned by an agnatic group and is sub-divided among the major segments of this group, and so on. In practice, the alienation of portions of land over a number of successive generations to other Suiei groups and to immigrants has to some extent obscured any basic pattern – if one ever existed. It is worth noting that although the Mathews Range covers some 360 square miles, or about two square miles per adult male Dorobo, there is a limit to the types of places in which bees can easily be cultivated, and land suitable for this purpose is not always superabundant.

Residence and close social ties tend to be with bilateral and affinal kinsmen among the Suiei, with a slight emphasis on paternal ties. Their 10 exogamous segments are each about as large as a Samburu lineage group, but they share no common interest sufficient to maintain any strong feelings of unity – even the joint ownership of property. It is frequent for an immigrant to consolidate his position by marrying a kinswoman of his new hosts and by giving away his own daughters or sisters in marriage to them. In this respect the Suiei differ from the Samburu, where an outsider who wishes to become accepted as a new member of the clan with which he now associates should avoid intermarriage with that clan, since this would only confirm his position as an outsider.

The age-set system of the Suiei is at first sight similar to that of the Samburu: they initiate new age-sets at about the same time and today give them the same names, and no Suiei would marry the daughter of an age mate. But there is no restriction placed on the age-set to which a boy may belong or on marriage. It does not matter if his father is a firestick elder and any Suiei moran may marry when it suits him, irrespective of the seniority of his age-set. Boys are circumcised as young as possible and then allowed to marry as soon as practicable. Apart from circumcision and the first *ilmugit* ceremony when they become moran, the Dorobo have no other age-set ceremonies.

Thus among the Suiei, men tend to marry early by Samburu standards and quickly become fully accepted adult males who associate with the older men on a more equal footing. This is consistent with their traditional way of life. In the first place, the Suiei were not a warrior tribe with a large number of unmarried men ready for action to defend their property: they only had bee-hives and land for cultivating bees and these were less of a liability than stock, even though it did entail a greater hardship in the dry season when honey and other foods were less easily obtainable. And secondly, apart from bee-keeping in the wet season which could be carried out by individual males, subsistence among the Dorobo called for collective action and pooling their combined resources. This was particularly true of hunting which tended to be carried out by teams and any food obtained was distributed widely.[1] It required the joint efforts of all active males living in the area, the older with their skill and the younger with their agility. It was possible for the pastoralist to manage his herds with the labour force of his homestead and certain outside help from time to time, but the Dorobo could never achieve quite the same measure of independence however large his family.

Among the Samburu, it has been shown that the desire for economic independence, the high rate of polygamy, and the strict subordination of young men to old were all related aspects of the society. Traditionally, various factors precluded them from arising among the Suiei. Polygamy on a wide scale would not increase a man's independence and it could only be achieved if young men were forced to marry late; and the absence of rigorously observed age-set restrictions as among the Samburu or of property controlled largely by the older men as among the Turkana hindered this. The Samburu and Turkana made use of young men as subordinates of social system. The

---

[1] For vivid accounts of hunting with the Dorobo, probably the Loliin who are now among the Leroghi Dorobo, see Chanler, pp. 358 ff., and Neumann, pp. 94 ff.

Dorobo allowed them to reach an earlier maturity where they participated more or less as equals.

The following figures, taken from the tax-book census, show how polygamy varies with age among the Suiei and the Samburu. The Suiei have a younger age of first marriage and a more even distribution of wives at all ages. The third column represents a Samburu phratry which conforms highly with Samburu ideals and it will be noticed that the difference between it and the Suiei is even more marked.[1]

Comparison between Polygamy Rates of Samburu and Dorobo

| Age-set | Approximate age range | Average Number of Wives | | |
		Suiei Dorobo	Samburu (total)	Lorogushu phratry
Merisho	58–71 yrs.	1·13	1·95	2·53
Kiliako	43–58 yrs.	1·28	1·67	1·73
Mekuri	32–43 yrs.	1·04	1·35	1·43
Kimaniki	18–32 yrs.	0·39	0·16	0·08
Sample size		190	5,736	820

Other Dorobo groups have similar figures to those recorded for the Suiei. Among the Elmolo there is an even lower rate of polygamy: of the 34 married men in 1958, only one had more than one wife.

On the whole, the Samburu prefer to limit their dealings with the Suiei. They are Dorobo; they have no sense of respect; their girls make notoriously bad wives, and marriages with them generally do not last; and above all, the Dorobo know the secrets of sorcery and will not hesitate to use it against their personal enemies. In short, the Samburu are looking at a society in which many of the factors which encourage conformity in their own society are absent. There is not the same general interest in maintaining the standards of the group and limiting the outrages of the mean man, for no kinship group emerges as a corporate unit; there is not the same general desire to retain

[1] To some extent these figures understate the differences between the Suiei and the Samburu as Suiei boys are circumcised younger and hence the age ranges will be younger for each age-set.

essential power in the hands of the older men and correspond-ing to this there is no developed belief in the power of the curse. The Dorobo make honey-beer and drink it regularly; this frequently leads to quarrelling among them, and this, possibly more than anything else, confirms the Samburu view of them that they have no sense of respect. Obviously, in a society where co-operation is necessary, there must be considerable conformity, but it is not the almost obsessive degree of con-formity discernible among the Samburu; it is more the modified conformity reported for the Turkana.[1] The Samburu see an element of competition in both societies which is absent or suppressed in their own, and this is most clearly expressed in their notion that the Turkana are witch-ridden and the Dorobo are sorcerer-infested: they are people who are prepared to use any mystical powers at their disposal for their own ends.

The Samburu-Dorobo

One feature of special interest in the previous section was that the Suiei have formed some sort of a relationship with the Samburu, and earlier had one with the Laikipiak Masai. What evidence I have collected from all sources suggests that the Dorobo groups in the area often formed uneasy alliances with their pastoral neighbours, and that when the latter moved to new areas, whether for reasons of strategy or economy, the Dorobo generally stayed where they were and formed new links with any new neighbours that presented themselves: their hunting and gathering economy did not encourage them to leave the areas with which they were thoroughly familiar. There was in addition a limited amount of intermigration between the tribes: after a serious defeat or epidemic one or two surviving pastoralists might temporarily or permanently settle down with their Dorobo neighbours, and conversely, certain Dorobo might cultivate social ties with the pastoralists and become members of these tribes as they built up herds of their own. This has certainly been true of the relations between the Dorobo groups and the Samburu, and it seems to have been true also of their relations with the Laikipiak Masai.

[1] Gulliver, 1955, pp. 196 ff.

The Samburu are rather critical of segments in their own society with Dorobo ancestry, for while they are fully accepted as Samburu, they may betray certain characteristics which other Samburu regard as 'Dorobo', although it is quite evident that their standards and values are closer to those of other Samburu than to those of the Suiei, for instance. These Samburu-Dorobo are atypical of Samburu in that there are among them a comparatively large proportion of men who do not conform closely with Samburu ideals and, significantly, there is less pressure on them from members of their local clan groups to encourage them to do so. Prominent among these groups are the Werkile of Loimusi phratry who live in the Ndoto mountains, Lanat clan living in the south-eastern region of the country, and certain portions of Masula phratry particularly those living around Mount Ngiro; each of these have remained in the country they previously inhabited as full Dorobo.

The Masula phratry are more closely associated with the Dorobo than any other Samburu phratry: there is their stronghold around Mount Ngiro where the inhabitants cultivate bees and are the only Samburu to claim exclusive ownership of land and water based on their local rights as bee-keepers; and they also have tenuous links with certain Suiei in the Mathews Range and other Dorobo groups formerly living on Leroghi. But it is not only their actual associations which marks the Masula off as quasi-Dorobo, it is also their disregard for the restrictions of phratry exogamy and of the age-set system, and their tendency to ignore a number of Samburu conventions. In short, the force of public opinion is comparatively low among the Masula and their prestige among other Samburu phratries is low.

Some figures substantiate this point. Normally, moran tend to marry late and the sons of firestick elders cannot be circumcised. At Mount Ngiro in July 1958, however, a sample revealed that among 121 moran, 26 were already married (of whom 19 had children), and 9 were sons of firestick elders. In the same sample 93 out of 166 recorded marriages (56%) occurred inside Masula phratry of which 75 infringed the prescribed limits of endogamy. This compared with figures collected among the Masula living at Ngelai (a more reputable section of the phratry) where only 21 out of 116 marriages (18%) were within the phratry and only 3 infringed the prescribed limits of endogamy.

For the other Samburu, the clan, and to a large extent the phratry is a corporate group in spite of its geographic dispersal. It is exogamous and anyone marrying into it is an outsider. The Masula, on the other hand, do allow a certain degree of marriage within the phratry, largely because they do not insist that outsiders who are attracted to them should observe new exogamous restrictions if they wish to become full members. Consequently, neither their clans nor the phratry as a whole emerge as distinctive groups; they have no exclusiveness maintained by an emphasis on exogamy. A Masula elder once boasted to me: 'We Masula do not know the word "outsider".' He was referring to the large number of groups from other Samburu phratries which have been absorbed by the Masula and regarded this as a source of strength in contrast to other Samburu phratries who regard their exclusiveness and solidarity as their real source of strength.

A different type of corporateness appears among the Masula in which locality and intermarriage play a more significant part and clanship, if anything, a less significant part. The term of address for an affine (*lautan*) might be used with a greater warmth to imply a more symmetrical relationship than is seen elsewhere: other Samburu phratries take care not to address an age mate in this way, but the Masula do not always see it as negating the closeness of age mates and may use it. The combination of Masula segments to perform *ilmugit* ceremonies and form Clubs varies in different parts of the country; so that what elsewhere are regarded as clans and are dispersed throughout the country, tend among Masula phratry to be less exclusive and more localized. To a modified extent, this also occurs among other Samburu phratries, as for instance among the Lorogushu of Lbarta where a few Makalilit moran belong to Pardopa Club (pages 91–94), but these are regarded as irregularities which should be avoided where possible. The Masula regard them as normal; they have a lower feeling of corporateness so far as the dispersed clan is concerned and a greater feeling of corporateness so far as the locality is concerned, and this is extended to any acretions from other

Samburu phratries who care to associate themselves and intermarry with them: the notion of exclusiveness is absent. At
Mount Ngiro in particular, owing to the modification of
exogamous restrictions, moran are frequently in a position to
marry their mistresses and often do. This, say many Samburu, is
why the girls of this area make notoriously self-willed wives and
why marriage there is so unstable. I was unable to collect
reliable figures to substantiate this point.

According to the official tax-books, Masula phratry constitutes just over 40% of the Samburu tribe, and this appears
to be largely due to the ability of this phratry to absorb outsiders. It becomes obvious that if the Masula are so large and so
unlike what has been referred to in this book as typically Samburu, then the book is not strictly speaking a study of a cross-
section of Samburu society. It may be noted that most of the
material presented here was collected inside Pardopa clan
(Lorogushu phratry) so that the opinions expressed are often
those of Pardopa men and many of the case examples quoted
concern this particular clan. A glance at the figures in the table
on page 285 makes it clear that Lorogushu is not altogether a
typical Samburu phratry: young men tend to marry later and
correspondingly there is a greater degree of polygamy among
the older men than in many other Samburu phratries (e.g. the
Masula). In a number of other respects the Lorogushu are
further from the Dorobo form of society than many other Samburu segments. Within the local clan groups of this phratry
there is constant moral pressure on individuals to conform with
the ideals of Samburu society. The reputation of worthiness of a
segment at any level stands to suffer when any of its members
are mean, when they show disrespect where respect is due, or
when they exploit their privileges unreasonably: they find it
harder to marry and their daughters will not be sought in
marriage by worthy men. This has been a major theme of this
study and it was demonstrated again and again while I was
working inside Pardopa clan. Among less worthy clans, there
was also a general pressure on individuals to conform, but lower
standards were permissible and there was a significant reduc-
tion in the rate of polygamy in these clans. Samburu society

as a whole can be thought of as existing on a scale where extremes are the ideal Samburu value of respect, worthiness and loyalty to clan, family and age-set on the one hand, and a lack of these values on the other. Close to the first extreme are segments such as Lorogushu phratry and close to the other extreme are the Dorobo groups such as Suiei. Between these two extremes, but much closer to the 'Samburu' than the 'Dorobo', lie the Samburu–Dorobo, and closer still to the 'Samburu' lie the Masula. The difference is not so much one of ideal as of the extent to which individuals are prepared to live up to that ideal and to interfere in the private affairs of those who do not.

The following table shows how polygamy rates vary between certain phratries.[1]

Comparison between Polygamy Rates of Certain Samburu Phratries

Age-set	Approx. Age Range		POLYGAMY RATES			
		(Suiei)	*Loimusi*	*Masula*	*Lorogushu*	*Lngwesi*
Merisho	58–71 yrs.	(1·13)	1·11	1·83	2·53	2·09
Kiliako	43–58 yrs.	(1·28)	1·42	1·67	1·73	1·85
Mekuri	32–43 yrs.	(1·04)	1·20	1·30	1·43	1·47
Kimaniki	18–32 yrs.	(0·39)	0·04	0·24	0·08	0·08
(Sample size)		(190)	(275)	(2,441)	(820)	(237)
Average rate (for married men)		(1·12)	1·30	1·44	1·65	1·67
			below average		above average	

This table shows quite clearly that differences in polygamy rates between the various phratries is not correlated with size. Thus if size is a criterion of prestige then the Masula are indisputably greater than all other Samburu phratries, and this is how they frequently try to present themselves. But if such aspects as the extent to which members of a phratry are polygamous are taken as a criterion for prestige then the Masula are comparatively low on the scale and the Lngwesi, the second smallest phratry, are the highest. The Lngwesi are, in fact, one of the most respected of all Samburu phratries and have a strong feeling of exclusiveness and solidarity. At the other

[1] These figures were taken from the tax-book census, see the appendix.

extremes, the Loimusi with the lowest degree of polygamy in the society are perhaps the most despised of all phratries for their failure to conform with Samburu ideals.

Thus, if one accepts that the Lngwesi and the Lorogushu are good examples of worthy phratries and that the Loimusi and the Masula are less worthy phratries then these differences are reflected in the extent to which they attain the Samburu ideal of polygamy, and the table may be regarded as a convenient one in which the various phratries can be placed in their correct position on a Dorobo–Samburu scale.[1]

III. The Rendille

The Rendille are the north-eastern neighbours of the Samburu. They own camels, sheep and goats and have a language of their own which has a certain affinity with Somali. The Rendille and the Samburu are traditionally firm allies and they claim to have lived side by side and to have migrated to new areas together for centuries. Today, there is still considerable overlap in their residential and grazing areas, even though they have been officially confined to separate districts since about 1914. Broadly speaking, they do not compete over natural resources as their needs are largely complementary: camels eat shrubs and prefer the hotter drier areas where there are good salt licks and where thick bush and tsetse fly are absent, and cattle prefer grass and areas where there are more convenient supplies of water.

In this account, I am confining myself to a description of the northern half of the tribe who number about 6,000 persons: the southern half have a number of characteristics in common with the Samburu not shared by those in the north, and the contrasts are less striking.

There is a considerable difference between camels and cattle, both in their performances and in their requirements. The camel is in many ways better adapted to a harsh environment than the cow. It may give two or three times as much milk in the

---

[1] The figure quoted for the Masula in this table include a large proportion of endogamous marriages. If they did not violate the custom of exogamy to the extent that they do, then these figures might well be substantially lower.

wet season and will continue to give adequate supplies during the dry season when a cow has almost completely dried up. In the dry season, camels can survive with water only once every 10 days to a fortnight, and in the wet season they do not need any water at all. If necessary they can travel up to 40 miles a day and this, taken together with their greater freedom from water supplies makes it possible for them to exploit areas which cattle cannot reach. They can also be used very successfully as pack animals, giving the Rendille a greater general mobility than the Samburu.

In order to exploit their resources to the full, the Rendille divide their stock between settlement and camp as do the Samburu. The settlement is normally not too far from a water point and small stock and a subsistence herd of camels are kept there. Camps are frequently many miles from any water point and young men who live in these camps may have to be without water for drinking or washing for a fortnight at a time. They do have copious supplies of milk, however, and this altogether precludes any hardship through thirst. This division between settlement and camp is only different from the Samburu in the extent to which it is practised, the distances it involves and the physical discomfort which young men suffer.

In managing camels, it is not merely that they can travel long distances, but that in order to thrive in Rendille country they *have* to travel these distances, and this places considerable liabilities on the camel-men. They do not know how to ride the camels and possibly the country is too rough to do so. The camel-men must accompany their herds on foot, and if taking them to water involves a 40-mile trek through hot and rough country then this is accepted as a matter of course. Only the fittest and most active members of the tribe – that is the fully grown boys and young men – are fit enough to do this daily. In other words, as compared with the Samburu, a smaller proportion of the population is actively engaged in stock management and a greater degree of co-operation between stock owners is entailed. This restricts the freedom of the young men to a greater extent than among the Samburu where a larger proportion of the population – including even girls and young wives – can herd cattle if necessary. One might almost say that the Samburu are hampered by the physical limitations of their cattle whereas the Rendille are hampered by the physical limitations of their human population to manage camels well in their type of country. Not only does a stock economy limit the size of the population according to the number of people a herd can feed, but each herd also requires at least a minimum number of people to manage it properly, and whereas among the Samburu cattle economy there seems to be a considerable tolerance between these two extremes, this is perhaps less true of the Rendille. In the 1890s when the Rendille were sadly reduced in numbers through a smallpox epidemic, they lost many of their stock, not merely because with fewer people they were more prone to attack from their enemies, but also because they simply did not have the manpower to maintain their herds efficiently.

Camels have one limitation which is a great liability to the general prosperity of the Rendille. Under their management, their herds only increase very slowly: so slowly, in fact, that some informants maintained that the overall number does not grow at all, the gradual increase of one man's herd being offset by the losses suffered by another. Diseases, in particular anthrax, are constantly infecting Rendille herds and reducing the general rate of increase, and even in ideal conditions this rate would be much slower than that for cattle, because of the longer period of gestation and the longer interval between pregnancies among camels.

This now raises important social problems. In the first place, a static stock population cannot support a human population which is increasing, and secondly, a set of brothers cannot all hope to be as rich as their father, unless his herd increases at an unusually fast rate or they are lucky enough to obtain further camels from elsewhere. The Samburu believe that their own cattle herds increase at a *faster* rate than their human population and their faith that the poorest of men can build up substantial herds is a basic incentive to prudence and conformity. The Rendille, on the other hand, believe that their camel herds, if they are growing at all, are growing at a *slower* rate than the human population, and this creates certain property problems.

293

The immediate solution to any increase in the human population is emigration to the cattle economy of the Samburu where they can easily be absorbed. Up to one-third of the Samburu segments claim descent from the Rendille and believe that their ancestors once lost or left their camels and decided to migrate. Immigration to these and other segments is still common today.

Those Rendille who remain inside the camel economy avoid dividing their stunted herds too widely so that the bulk of the family wealth remains intact. A man should comply with his social obligations to give away certain camels on occasion, and he must, of course, use some of his herd to pay the bridewealth of his own marriage. But he does not divide his herd among different wives, and at his death his sons do not share the herd between them. The herd remains intact and is inherited entirely by this senior son. Junior sons can expect enough help from their father or guardian to enable them to pay the necessary eight camels as bridewealth for their first marriages, and in seeking these they may have considerable public support. But they have no claim to further camels from him, and would obtain no general support if they tried to exercise such a claim.

The obligations of a young man towards his elder brother are similar in Rendille to Samburu, but there is a shift in emphasis. He should help his elder brother in herding camels and respect him and in return the senior brother should help the younger at his first marriage. But the relationship between them is more formal than among the Samburu and the unequal distribution of property in favour of the senior is a recognized source of tension. If the junior were to flout his obligations or show too little respect then the senior would not be generally criticized if he in his turn refused to help him at his marriage.

Mystical beliefs which suggest a certain tension between brothers among the Rendille are not shared by the Samburu: for instance, a woman's younger sons born on a Wednesday or born after her eldest son has been circumcised are thought to be jealous of their elder brothers and should be killed at birth, before they cause deaths in the family. There is also a Rendille saying that when a man's brother dies he cries with one eye and counts the dead man's camels he will inherit with the other eye.

III. The Rendille

The Samburu have an exaggerated notion of the bitterness between Rendille brothers which the unequal distribution of wealth produces. This is partly due to their willingness to believe the worst of any other tribe, and it is also due to the fact that they form their opinions of the Rendille from recent immigrants among whom there are several who have, in fact, been disinherited by their elder brothers. The life histories of these immigrants are not perhaps quite as typical as some Samburu seem to think.

The principle that a herd should not be divided between wives affects the degree of polygamy. A limited census of 117 elders revealed that only 11 had more than one wife, none had more than two, and four had no wives at all. This gave a polygamy rate of about 1·06 as opposed to the Samburu figure which is of the order of 1·5. This confirms to some extent the Samburu notion that the Rendille are monogamous.

This immediately suggests that the Samburu age-set system, which was earlier related to their high preference for polygamy, cannot be observed in an unmodified form by the Rendille. In fact, the Rendille age-set system, although basically similar to the Samburu one, is modified by a number of customs which in effect lower the age at which men may marry and increase the age at which women may be married so that there is a greater balance in numbers between married men and married women than among the Samburu.[1] In addition, there is a considerable demand among the Samburu, especially among families with close Rendille connections, for Rendille wives, and so the slight excess of women created by the Rendille preference for monogamy helps to counteract the shortage of women created by the Samburu lust for polygamy.

Both the Rendille and the Samburu acknowledge the same age-set system with the same interval between successive age-sets; these modifications in custom not only narrow the difference in age between the marriage of Rendille men and women but also modify the character of the age-set system. The Rendille do not have moran: their circumcised youths, although they belong to a well regulated age-set system, do not traditionally observe any food prohibitions or grow their hair long, and

---

[1] These customs are described elsewhere in detail (see *The Survey*, Chapter Four).

there is no ritual association between them and the bush. Altogether there is a blurring of the system acknowledged by the Samburu: the boundaries which separate boys from youths or youths from elders are less apparent. Custom allows certain boys to have mistresses, and certain youths to marry. It is not easy to distinguish between a fully clothed Rendille boy and a circumcised youth or between a youth and an elder without actually speaking to them. Among the Samburu, there is never any difficulty in distinguishing between fully clothed moran and other males. The Rendille age-set system certainly regulates the behaviour of the total society and in particular of the young men, but it does so less positively than the Samburu age-set system.

It is, at first sight, a paradox that the Samburu moran, who are ritually identified with the bush, spend much of their time inside and close to settlements, whereas the Rendille youths, who are not ritually associated with the bush, actually spend most of their time in camel camps many miles from the settlements. The explanation for this seems to be that the Rendille youths are under a different set of constraints to the Samburu moran. The camel economy is more exacting than the cattle economy. The Samburu moran may absent themselves from herding duties to visit distant parts of the district for purely social reasons, and they may be away for months at a time. In some cases such behaviour has led to severe losses in their family herd because there has been no one left behind with the capacity to manage the cattle properly. *But*, provided that they are prepared to alter their way of life and their attitude towards cattle, it is always possible for such men to rebuild their herds. This would never be possible among the Rendille: no one can expect to regain a lost herd. From early boyhood, Rendille youths are subjected to family discipline, especially where this concerns the tending of camels. They remain for extended periods in camel camps in the remoter parts of the country; the bulk of the herding duties is carried out by them, as the older men are not active enough to face the daily task.

The Rendille youths are kept away from the settlements in a very real sense while living in the camel camps, but they remain under the authority of their guardians – whether their fathers or elder brothers – and learn to accept this authority and to value the prime importance of the camel herds unconditionally. Any youth who tries to rebel against these restrictions may be faced with harsh economic privations when his guardian and close kinsmen, with the complete sympathy of the other elders, refuse to help him build up even a small herd of his own with which to marry. The Rendille have very effective economic sanctions in their hands which are not shared by the Samburu with a somewhat easier cattle economy.

It is hardly surprising, then, that the age-set system does not have so much importance for the Rendille as it does for the Samburu. Instead of the education and discipline of young men after initiation being largely in the hands of the firestick elders who subject them to a formal control, these aspects of their life remain the responsibility of their guardians and close kinsmen. The Rendille acknowledge the existence of the firestick relationship, but they do not stress its importance. The age-set of unmarried men does not emerge as a distinct and in some respects a delinquent group, a persistent source of social disorder and resentment. Strains caused by the anomalous position in which young men find themselves are contained largely within the family, and are not transferred from the family to the wider society.

Among the Rendille, the camel economy encourages large settlements, and these correspond more or less in size and composition with the Samburu local clan groups. But inevitably they are more permanent: they migrate together and only disperse into smaller settlements when forced to do so by the hardships of an unusually harsh dry season. The magnitude of the local group sharing residence gives one the impression of a greater intensity of life where public opinion is even more important than among the Samburu. Once again there is an emphasis on conformity, an elaborate variety of important collective ceremonies attached to many aspects of their lives, and a developed belief in the curse.

But the general attitude towards the curse is different from that among the Samburu. Men are more willing to threaten to use it directly. Possibly as many as two-thirds of the Rendille families are thought to have some particularly potent curse; and it is significant that when members of these families emigrate to the cattle economy of the Samburu, they often surreptitiously cease to perform the ceremonies which maintain this power to curse: it is a power which is contrary to the general ethos of Samburu society. That the Rendille should retain a more tolerant attitude towards the curse may be due to their inability to use it more indirectly: waiting on a col for an adversary is an accepted form of reprisal among them, but it may be less effective than among the Samburu: there is no shortage of marriageable girls and hence if any man finds his proposed marriage to one girl barred by an adversary then he can more easily seek to marry another. The Samburu speak of the curse as if it should only be used as a final resort; the Rendille speak of it as if it is fully justified under any circumstances of genuine provocation.

In both societies public opinion is strong and the accent is on conformity rather than on competition, but one has the impression of a greater intensity of life among the Rendille, a less easygoing society, severer property problems and tensions within the family. All these seem to be consistent with the greater readiness to resort to the curse.

A characteristic feature of the general Rendille attitude is their concern for their camels. On each of my three visits to the country, there had been persistent deaths among their camels through disease; they were faced with a problem that they felt themselves powerless to cope with, and they gave the impression of a tribe with a sense of persistent misfortune dogging them. Camels were often herded in a distant camp, and even those of the subsistence herds could only be tended by the younger more active men. The older men, owners of these herds, were constantly worrying about their camels but were not fit enough to work off their anxieties by joining in the herding. In this respect, the Samburu living in the less demanding cattle economy where older men could participate seemed to be in a happier position. I think it would be fair to say that whereas a Samburu elder constantly worries about his youngest wife when she is out of his sight, the Rendille worries about his camels. It is hardly surprising that much of the Rendille ceremonial activity is focused on the welfare of their camels, just as much of the Samburu activity is focused on the behaviour of the moran. These are the main problems which face the two societies based on the shortage of camels in the one and the shortage of marriageable women in the other.

The Gerontocratic Index

This chapter would be incomplete without some reference to more distant tribes with comparable social systems. Thus, on the basis of the present study, it is tempting to assume that wherever an age-set system restricts and regulates men's first marriages, this is related in some way to a high degree of polygamy and it protects the family from intense competition. One would also expect the same disruptive forces that are diverted from the family to reappear in some form in the age-set system. This may well have been characteristic of the southern tribes of the Nilo-Hamitic cluster: besides the Samburu, we also know that the Masai, Kipsigis and Nandi had age-set systems based on warriorhood which restricted the first marriages of young men.[1] Further afield, the Zulu were also in this category.[2]

A full cross-cultural survey would be too ambitious in the present context, but it would certainly include such tribes as the Nyakyusa and Lele of Central Africa, and the Tiwi and Groote Eylandt aborigines of north Australia.[3] All these were societies where the rate of polygamy was high and the age of marriage for young men was delayed. Corresponding to this delay were the sorts of strain we should expect. Among the Nyakyusa, young men were brought indirectly into competition with their fathers and senior kinsmen, but the strain was alleviated to some extent by their living apart in different age-set villages and avoiding one another; an emphasis on ritual served to instil a general acceptance of the system. Among the Lele, tension between the older debilitated polygamists and the younger virile bachelors who could not marry until they

---

[1] Fosbrooke, 1948; Peristiany, 1939; and Huntingford, 1953.

[2] Krige, 1936; and Gluckman, 1950.

[3] Wilson, 1950, 1951 and 1957; Douglas, 1963; Hart and Pilling, 1961; and Rose, 1960.

were perhaps 38 years old, was expressed in the widespread fear of sorcery directed at the older men and the general concern over adultery directed at the younger men; the situation was eased by allowing young men of an age-set to share a wife. Among the Tiwi, youths were taken away from their homes and lived in semi-seclusion for 10 years under the strict supervision of elders who instructed them on ritual matters; following this oppressive period in their lives, they entered a 'prestige race': by creating debts, manipulating their rights over kinswomen's marriages and becoming satellites to much older men they might be able to marry by the age of 40 and continue the race from a position of greater strength. The Groote Eylandt aborigines seem to have had a similar system.

Such is the variety among societies of this type, and they have come to be known as *gerontocracies* in Melanesian and Australian studies. Literally, the term gerontocracy means government by old men; but by defining power as the possession of wives, all those societies in which the older men are polygamists and the younger men are bachelors become gerontocracies. My own personal impression is that among the societies cited in this chapter, the Samburu, Rendille and Nyakyusa are the closest to gerontocracies in the literal sense: social values point upwards to respect for the older men, there is an emphasis on collective ritual practices, and a developed concept of the curse which acts as a sanction against competition. In the other societies, there appears to be rather more overt competition between men of different ages even if lip service is paid to respect for the old, the competitive notions of sorcery and witchcraft seem to be more developed than the conformist notion of the curse,[1] and polygamy in old age is achieved by the successful man, rather than ascribed to the worthy man. These are shifts in emphasis rather than absolute distinctions.

Accepting the derivative sense of gerontocracy, it is possible to construct an index for ranking these tribes according to the extent to which polygamy is a privilege of old age. Marriage figures are available for the Samburu, Dorobo, Turkana and

---

[1] Nyakyusa beliefs in witchcraft are largely centred on the age-village and do not therefore imply overt competition between young and old to the extent, for instance, that this is implied in Lele sorcery.

Groote Eylandt aborigines.[1] The following table is an attempt at such a ranking, in which the *gerontocratic index* is simply arrived at by dividing the polygamy rate for the men above 40 years old by that for younger men. A high value for this index suggests that regardless of the actual rate of polygamy, remarriage of widows, etc., the older men have a large number of wives compared with the younger men.

The Gerontocratic Index for Several Tribes

Tribes and number of adult males in the sample	Gerontocratic Index (*polygamy rate for older men ÷ polygamy rate for younger men*)
Samburu	
Pardopa (566)	5·4
Lorogushu (820)	3·9
Loimusi (275)	3·7
Lngwesi (237)	3·5
Masula (2,441)	3·1
Groote Eylandt (82)	2·7
Turkana (1,027)	2·5
Dorobo (190)	1·9

It will be seen that apart from Pardopa clan, the indices for the various Samburu segments are fairly constant in contrast to the broad range of their polygamy rates (see table, page 290). In other words, the gerontocratic aspects of Samburu society are more uniform than the ability to marry a large number of wives. The differences between the indices for these various Samburu segments is largely because they were collected at different points in time with regard to age-set development. The Pardopa clan census was conducted just before any moran started to marry, and gerontocratic restrictions on marriage were at their peak. The other figures were collected rather later when a number of moran had begun to marry. In the case of Masula phratry, with the lowest index, the moran had been marrying for a considerable period. Thus, the age-set cycle can be thought of as one in which the gerontocratic aspects of

---

[1] The figures have been taken from the clan census (Pardopa), the tax-book census (other Samburu segments, Turkana and Dorobo) and Rose's tables (Groote Eylandt).

Samburu society build up to a peak before being released at the time of change-over: the marriage of just 10 % of the moran who have been waiting for this point may lower the value of the index substantially.

Marriage statistics for the Tiwi and Lele are not available, but with their exceptionally late ages for marriage, one would expect them to have much higher indices than any of the Samburu segments.

Appraisal and Summary

The Samburu also make comparisons between themselves and their neighbours; and the ways in which they interpret certain differences throw additional light on their own social values. Inevitably, they all seek to justify behaviour which typifies their own society and condemn in others behaviour which seems untenable; and this is presumably as true of the Turkana as it is of the three tribes among whom I have worked. The Samburu regard the casual lack of concern for age and age-set obligations displayed by the Dorobo and Turkana as signs of an utter lack of a sense of respect; and they regard the tightfistedness of the Rendille over their camels and their greater willingness to resort to the curse as signs of meanness. In fact, they have the same sorts of criticisms for these tribes as for the less worthy members of their own society.

Conversely, the unpredictable and at times delinquent behaviour of their moran is the one aspect of Samburu society which others criticize them for. Turkana, Dorobo and Rendille have all drawn my attention to it repeatedly. The various factors which combine to produce a rift between the young men and the remainder of the society have been discussed at length in this study, and it is a combination which is absent in any of the other three. None of these other societies has *both* a restrictive age-set system *and* a high degree of polygamy as the Samburu have, and none of them has anything quite comparable with the Samburu moran. The Dorobo, it is true, have moran and they were at the time of my study among the most notorious stock thieves in the area; but this seemed largely explained by the fact that most of them had been confined to land bordering on the European settled area, and the Europeans were the most notorious people for not guarding their stock carefully and they had, in addition, some of the finest cattle on the finest land in northern Kenya. The Dorobo stole largely to supplement the herds which they had only recently begun to acquire, whereas the Samburu moran stole largely for the sake of stealing and all that it might bring them in the way of enhanced prestige in their Clubs.

There are certain superficial parallels between the Rendille and the Turkana based on the scarcity of property, which engenders greater tension between brothers. For both societies one has the impression of a stock economy which presents serious problems of management, whether this is due to limitations in their stock, their environment, their techniques of husbandry or a combination of these various factors. Gulliver's account of Turkana stock-keeping reveals a far lower proportion of stock to human population than the Samburu and generally more concern over their stock; and in this they appear to have much in common with the Rendille.

Pervading each of these four societies there are certain cultural values which are not determined by ecological considerations. There appears to be no obvious reason, for instance, why the notion of the curse or a sense of respect should be more developed among the Samburu and Rendille than among the Dorobo and Turkana, or why there should be a greater emphasis on conformity, which tends to inhibit open competition. In other words, the superficial similarity between Rendille and Turkana with regard to scarcity of property does not correspond to a similar degree of open competition in the society: competition between Rendille brothers is condemned by public opinion and is generally suppressed. On the other hand, the Dorobo, who do not have intense property difficulties and have a substantial number of men working for wages which brings them a useful supplementary income, pay less attention to social convention, and the very fact that they do take on any work offered illustrates a certain enterprise among them that is generally absent from the Samburu and Rendille.

The emphasis on large collective ceremonies by both Samburu and Rendille is not shared by the Dorobo or, judging from Gulliver's account, by the Turkana. In other words, ceremony is more organized in the two societies in which the accent is on conformity and respect. The function of ceremony in maintaining social conventions was examined in Chapter Nine, and the general conclusions of that chapter would appear to be as valid for the Rendille as for the Samburu. The social structure of the two conformative societies is more clearly defined: individual enterprise and competition are more discernible in the other two and this is consistent with a more fluid social structure.

Van Gennep himself refers to the importance of rites of passage in 'semi-civilized' societies where the differentiation between social groups is more accentuated.[1] The only modification to this view suggested here is that various primitive societies are internally differentiated to varying extents irrespective of economic considerations. A survey of the extent to which a large number of egalitarian societies conform or compete, have rigid or fluid social structures, and perform or do not perform regular collective ceremonies would be most interesting.

The broad differences between the four societies discussed here are summarized in the following table:

Relative Degree of Differentiation and Scarcity in
Four Societies

| | *Type of Society* | |
Nature of property	*Highly differentiated* (*rigid social structure, emphasis on conformity and respect, ceremony important*)	*Less differentiated* (*fluid social structure, more emphasis on competition and enterprise, ceremony less important*)
Adequate	Samburu	Dorobo
Scarce	Rendille	Turkana

---

[1] Van Gennep, pp. 1–3.

Chapter Eleven

CONCLUSION: THE GERONTOCRATIC SOCIETY

IN this study considerable attention has been paid to the ways in which the Samburu cope with problems created by their particular type of social system. The principal problems which have appeared in one form or another in every chapter have been related to marriage and in particular to polygamy. Biologically, human societies are well adapted to monogamy: there are approximately equal numbers of each sex, and each sex reaches maturity at about the same age. But the Samburu prefer to practise polygamy, and as a result there is a large number of unmarried men, and a large number of women married to men many years older than themselves. These are liable to cause resentment and even open rebellion unless the strains can be contained within the institutions of the society. The egalitarian principle which pervades the whole society ensures that every man – even the stockless immigrant – can marry if he waits long enough. Clearly, not every man can have as many wives as he might like, and the rate of polygamy is ultimately determined by the extent to which the older men can retain the monopoly in marriage over the younger men, which in turn is determined by the means at their disposal.

It was a Samburu who drew my attention to the fact that this problem of polygamy is not confined to the human race: it is also to be seen in herds of such animals as gazelle. Darwin also made the same observation, and from behaviour reported in baboons and gorillas he postulated that Man's ancestor, the Brute, lived with as many wives as he could retain by force and would expel the younger males from the family, until they successfully rebelled against this tyranny. This conjecture was fully accepted by both Atkinson and Freud who separately developed it to account for the origins of human society.[1]

The Samburu could, for that matter, point to similarities with their own herds of cattle, by comparing the bulls with the elders, the oxen and immature bulls with the moran, and the milch cows with the wives. In addition, there is a periodic change-over in which the reigning bull is outfought by a more powerful rival and the latter then acquires supremacy over the females; this could be thought to resemble the change-over of age-sets when the moran are permitted to enter into the competition for wives. The Samburu do not, however, consciously try to model their society on that of animals or see any significant resemblance. They do not have any apt explanations as to why it should be an ox, a castrated animal, which is killed during the *ilmugit* ceremonies they perform during their prolonged bachelorhood and when they are being deprived of a mistress at marriage, or why, when they are given permission to marry at the *ilmugit of the bull* ceremony, they should kill a bull provided by the ritual leader. They do not suggest, for instance, that by suffocating the bull they are symbolically breaking the monopoly which the elders have in marriage (as Freud might have suggested: cf. killing the father for his wives), or conversely that they are symbolically renouncing their own bull-like qualities of assertiveness and fearlessness associated with moranhood in order to settle down to the more placid life of elderhood (see page 108). Similarly, there is no hint that circumcision is a form of symbolic castration before they enter the period of enforced bachelorhood. There is almost a complete dearth of conscious symbolism in Samburu ceremony and belief: they only maintain that certain things are propitious and that others are unpropitious. It is because of this lack of explanation and the unlimited number of possibilities for conjecture that no attempt has been made to consider symbolic interpretations of their ceremonies as a complement to the chapter on the social function of ceremony. It is interesting to note that Freud was strongly influenced by Robertson Smith's work on ancient Semitic religion; and yet, this religion appears to have been of the sort which does not readily lend itself to

[1] Darwin, 1871, p. 590; Atkinson, 1903, Chaps. 1–3; Freud, 1913, p. 125.

symbolic analysis. Robertson Smith writes that: '. . . the antique religions had for the most part no creed; they consisted entirely of institutions and practices'; the worshipper 'was often offered a choice of several accounts of the same thing, and, provided he fulfilled the ritual with accuracy, no one cared what he believed about its origin'; and in religious as in political institutions 'the rules of society was sufficient reason why precedent once set should continue to be followed'.[1] These remarks might almost have been written about Samburu society.

Polygamy is only one aspect of Samburu society; another which is related to it in a particular way is the age-set system. Eisenstadt has expressed very clearly a number of problems raised here in his book *From Generation to Generation*.[2] He considers the function of 'age-groups' in transmitting social values to new generations, the relationship between age-groups and various types of family structure, and certain deviant tendencies within these age-groups. But unfortunately, by 'age-groups' he understands any form of differentiation between persons of different ages so that no obvious distinction is made between, for instance, the formalized structure of age-villages of the Nyakyusa and the tacit tension between successive generations in European peasant societies. As a result, many of his conclusions are too broad to have any real interest, and are sometimes based on circular arguments, such as one to the effect that age-groups tend to arise where there is tension between young and old (having previously *defined* age-groups with reference to such tensions). There is, moreover, no adequate attempt at correlating different *kinds* of age-set system with other aspects of each society, although this is one of the primary aims of his book.

Here, I have tried to make such a correlation. I have suggested that by restricting a man's first marriage, the Samburu age-set system shields the family from some of the strains entailed by polygamy: forces which could disrupt the bonds between brothers and between fathers and their sons, as occurs among the

---

[1] Robertson Smith, pp. 16, 17 and 20. These quotations may be compared with the following references in the present study: p. xxv, line 4, p. 91, line 28, p. 180, line 29 and p. 185, line 17.

[2] Eisenstadt, 1956.

Turkana, are diverted and reappear inside the age-set system itself.

In any society of this sort, whatever the pressures against competition, the unequal distribution of privileges between men of different ages is almost certain to generate some resentment among the younger members. The privileges are largely expressed in terms of polygamy, but even in mono-gamous societies there is every reason to suppose that a similar situation arises when an excessive amount of power of any kind is retained in the hands of the older men. One is tempted to look for institutions comparable with that of moranhood even in our own society and on finding them to try to relate them to other similarities with the Samburu.

The English public school comes immediately to mind, and further examination reveals that it was at its most characteristic phase during the first half of the nineteenth century before the public school reforms had taken place. A useful account of the public school system of this period has been written by G. F. Lamb.[1] In the course of his book, Lamb draws attention to the following aspects of school life: the ordeals to which new boys were subjected, among other things to test their personal courage, which he himself refers to as their initiation; the notion of honour, both of the school with respect to outsiders and of the inmates with respect to each other, and the high regard for prowess at fighting; the policy that boys should be allowed to govern themselves with as little outside interference as possible and the state of affairs that this could give rise to; fagging; rebellions against authority; the position of the headmaster as ultimate disciplinarian and the ruthless use of flogging to maintain discipline and induce a will to learn; the utter use-lessness of what was taught and the ineffectiveness of the ways in which it was taught; and the feeling that some boys later expressed of having been unnaturally torn away from their homes because the parents had followed convention.

The similarities of many of these aspects to Samburu moran-hood are obvious: initiation, honour, self-government and fagging (i.e. clientship) need no further comment – they were all discussed in Chapter Five. The relationship of schoolboys to

[1] Lamb, 1959.

their families on the one hand and to the headmaster on the other is especially interesting. Holidays were short and the boys were kept away from their families for long periods (cf. especially, the camp life of the Rendille youths) and were submitted to the ultimate authority of a disciplinarian who stood outside the family in the form of the headmaster (cf. the firestick elders). Schoolboys lived in the constant fear of flogging (cf. the curse). It is hardly surprising that regimes of this sort should have occasionally given rise to revolts against the authority of the school as they have done from time to time among the Samburu. One has the impression from this book that the closed society of public school life and the situation which forced the same sets of boys to remain in each other's company for lessons, for sport, for meals, for recreation and at night during a period of years gave an added intensity to the social relationships between them: these were in a sense multiplex relationships.[1] This may account for many of the similarities between the social life developed by schoolboys among themselves and that among the moran who are also forced to share one another's company almost without respite.

The time that was used in ineffectively teaching the boys subjects which had no practical bearing on life bears some resemblance to the way in which moran are prevented from obtaining any useful insights into the dynamics of the Samburu society. Both Samburu moran and nineteenth-century English public schoolboys were in effect in a state of social suspension for a number of years, although admittedly the latter tended to be 10 years younger than the former. In 1809 Sydney Smith wrote: 'A young Englishman goes to school at 6 or 7 years old, and he remains in a course of education till 23 or 24 years of age. In all that time his sole and exclusive occupation is learning Latin and Greek: he has scarcely a notion that there is any other kind of excellence. ... The present state of classical education ... trains up many young men in a style of elegant imbecility, utterly unworthy of the talents which nature has endowed him.'[2] And 50 years later Herbert Spencer criticized

[1] Gluckman, 1955(*a*), p. 19.
[2] Smith, 1809, *Edinburgh Review*.

methods of education, the public school system and the years 'spent by a boy in gaining knowledge of which the chief value is that it constitutes "the education of a gentleman" ' as utterly inadequate to train him to participate fully as an adult and a parent.[1]

The puritanical notion that children were by nature sinful and had to be purged by a strict religious upbringing was well developed in these schools and it bears some resemblance to the Samburu notion that moran are only children and have no sense of respect. In some of these schools punishment (public flogging) was deliberately delayed to give the offender time to meditate on his shortcomings, and this is reminiscent of the interval of suspense between a curse pronounced on the moran and the subsequent blessing which the elders insisted on in order to convince them of their lack of respect and possibly to demonstrate their power and keep them in subjection.

And just as Tom Brown's father maintained that the importance of school was not the subjects that were taught, but the means of making schoolboys 'brave, helpful, truth-telling Englishmen and gentlemen and Christians', so the Samburu elders maintain that moranhood with its prohibitions and obligations is a means by which young men may gain a sense of respect. Education in both societies is openly regarded as necessary in social virtues rather than in practical matters.

While it is fairly safe to assume that boys who were sent to these public schools came from upper and upper-middle-class families, it is not so easy to assess whether theirs were typical families of these classes. Nor can we be certain of all the motives involved in sending boys to school: convention, prestige and a desire to bring them up as gentlemen seem to have been present; but what of the desire to keep them in subjection or to protect the family from strains which their continual presence might engender? It is not easy to make generalizations. Considerable changes occurred in English society during the first half of the nineteenth century: middle class morality was spreading to the upper classes,[2] and new public schools were attracting large numbers of pupils at the expense of the older ones, although

[1] Herbert Spencer, 1861, pp. 105–11.
[2] Rattray Taylor, 1958, Chaps. 1 and 2.

they do not at first seem to have had more to offer.[1] It is tempting to assume that the public school system as described by Lamb represented an upper class institution before pressure from the middle class gave rise to reform; but again we do not know.

It is, nevertheless, evident that public school education became quite popular during the nineteenth century,[2] and this does suggest that quite apart from the need for education there could have been other reasons connected with the structure of the family. Was Samuel Butler really expressing a general reaction to the family of this period when he bitterly attacked the way in which children were kept in subjection and ignorance by a jealous patriarchal father?[3] Rattray Taylor certainly accepts that the increase in the popularity of educational institutions, in the age at which boys left school and university, and in the age of marriage at this time were all correlated with an extension of family influence 'which seems to betray a desire to keep children in subjection and perhaps a resentment of the competition of the younger generation'.[4] It is, however, by no means clear whether economic influences, such as the spread of the industrial revolution, or political influences, such as the shadow of the French revolution, were direct causes of this state of affairs.

If the present conjectures are valid, then they may be summarized as follows. Regardless of the differences in culture, social values and religious beliefs of the Samburu today and of the English upper and upper-middle classes more than a century ago, both societies attach a great importance to conformity with social conventions.[5] The exclusion of young men from the family among the Samburu corresponds broadly to the segregation of youths in public schools, and behind both institutions is the notion that this is manifestly a means whereby social virtues can be acquired. But it also serves to exclude such

[1] Ogilvie, 1957, pp. 123–36.
[2] Among existing public schools in this country, 86 were founded during the nineteenth century, as opposed to 15 during the eighteenth century and 17 during the seventeenth century. (Ogilvie, pp. 8–10.)
[3] Butler, 1912.
[4] Rattray Taylor, 1953, pp. 220–1: the writer is elaborating a view expressed by Beales, 1950.
[5] Taylor, 1958, Chap. 13.

persons for a time from full participation in society, for even when they cease to be segregated from it they still must learn how to participate fully within it; and in doing so it maintains the balance of power in the hands of the older generation.

The Samburu are an example of a gerontocracy. In this study, I have tried to show many of the strains which are liable to develop in such a society. In relation to this general theme, I have examined the statuses of both sexes at different ages, the social function of ceremony and the extent to which individuals are influenced by economic and social factors in making decisions.

The stability of this system and its capacity to survive the complete change in its political environment that followed the coming of the British without any radical modification is striking. It is fully consistent with the extent to which the Samburu have turned their backs on the changes that are occurring elsewhere in Kenya and in Africa generally. Many Europeans argue that theirs is not a far-sighted attitude, that the change is bound to affect them eventually. But it is an attitude which shows no definite sign of weakening, for as yet no one has suggested a mode of existence which is more congenial to them or better suited to the country in which they live.

Summary

Chapter One. The Samburu are a Masai-speaking tribe of some 30,000 people living in northern Kenya. They are nomadic and rely for their livelihood on their cattle, sheep and goats. The country and climate over most of the district are too dry to allow any form of agriculture. The stock economy is exacting in that it entails constant attention by the owner of each herd if he is to avoid sudden and drastic loss. But it is also rewarding: even a poor man who is willing to devote his energies to his herd can with luck build it up quite rapidly, marry several wives and achieve a measure of independence. Even so, he is still dependent on others to some extent, especially during the dry season when milk supplies are low and the demands on the community are heavy. At such times he is expected to turn to his own clansmen for support.

Chapter Two. The interdependence of clansmen encourages conformity. This goes further than the purely economic aspects of their lives: clansmen help one another to marry, and conversely they restrain one another from behaviour which might tarnish the reputation of the clan and prejudice its chances in future marriage suits; these entail considerable competition because of the high degree of polygamy. Following each marriage there is an unresolvable strain between the husband and his affines, as they try to exploit his herds holding the threat of a curse over his children on the one hand, and trying to preserve the reputation of their clan on the other. Inter-marriage between clans maintains a social barrier between them, and clan exogamy protects the unity of each clan.

Chapter Three. A Samburu allots a portion of his herd to each wife on marriage. Her children use this allotted herd to build up herds of their own, and the husband uses the remainder for his future marriages. Whenever a clansman or an affine begs a cow from him, he takes it from one of his wives' herds; whereas when he begs a cow, he adds it to his own herd. In this way, he builds up his herd at a much faster rate and prepares for his next marriage. These manipulations consolidate his external ties, especially with his clansmen, but only at the cost of resentment within his own home. Once again, his close ties with his clan are correlated with marriage strains.

Chapter Four. The clan emerges as the most important level of the segmentary descent system. Cross-cutting this is an age-set system which is largely focused on the *moran*, the most junior age-set of young men who are forbidden to marry until they can be replaced by a new age-set, by which time many of them are well over 30 years old. It is through this prolonged bachelor-hood, and not through any imbalance in numbers between men and women, that the high degree of polygamy is achieved in the society; a higher degree could be attained by increasing the periodic interval (about 13 years) between age-sets, and thereby delaying the age of marriage of young men still further.

Chapter Five. The moran are associated with the bush and encouraged to form a society of their own, with their own values, structure and strains. The unmarried girls who associate with them are relatively few because of the heavy demand for them in marriage to the elders. This leads to various forms of competition for the favours of these girls and occasionally to affrays between the moran. Notions of honour and clanship are developed to a brittle extreme which brings them against one another in what might be described as gang warfare between the clans. A wide range of activities from dancing to fighting and stock theft becomes intelligible in the context of their relationship with these girls and their prolonged bachelorhood.

Chapter Six. Ultimately, the moran are held in check by the elders, who also keep them in a state of delayed adolescence until they are replaced by a new age-set. The responsibility of holding the moran in this state of social suspension and drawing them up to elderhood is delegated to one particular age-set who hold a powerful curse over the moran and play a leading part in haranguing them and supervising their ceremonies. The age-set system is seen as protecting the family: in preventing the moran from marrying, it inhibits competition over marriage between them and their close kinsmen. The strains that are diverted from the family reappear in the age-set system, accounting for the delinquent tendencies of the moran and the fear of the curse of the elders.

Chapter Seven. Real power in the society is vested in the elders and their control over the moran in particular rests entirely on the general belief in their curse. The ability to curse gives each man a power of a sort, but real prestige among the elders is obtained by not resorting to it in the interests of social harmony, especially within the clan. No man who often makes use of his curse could enjoy any measure of influence, either privately or in formal discussions when decisions have to be made. A man who wishes to score off an adversary normally prefers to use his curse indirectly, such as by threatening to curse him only when he is negotiating for marriage: until reparations have been made, no one would allow the marriage to take place.

Chapter Eight. Marriage is a constant theme throughout this study: women are the pawns in a game played by the elders. For a girl, her marriage is the major crisis of her life: she must go to live among strangers who stand in completely unfamiliar relationships to her. Before her marriage, she avoided elders,

314

was a sister and a daughter in a family and enjoyed a special place among the moran of her clan. After her marriage, she must avoid moran, she is married to an elder much older than herself and she must learn to be a wife and mother. It is through the family that she rears that she finds a new niche in society.

Chapter Nine. A marriage ceremony is analysed as a means of preparing the bride for this complete change in her life. By reference to Pavlovian psychology, anxiety is seen as increasing suggestibility which induces a change in attitudes consistent with the change in status. The prospect of a marriage in itself generates some anxiety, but the form of the ceremony is so intense for the bride that this increases her anxiety and her readiness to accept her change in status. Ordeals in other ceremonies are seen as having a similar function. The general argument is extended to material presented in previous chapters, including the ceremonies of the moran, dancing, harangues and the belief in the curse.

Chapter Ten. The ways in which certain variables are correlated in this study are confirmed by reference to the social systems of the Turkana, Dorobo and Rendille tribes when compared with the Samburu. An index is constructed in which the extent to which polygamy is the prerogative of the older men is compared between various societies.

Chapter Eleven. Gerontocracy in its broadest sense is a society where an inordinate amount of power is vested in the older men, whether this is marriage or other privileges. For the Samburu, the monopoly of marriage among the elders corresponds to all the different advantages and privileges discussed in the previous chapters. It also leads to the resentment among the younger men, who nevertheless subscribe to the system since they in their turn may acquire the privileges of elderhood when *they* become elders.

Appendix

CENSUS TECHNIQUES AND DATA

Census techniques

THREE censuses were undertaken during the study; these were the *settlement census* (March to July 1958, carried out in the course of other field work), the *clan census* (August 1958) and the *tax-book census* (June 1959 to June 1960).

I. *The settlement census* was only made among Samburu settlements outside government grazing schemes. An attempt was made to include as many settlements as possible in three different areas (Upper Seiya, Lenkosaka, and the south-west of Mount Ngiro). If any information was suspect or inconsistent then data for the whole settlement was disregarded. A check was made between information concerning wives and stock owners on the one hand, and the actual gateways and huts in each settlement on the other; and a sketch map was drawn for each settlement with these details marked. It was impossible, however, to include any cattle counts in the census as this would have met with strong opposition and would almost certainly have been inaccurate. When collecting data seemed likely to arouse suspicion, it was suspended for a time. But in point of fact, the sort of questions I asked were similar to those which the Samburu visiting the area would ask each other, and a number of people were most insistent that I wrote down far more information than I had asked them for, and would want to know what I had written down for other settlements so that they could check my information for me. People were also very willing to give the information in exchange for tea, sugar, tobacco and medicines. Members of my own clan commonly held that I had a right to know things that they already knew about each other anyway and constantly wanted to know the census data of my own family in England. By July it became evident that while my sample was not as large as originally planned, I could not afford to spend so much time and energy on it in future as new interests of research were opening up. Furthermore, there were still many Samburu who were rather suspicious of my direct questions and lied blatantly to me; it

317

seemed that it would only be possible to improve my relationship with them by adopting a more reserved attitude in my field work. No assistants were employed in collecting the material.

Altogether 66 settlements were included in the census. It has become evident since collecting this material that the Mount Ngiro data is not altogether typical of Samburu, but the difference between figures collected here and elsewhere is marginal: men tend to marry their first wives when they are younger and elders generally have fewer wives, but the figures in the census do not bring out these points to any great extent.

In instances where a man's compound family was divided between several settlements, it was necessary to regard him for the purpose of the census as being divided between them.[1]

II. A second census, referred to here as *the clan census* is based on as full a genealogy of Pardopa clan as I was able to collect. As with the settlement census it was assumed that the figures obtained would be representative of the tribe as a whole. In compiling this genealogy, I relied on a few exceptionally reliable informants of the clan. The extensive knowledge of these persons in many small details, sometimes concerning clansmen who lived almost 100 miles away was an ample demonstration of the corporateness of the clan. They were so highly consistent with one another and with what other data I had collected in the course of my work in this clan, that I now regard this census as the most reliable of the three.

Informants admitted that they were not too certain of the exact number of children of distant clansmen and these were therefore left out of the census. In addition, it seemed possible that there might be confusion in counting wives: informants might regard the wives of a man as including both those who were now living with other men and those that had never actually been married; thus women with irregular marriages might tend to be counted more than once in such a census. This could not occur in the settlement census where a woman was counted as a wife if she had a hut and hence could not be recorded as living in two places at once. But once again, there was great consistency between the information given by informants and data I had collected living with this clan in various areas.

It is also perhaps important to note here that the model I have built up of Samburu society, as presented in this study, is predomi-

---

[1] i.e. if he has two wives in one settlement (in the sample) and one wife elsewhere, then he is counted as two-thirds of an elder in that settlement. Barnes (1949) has elaborated the logic behind this device, pointing out that men with several wives in certain circumstances are more likely to be chosen in a random sample than men with only one wife.

nantly based on information collected and incidents which have occurred inside this clan, and so the results of this census are of greater significance for this study than the other two censuses, which give the impression that in the total society, polygamists tend to be fewer and men tend to marry younger than in Pardopa clan.

III. *The tax-book census* was carried out with the permission of the district commissioner. The inconsistencies between the settlement census and the clan census were sufficient to warrant a third census based on rather larger numbers. Tax clerks were asked to record the age-sets and numbers of wives of all Samburu men as they came to pay their taxes. Information collected in this way could not be as detailed as in the other two censuses and there was every reason to expect that it would be less accurate.

Data of the tax-book census for Pardopa clan was checked with that of the clan census (above) and considerable discrepancies were found. However, where there were errors, there seemed to be no consistent tendency to err in any direction, and no corrections have been made to allow for these.

The settlement census indicates a rate of polygamy of 1·47 wives per elder which is consistent with the figure of 1·49 obtained from the tax-book census, but inconsistent with the figure obtained from the clan census of 1·64 wives per elder. But as noted elsewhere, Pardopa clan is not altogether typical of Samburu and detailed examination of the tax-book census revealed a rate of 1·69 for Pardopa. Whatever the difference between the census results, (and these could have been largely due to the small size of the samples), the statistical pattern is fairly consistent, and suggests that the techniques were in themselves valid.

Comparison of data collected in the three censuses

A. Frequency of polygamy at different ages.

I. Settlement Census (March–July 1958)

Age-set and approx. age		Number of Wives						Total men	Total wives	Wives/ men
	0	1	2	3	4	5	6			
Marikon and										
Terito 80	1	6	5·5	2·7	–	–	–	15·2	25	1·65
Merisho 65	–	10	7·5	5·3	1	1·2	–	25	51	2·04
Kiliako 50	3	36	26·5	7·3	1	–	–	73·8	115	1·56
Mekuri 40	2	48	9·5	2	–	–	–	61·5	73	1·19
Kimaniki 25	161	16	1	–	–	–	–	178	18	0·10
Total	167	116	50	17·3	2	1·2	–	353·5	282	

II. Clan Census (August 1958)

Age-set and approx. age		Number of Wives						Total men	Total wives	Wives/ men
	0	*1*	*2*	*3*	*4*	*5*	*6*			
Marikon and										
Terito 80	2	3	7	3	–	–	–	15	26	1·73
Merisho 65	–	13	8	13	5	1	1	41	99	2·41
Kiliako 50	5	48	46	11	4	–	–	114	189	1·66
Mekuri 40	7	61	29	5	–	–	–	102	134	1·31
Kimaniki 25	293	1	–	–	–	–	–	294	1	0·003
Total	307	126	90	32	9	1	1	566	449	

III. Tax-book Census (December 1959)

Age-set and approx. age		Number of Wives						Total men	Total wives	Wives/ men
	0	*1*	*2*	*3*	*4*	*5*	*6*			
Marikon and										
Terito 80		no figures available						–	–	–
Merisho 65	4	143	129	68	25	1	3	373	728	1·95
Kiliako 50	10	569	495	128	19	1	–	1,222	2,024	1·67
Mekuri 40	28	828	381	34	7	–	–	1,278	1,720	1·35
Kimaniki 25	2,435	389	39	–	–	–	–	2,863	467	0·16
Total	2,477	1,929	1,044	230	51	2	3	5,736	4,939	

B. Distribution of population in different age grades.

Census	Settlement		Clan		Tax-book	
	Males	Females	Males	Females	Males	Females
Elders*	192·5		273		3,301	
Wives		282		449		4,939
Moran	161		293		2,435	
Widows		79†		150		no fig.
Total adults	(353·5)	(361)	(566)	(599)	5,736	–
Boys	427		no figures		no figures	
Girls		438				
Total population	780·5	799	–	–	–	–

C. The average number of wives per elder.

I	Settlement census	1·47
II	Clan census	1·64
III	Tax-book census	1·49

D. Distribution of population with sex and age (based on clan census).

Age-set and sub-age-set	Men Est. age (*1958*)	Numbers recorded		Lovers' age-set	Women Est. age (*1958*)	Wives	Wid- ows	Total
Marikon	over 88	2						
Terito			7	Marikon	over 79	–	5	5
Chong'onopir	84	5						
Palgoso	79	3						
Timisho	72	5						
Merisho			23	Terito	61–78	1	30	31
Chong'onopir	66	15						
Lgelayo	61	11						
Laitoro	58	15						
Kiliako			63	Merisho	50–60	38	56	94
Chong'onopir	55	37						
Riangiyo	50	50						
Lkichik	46	5						
Marakoma	42	22	114	Kiliako	36–49	105	43	148
Mekuri								
Chong' I	41	37						
Chong' II	36	38						
Langoda	32	27						
Kimaniki			179	Mekuri	24–35	176	14	190
Chong'onopir	29	114						
Kimatisho	24	82						
Ngusungus	20	65	180	Kimaniki	17–23	129	2	131
Lmuri	17	33						

* For the purpose of compiling these tables the elder age grade has been taken as being composed of married men of the Kimaniki age-set and all living members of the other age-sets.

† This figure includes seven women who had no acknowledged husbands at the time the census was made, and who were not concubines. Concubines, who may later become full wives, are treated in the settlement census as wives – it was not possible always to distinguish between them while the census was being compiled.

E. Comparison between age of husband and that of wives (based on the clan census).

Age of husband	Ages of wives					Ages of widows						Ages of all women						Total
	20	30	43	55	70	20	30	43	55	70	85	20	30	43	55	70	85	
115?	–	–	–	–	–	–	–	–	4	11	1	–	–	–	4	11	1	16
Over 90	–	–	–	3	–	–	–	6	11	11	4	–	–	6	14	11	4	35
77	–	3	5	14	1	–	2	13	24	8	–	–	5	18	38	9	–	70
65	25	21	32	21	–	1	5	19	17	–	–	26	26	51	38	–	–	141
50	50	71	68	–	–	1	5	5	–	–	–	51	76	73	–	–	–	200
40	53	81	–	–	–	–	2	–	–	–	–	53	83	–	–	–	–	136
33	1	–	–	–	–	–	–	–	–	–	–	1	–	–	–	–	–	1
Total	129	176	105	38	1	2	14	43	56	30	5	131	190	148	94	31	5	599

All these ages are very approximate and have been estimated from the age-sets of the husbands (vertical scale) and of the former lovers of the wives (horizontal scale). The age-set whose age is estimated at 115 is Tarigirik which has since died out.

Notes on Chapter One (pages 12 to 20).

In the four tables on pages 13 to 16 considerable use was made of the settlement census. The following notes amplify this further.

In the 66 settlements of the census, a homestead was taken as consisting of all those huts whose stock used one gateway. But it should be emphasized that when a man first builds his own gateway, this is only one stage in his efforts to be self-contained: even at this time he and his brothers may still be quite dependent on one another. Building a separate gateway is not a proclamation that complete economic independence has been achieved, but rather it is a positive indication of the lines along which fission will occur in the future, and it does suggest a certain social autonomy.

With regard to the various types of homestead, the following points should be noted:

Type A. In addition to the eight widows with uncircumcised children who had homesteads of their own, there were 29 widows attached to other homesteads of whom 14 were living with their married sons. There were also seven women living away from their husbands attached to the same homesteads as their mothers in every case.

Type C. In 10 of these 12 instances, the stock owner was a full brother of the others, and in two instances he was a half brother.

Type E. In the sample, 10 stock owners had split homesteads which shared residence in the same settlement (21 homesteads), and 23 stock owners had split homesteads divided between settlements: of the latter, 30 homesteads lay inside the sample area and were included in the census and 16 lay outside it and were excluded.

There were in addition eight families which at other times would have had gateways of their own (two of type B, five of type D and one of type E). But at the time of the census they were temporarily dependent on other stock owners and are not included separately.

In the first of these tables, it should be noted that the number of persons in a homestead is not a good indication of its ability to cope with stock. Unfortunately, more refined figures relating size, skill and fitness of the *active* labour force of each homestead to the size of its herd and food supply were too difficult to collect in sufficient numbers for use here. These tables have been compiled from data which the people were very willing to give, but they would have been less frank about further details, especially where these concerned the sizes of their herds.

None of the settlements in this sample were of the ceremonial type outlined in Chapter Four.

Notes on Chapter Six (page 170).

In the table on page 170, the first column on the proportion of moran to the total male population was arrived at by a very indirect path in which the main assumption was that the shape of the age distribution among males has remained constant for the last half century, regardless of the extent to which the tribe has grown and regardless of the number of men who have died since these age-sets were moran.

The first task was to draw a graph of the age distribution for the male population. It will be seen from chart D that at first sight the male population did not decrease uniformly with age owing to the extent to which they tended to cluster in popular age-sets. However, due to the custom of dividing those circumcised at the beginning of an age-set into those who are fully grown (*Chong'onopir*) and the remainder, the gap between these two sub-age-sets provided a natural and more reliable limit to an age range: there was little chance of a substantial overlap in true ages between the junior and the senior sub-age-set. This gave six fairly reliable points for constructing an age distribution curve for the total male population. In order to assess the number of boys (not collected in the clan census), data was extrapolated from the settlement census, giving a total male poulation of 1,249.

Using this graph and assuming that the age distribution of the society has not radically altered in the last 50 years, it was possible to assess the proportion of each sub-age-set 10 years after the initiation of the whole age-set. Thus, for the senior sub-age-set of the Kiliako, there were 37 members alive in 1958 out of 1,249 males in Pardopa clan, and their average age was estimated at 55 years. According to the age distribution graph, the proportion of males between the ages of 54·5 and 55·4 was 0·48%. In 1932 when the Kiliako had been initiated for 10 years these same men would have been 29 years old, and the corresponding proportion of males between the ages of 28·5 and 29·4 was 1·21%. Hence, a reasonable estimate for the proportion of this group to the total male population in 1932 was:

$$\frac{37 \times 1·21}{1249 \times 0·48} = 7·48\%$$

This calculation was repeated for the other sub-age-sets of the Kiliako age-set and the total proportion of 21·6% was obtained. It should be noted that by considering proportions of the total population the problem of how fast the population has been increasing was avoided.

BIBLIOGRAPHY

ARGYRIS, C., *Understanding Organizational Behaviour*, Dorsay Press, Illinois, 1960.

ARKELL-HARDWICK, A., *An Ivory Trader in North Kenya*, Longmans, London, 1903.

ATKINSON, J. J., 'Primal Law' (in A. Lang, *Social Origins*, Green & Co., London, 1903).

BARNES, J. A., 'Measures of Divorce Frequency in Simple Societies', *Journal of the Royal Anthropological Institute*, vol. 79, 1949.

BEALES, H. L., 'The Victorian Family' (a contribution to a series of B.B.C. talks), *Ideas and Beliefs of the Victorians*, Sylvan Press, London, 1950.

BUTLER, SAMUEL, (ed. Jones), *The Notebooks of Samuel Butler*, Dutton, New York, 1912.

CHANLER, W. A., *Through Jungle and Desert, Travels in Eastern Africa*, Macmillan, London, 1896.

CHAPPLE, E. D., and COON, C. S., *Principles of Anthropology*, Holt, New York, 1947.

DARWIN, C. R., *The Descent of Man, and Selection in Relation to Sex*, Murray, London, 1871.

DOUGLAS, M. *The Lele of the Kasai*, Oxford University Press, 1963.

DURKHEIM, E. (trans Simpson), *Suicide*, Routledge & Kegan Paul, London, 1952.

EISENSTADT, S. N., *From Generation to Generation*, Routledge & Kegan Paul, London, 1956.

EVANS-PRICHARD, E. E., 'The Dance', *Africa*, vol. 1, no. 1, 1928.

—— *Nuer Religion*, Clarendon Press, Oxford, 1956.

FORTES, M., *The Dynamics of Clanship among the Tallensi*, Oxford University Press, 1945.

—— *The Web of Kinship among the Tallensi*, Oxford University Press, 1949.

—— 'The Structure of Unilineal Descent Groups', *American Anthropologist*, vol. 55, no. 1, 1953.

FOSBROOKE, H. A., 'An Administrative Survey of the Masai Social System', *Tanganyika Notes and Records*, no. 26, 1948.

FREUD, S. (trans. STRACHEY), *Totem and Taboo*, Routledge & Kegan Paul, 1950.

Bibliography

GLUCKMAN, M., 'Kinship and Marriage among the Lozi of Northern Rhodesia and the Zulu of Natal' (in Radcliffe-Brown and Forde, 1950).

—— *The Judicial Process among the Barotse of Northern Rhodesia*, Manchester University Press, Manchester, 1955a.

—— *Custom and Conflict in Africa*, Blackwell, Oxford, 1955b.

GOODY, J., 'The Mother's Brother and the Sister's Son in West Africa', *Journal of the Royal Anthropological Institute*, vol. 89, 1959.

GULLIVER, P. H., *A Preliminary Survey of the Turkana*, sm. fol. School of African Studies, University of Capetown, 1951.

—— *The Family Herds*, Routledge & Kegan Paul, London, 1955.

HART, C. W. M., and PILLING, A. R., *The Tiwi of North Australia*, Holt, New York, 1961.

HOMANS, G. C., *The Human Group*, Routledge & Kegan Paul, London, 1950.

HUNTINGFORD, G. W. B., *The Nandi of Kenya*, Routledge & Kegan Paul, London, 1953.

Kenya Land Commission: Evidence and Memoranda., H.M.S.O., London, 1933.

KRIGE, E. J., *The Social System of the Zulus*, Longmans, London, 1936.

LAMB, G. F., *The Happiest Days*, Collins, Toronto, 1959.

LEACH, E. R., *Political Systems of Highland Burma*, Bell, London, 1954.

MALINOWSKI, B., *Magic, Science and Religion, and Other Essays*, Free Press, Illinois, 1948.

MPAAYEI, J. T. OLE, *Inkuti Pukunot oo Lmaasai*, Oxford University Press, 1954.

NEUMANN, A. H., *Elephant Hunting in East Equatorial Africa*, Ward, London, 1898.

OGILVIE, V., *The English Public School*, Macmillan, New York, 1957.

PARSONS, TALCOTT, *Essays in Sociological Theory, Pure and Applied*, Free Press, 1949.

PERISTIANY, J. G., *The Social Institutions of the Kipsigis*, Routledge, London, 1939.

RADCLIFFE-BROWN, A. R., *The Andaman Islanders*, Cambridge University Press, 1922.

—— 'Introduction' to Radcliffe-Brown and Forde, 1950.

—— *Structure and Function in Primitive Society*, Cohen and West, London, 1952.

—— and FORDE, D , *African Systems of Kinship and Marriage*, Oxford University Press, 1950.

ROSE, F. G. G., *Kin, Age Structure and Marriage amongst the Groote Eylandt Aborigines*, Pergamon Press, Oxford, 1952.

SARGANT, W. W., *Battle for the Mind: a Physiology of Conversion and Brain-washing*, Heinemann, London, 1957.

SIMMEL, G. (trans. WOLFF), *Conflict*, Free Press, 1955.

SMITH, W. ROBERTSON, *Lectures on the Religion of the Semites* (Burnett Lectures 1888–9), Black, Edinburgh, 1907.

SMITH, SYDNEY, Letter to the *Edinburgh Review* (October, 1809).

SPENCER, HERBERT, *Education: Intellect, Moral, and Physical*, Norgate, London, 1861.

SPENCER, P., 'Dynamics of Samburu Religion' (paper read at a conference at the East African Institute of Social Research, July, 1959 (cyclostyled)).

—— *A Survey of the Samburu and Rendille Tribes of Northern Kenya* (unpublished draft of separate report, 1961):
Chapter 1. 'A History of the Samburu and Rendille.'
Chapter 2. 'Ecology and Economy.'
Chapter 3. 'An Outline of Samburu Society.'
Chapter 4. 'An Outline of Rendille Society.'
Chapter 5. 'The Ariaal and Samburu-Rendille Relations.'
Chapter 6. 'The Dorobo of Northern Kenya.'
Chapter 7. 'The Samburu and the Administration.'
Chapter 8. 'Discussion and Conclusions.'

TAYLOR, G. RATTRAY, *Sex in History*, Thames, London, 1953.

—— *The Angel-Makers, a Study in the Psychological Origins of Historical Change*, Heinemann, London, 1958.

THOMSON, J., *Through Masai Land: A Journey of Exploration among the Snow-clad Volcanic Mountains and Strange Tribes of Eastern Equatorial Africa*, Samson Low, London, 1885.

TUCKER, A. N., and MPAAYEI, J. T. OLE, *A Masai Grammar*, Longmans, London, 1955.

TURNER, V. W., *Schism and Continuity in an African Society*, Manchester University Press, Manchester, 1957.

VAN GENNEP, A. (trans. VIZEDOM AND CAFFEE), *The Rites of Passage*, Routledge & Kegan Paul, London, 1960.

WILSON, M., 'Nyakyusa Kinship' (in Radcliffe-Brown and Forde, 1950).

—— *Good Company: A Study of Nyakyusa Age-Villages*, Oxford University Press, 1951.

—— *Rituals of Kinship among the Nyakyusa*, Oxford University Press, 1957.

INDEX

abortion, 112, 185, 191

abreaction, 261–9

address, forms of: affines, 30, 82, 241, 288; age mates, 74, 82, 256, 288; bond brothers, 77; clansmen, 77; firestick elders, 82–3; mother's brothers, 37; mother's sisters' sons, 227; with privileged familiarity, 79, 94

administration: attempt to accelerate age set system, 154–5, 171; attempt to cull stock, 155; attitudes of moran towards, 146, 151; ban song, 147; control over district, xxvi–xxviii, 154–5; courts used to confirm irregular marriages, 46; levies imposed by, 144; peace maintained by, xxvi, 148, 149; views expressed by, 182

adoption into clan, 50; and Masula phratry, 288–9; precipitated by misfortune, 192

adultery between moran and wives, 148, 199; elders' attitude towards, 100, 141, 199, 228, 266; and junior elders, 137, 158; moran attitude towards, 146; women's attitude towards, 146, 227–8

affines: in an asymmetrical relationship, xxxiii, 30, 35–7, 212, 234; contrasted with clansmen, 29, 279–81; strain between, 29, 35–7, 47–8, 52, 70, 192, 200, 207, 279–80; terms of address, 30, 82, 241, 288; and the Turkana, 278–81

affrays: averted at a circumcision, 105; and competition among moran for girls, 113–19, 215; at dances, 124–5, 262–3, 264; between moran and elders at Ngelai,

158–61, 176, 272–3; between Pisikishu and Lorogushu moran, 117, 124, 148, 157; precipitated by notions of honour, 111, 113–17

age grades, **80–1**; behaviour associated with, 85–9; outline of system, 80–5

age mates: avoid daughters, 82, 213; avoid personal names, 74, 145; as classificatory fathers, 33–4, 57, 175, 213, 217–18; curse, 160, 188; equality of, 26, 81–2, 107–10, 288; as neighbours, 16, 188; norms of hospitality, 82, 160, 244; 'share hair', 74; support marriages, 44, 235; terms of address, 74, 82, 256, 288

age-sets, **80**; association of alternates, 151–2, 167–72, 323–4; breach of etiquette, 129; and gerontocratic index, 301; life cycle of, 85–90; period associated with polygamy rate, 95–9, 139, 154, 295, 299; relationships between, 81–3, 136–8, 149–53, 156; solidarity, 82, 107, 160; strains in a large age-set, 167–8; sub-age-sets, 91, 118–19, 143, 157, 170, 321. (*See also* change-over)

'age-set seniority', **91**

age organization: function of, **134**, 172, 307; and gerontocracy, xxx and *ilmugit* ceremonies, 87–9, 161–6, 256–9; outline of, 80–5; and Rendille, 99, 295–7; and Suiei Dorobo, 283–4; and Turkana, 134, 277

agriculture, lack of, 2, 22

allotted herd of wife, **53–8**; exploited by husband, 55–7, 62–3, 66–70; inherited by youngest son, 62; and

329

allotted herd of wife–*contd.*
Rendille, 294; son's interest in, 59,
61, 224–5; used to gratify affines,
56–8, 70
alternations, **95**, 193, 219; and standards of respect, 221–2
ancestry, beliefs in, xxxii–xxxiii, 76–7, 91
anger: associated with shaking, 124,
263–4, 268; of moran at a dance,
124
axomie and the moran, 162–3, 257
anxiety: at boys' circumcisions,
104–6, 254; at dances, 261–3; at
discussions, 271; at marriage
ceremonies, 236, 238, 247–54;
and moranhood, 264–8; and
suggestibility, 247–74
Arkell-Hardwick, A., 148
Atkinson, J. J., 306
avoidance: between bond brothers,
78–80, 208, 212–13; between
fathers and daughters, 82, 212–15,
217–18; between girls and elders,
90, 173, 212–13, 219; between
moran and married women, 87,
100, 219, 223, 266; and polygamy, 213; and sentiment, 214

barrenness, cured by women's songs,
228–9
Barnes, J. A., 49, 318
bachelorhood: and polygamy, 96,
133, 305. (*See also* moran)
best man, 238–45
beer drinking, compared with dancing, 215
birth ceremony, 211
blacksmith, 239
blessing: of bond brothers, 157;
contrasted with cursing, 41, **166**,
196, 268; by elders during
discussion, 177–8; by elders for the
moran, 141, 153, 160, 166, 267–8; of
mother's brother, 41, 187, 200; to
settle a curse, 38, 153, 160, **187**,
194, 195, 202, 203, 204
bloodwealth, 80

boasting: before battle, 106; at
circumcision, 105–6; in songs,
123, 124
bond brothers, **78–80**; avoidance
between, 78–80, 208, 212–13;
blessing, 157; curse, 156–7, 186,
187, 190, 193; imputed curse, 78,
191, 192, 199; and Rendille, 79n.;
and ritual partners, 87; settle
disputes, 79, 156, 157; terms of
address, 77
Boran: as enemies of the Samburu,
xxiii, xxv, xxvi, xxviii, 49; Warta, 281
boys: herding activities, 10; learn
idiom of moran songs, 147; upbringing compared with girls',
215; valued more highly than
girls, 211
boys' circumcision: anxiety shown
at, 104, 254–6; boasting at, 105–6;
ceremony, 85–7, 104–5; flinching
at, 103–6; preferably at change
over of age-sets, 169; settlement,
104; similarity with *ilmugit* ceremonies, 91, 268; song, 39, 87,
104, 228; symbolic implications,
255, 306
'boys' dances', 122, 261
brain-washing, 142, 246, 247, 249
breakdown, 247, 248, 260. (*See also*
shaking)
bride: allotted cattle, 53–4; harangued, 241–2, 248–9, 251; life
crisis, 215–16, 219–20, 247–9;
ordeal during marriage, 237–45;
247–9, 253
bridegroom: anxiety displayed during wedding, 249–53; role in
marriage ceremony, 236–45; role
in marriage negotiations, 29–32,
233–6
bridewealth, **46**; comparatively
small, 69, 134, 277; is followed by
further marriage payments, 30,
35, 46, 278; handed over during
wedding, 238–9; and lineage